McGraw-Hill's
GED
Language Arts, Writing

The Most Comprehensive and Reliable
Study Program for the GED Test

Ellen Carley Frechette (Part I)
Tim Collins, National-Louis University (Part II)

Reviewers

Walter L. Dunn, Ed.D., Adult Literacy Director, Griffin Technical College, Griffin, Georgia

Pauline Geraci, Literacy Instructor, Stillwater Correctional, Bayport, Minnesota

Andrea Holt, GED Instructor, Adult Education,
Grand Ledge Public Schools, Grand Ledge, Michigan

Ann Jackson, Chief Examiner, GED Test Center,
Los Angeles Unified School District, Los Angeles, California

Beverly Klausner, Counselor, Clark County School District,
Adult High School, Las Vegas, Nevada

Stanley Levin, Ed. D., Alternate Chief Examiner, GED Test Center,
Los Angeles Unified School District, Los Angeles, California

Federico Salas, Director, Adult Education Department, North Harris College, Houston, Texas

McGraw-Hill

New York   Chicago   San Francisco   Lisbon   London   Madrid   Mexico City
Milan   New Delhi   San Juan   Seoul   Singapore   Sydney   Toronto

5 6 7 8 9 0   QPD/QPD   1 0

ISBN 0-07-140708-1

McGraw-Hill books are available at special quantity discounts to use as premiums and sales promotions, or for use in corporate training programs. For more information, please write to the Director of Special Sales, Professional Publishing, McGraw-Hill, Two Penn Plaza, New York, NY 10121-2298. Or contact your local bookstore.

This book is printed on acid-free paper.

Table of Contents

PART II: THE ESSAY

To the Student

If you're studying to pass the GED Test, you're in good company. In 1999, the most recent year for which figures are available, the American Council on Education GED Testing Service reported that over 750,700 adults took the GED Test battery worldwide. Of this number, more than 526,400 (70 percent) actually received their certificates. About 14 percent of those with high school credentials, or about one in seven, have a GED diploma. One in twenty (5 percent) of those students in their first year of college study is a GED graduate.

The average age of GED test-takers in the United States was over 24 in 1999, but nearly three-quarters (70 percent) of GED test-takers were 19 years of age or older. Two out of three GED test-takers report having completed the tenth grade or higher, and more than a third report having completed the eleventh grade before leaving high school.

Why do so many people choose to take the GED Test? Some do so to get a job, to advance to a better job, to attend college, or to qualify for military service. More than two out of every three GED graduates work toward college degrees or attend trade, technical, or business schools. Still others pursue their GED diplomas to feel better about themselves or to set good examples for their children.

More than 14 million adults earned the GED diploma between 1942 and 1999. Some well-known graduates include country music singers Waylon Jennings and John Michael Montgomery, comedian Bill Cosby, Olympic gold medalist Mary Lou Retton, Delaware Lieutenant Governor Ruth Ann Minner, Colorado's U.S. Senator Ben Nighthorse Campbell, Wendy's founder Dave Thomas, Famous Amos Cookies creator Wally Amos, and Triple Crown winner jockey Ron Turcotte.

This book has been designed to help you, too, succeed on the test. It will provide you with instruction in the skills you need to pass and plenty of practice with the kinds of test items you will find on the real test.

What Does GED Stand For?

GED stands for the Test of **General Educational Development.** The GED Test Battery is a national examination developed by the GED Testing Service of the American Council on Education. The certificate earned for passing the test is widely recognized by colleges, training schools, and employers as equivalent to a high school diploma. The American Council reports that almost all employers in the nation (more than 95 percent) employ GED graduates and offer them the same salaries and opportunities for advancement as high school graduates.

The GED Test reflects the major and lasting outcomes normally acquired in a high school program. Since the passing rate for the GED is based on the performance of graduating high school seniors, you can be sure your skills are comparable. In fact, those who pass the GED Test actually do better than one-third of those graduating seniors. Your skills in communication, information processing, critical thinking, and problem solving are keys to success. The test also places special emphasis on questions that prepare you for entering the workplace or higher education. Much that you have learned informally or through other types of training can help you pass the test.

Special editions of the GED Test include the French language, Spanish language, Braille, large print, and audiocassette formats. If you need special accomodations because of a learning or physical disability, your adult education program and testing center can assist you.

What Should You Know to Pass the Test?

The GED Test consists of five examinations, called Language Arts, Writing; Social Studies; Science; Language Arts, Reading; and Mathematics. On all five tests, you are expected to demonstrate the ability to think about many issues. You are tested on knowledge and skills you have acquired from life experiences, television, radio, books and newspapers, consumer products, and advertising. Your work or business experiences may be helpful during the test. You can expect the subjects to be interrelated. This is called *interdisciplinary* material. For example, a mathematics problem may include a scientific diagram. Or a social studies question may require some mathematical skills.

In addition to the previous information, keep these facts in mind about specific tests:

1. The **Language Arts, Writing Test** requires you in Part I to recognize or correct errors, revise sentences or passages, and shift constructions in the four areas of organization, sentence structure, usage, and mechanics (capitalization and punctuation). Letters, memos, and business-related documents are likely to be included.

   In Part II you will write a well-developed essay presenting an opinion or an explanation on a topic familiar to most adults. You should plan and organize your ideas before you write, and revise and edit your essay before you are finished.

2. Three of the five tests—**Social Studies, Science,** and **Mathematics**— require you to answer questions based on reading passages or interpreting graphs, charts, maps, cartoons, diagrams, or photographs. Developing strong reading and critical thinking skills is the key to succeeding on these tests. Being able to interpret information from graphic sources, such as a map or cartoon, is essential.

3. The **Language Arts, Reading Test** asks you to read literary text and show that you can comprehend, apply, analyze, synthesize, and evaluate concepts. You will also read nonfiction and show that you can understand the main points of what you are reading.

4. The **Mathematics Test** consists mainly of word problems to be solved. Therefore, you must be able to combine your ability to perform computations with problem-solving skills.

   Part I of the Mathematics Test will permit the use of the Casio fx-260 calculator, which will be provided at the test site. The calculator will eliminate the tediousness of making complex calculations. Part II will not permit the use of the calculator. Both parts of the test will include problems without multiple-choice answers. These problems will require you to mark your answers on bubble-in number grids or on coordinate plane graphs.

Who May Take the Test?

About 3,500 GED Testing Centers are available in the fifty United States, the District of Columbia, eleven Canadian provinces and territories, U.S. and overseas military bases, correctional institutions, Veterans Administration hospitals, and certain learning centers. People who have not graduated from high school and who meet specific eligibility requirements (age, residency, etc.) may take the test. Since eligibility requirements vary, you should contact your local GED testing center or the director of adult education in your state, province, or territory for specific information.

What Is a Passing Score on the GED Test?

A passing score varies from area to area. To find out what you need to pass the test, contact your local GED Testing Center. However, you should keep two scores in mind. One score represents the minimum score you must get on each test. The other is the minimum average score on all five tests. Both of these scores will be set by your state, and you must meet them in order to pass the GED Test.

Can You Retake the Test?

You are allowed to retake some or all of the tests. The regulations governing the number of times that you may retake the tests and the time you must wait before retaking them are set by your state, province, or territory. Some states require you to take a review class or to study on your own for a certain amount of time before retaking the test.

THE GED TESTS

Tests	Minutes	Questions	Content/Percentages
Language Arts, Writing Part I: Editing (multiple choice) Part II: the Essay	75 45	50 1 topic: approx. 250 words	Organization 15% Sentence Structure 30% Usage 30% Mechanics 25%
Social Studies	70	50	World History 15% U.S. History 25% Civics and Government 25% Economics 20% Geography 15%
Science	80	50	Earth and Space Science 20% Life Science 45% Physical Science 35% (Physics and Chemistry)

Language Arts, Reading	65	40	Literary Text 75%
			    Poetry 15%
			    Drama 15%
			    Fiction 45%
			Nonfiction 25%
			    Informational Text
			    Literary Nonfiction
			    Reviews of Fine and Performing Arts
			    Business Documents

Mathematics Part I Calculator Part II No Calculator	 45 45	 25 25	Number Operations and Numbers Sense 20–30% Measurement and Geometry 20–30% Data Analysis, Statistics, and Probability 20–30% Algebra, Functions, and Patterns 20–30%
	Total: $7\frac{1}{4}$ hours	Total: 240 questions and 1 essay	

How Can You Best Prepare for the Test?

Many community colleges, public schools, adult education centers, libraries, churches, community-based organizations, and other institutions offer GED preparation classes. While your state may not require you to take part in a preparation program, it's a good idea if you've been out of school for some time, if you had academic difficulty when you were in school, or if you left before completing the eleventh grade. Some television stations broadcast classes to prepare people for the test. If you cannot find a GED preparation class locally, contact the director of adult education in your state, province, or territory.

What Are Some Test-Taking Tips?

1. **Prepare physically.** Get plenty of rest and eat a well-balanced meal before the test so that you will have energy and will be able to think clearly. Intense studying at the last minute probably will not help as much as having a relaxed and rested mind.

2. **Arrive early.** Be at the testing center at least 15 to 20 minutes before the starting time. Make sure you have time to find the room and to get situated. Keep in mind that many testing centers refuse to admit latecomers. Some testing centers operate on a first come, first served basis, so you want to be sure that there is an available seat for you on the day that you're ready to test.

3. **Think positively.** Tell yourself you will do well. If you have studied and prepared for the test, you should succeed.

4. **Relax during the test.** Take half a minute several times during the test to stretch and breathe deeply, especially if you are feeling anxious or confused.

5. **Read the test directions carefully.** Be sure you understand how to answer the questions. If you have any questions about the test or about filling in the answer form, ask before the test begins.

6. **Know the time limit for each test.** The Language Arts, Writing Test, Part I, has a time limit of 75 minutes (1 hour 15 minutes). Work at a steady pace; if you have extra time, go back and check your answers. Part II, the essay, has a time limit of 45 minutes. Take the time to organize your thoughts and ideas before you begin to write; when you finish writing, reread your essay and correct any errors you find.

7. **Have a strategy for answering questions.** You should read through the reading passages or look over the materials once and then answer the questions that follow. Read each question two or three times to make sure you understand it. It is best to refer back to the passage or graphic in order to confirm your answer choice. Don't try to depend on your memory of what you have just read or seen. Some people like to guide their reading by skimming the questions before reading a passage. Use the method that works best for you.

8. **Don't spend a lot of time on difficult questions.** If you're not sure of an answer, go on to the next question. Answer easier questions first and then go back to the harder questions. However, when you skip a question, be sure that you have skipped the same number on your answer sheet. Although skipping difficult questions is a good strategy for making the most of your time, it is very easy to get confused and throw off your whole answer key.

    Lightly mark the margin of your answer sheet next to the numbers of the questions you did not answer so that you know what to go back to. To prevent confusion when your test is graded, be sure to erase these marks completely after you answer the questions.

9. **Answer every question on the test.** If you're not sure of an answer, take an educated guess. When you leave a question unanswered, you will always lose points, but you can possibly gain points if you make a correct guess.

    If you must guess, try to eliminate one or more answers that you are sure are not correct. Then choose from the remaining answers. Remember that you greatly increase your chances if you can eliminate one or two answers before guessing. Of course, guessing should be used only when all else has failed.

10. **Clearly fill in the circle for each answer choice.** If you erase something, erase it completely. Be sure that you give only one answer per question; otherwise, no answer will count.

11. **Practice test-taking.** Use the exercises, reviews, and especially the Posttest and Practice Test in this book to better understand your test-taking habits and weaknesses. Use them to practice different strategies such as skimming questions first or skipping hard questions until the end. Knowing your own personal test-taking style is important to your success on the GED Test.

How to Use This Book

This book will guide you through the types of questions you can expect to find on the Language Arts, Writing Test. To answer some questions successfully, you will need to focus on sentence structure, grammar, and the mechanics of punctuation and capitalization. For others, you will need to concentrate on the organization of sentences within a paragraph or an article. Finally, you will need to develop your ability to organize your thoughts from paragraph to paragraph. This skill is important for success on the essay portion of the test.

Before beginning this book, you should take the Pretest. This will help you identify which skill areas you need to concentrate on most. Use the chart at the end of the Pretest to pinpoint the types of questions you have answered incorrectly and to determine which skills you need special work in. You may decide to concentrate on specific areas or to work through the entire book. We strongly suggest you *do* work through the whole book to best prepare yourself for the GED Test.

This book is divided into two sections.

- **Part I: Editing** contains seven chapters, which focus on organization, sentence structure, usage, and mechanics.

- **Part II: the Essay** contains six chapters covering the four steps of the writing process: gathering ideas, organizing, writing, and revising.

In addition, this book has a number of features designed to make the task of test preparation easier and more effective.

- Each chapter in Part I: Editing concludes with a **Chapter Review** and a **Cumulative Review.** Both reviews are written in GED format to give you practice in taking the GED Test.

- The chapters in Part I include three special features:
  1) **Mind on Mechanics,** which gives information on capitalization and comma usage
  2) **Editing Tips,** which give information about sentence structure and correct sentence usage
  3) **Evaluate Your Progress,** which allows students to periodically check their knowledge of skill areas they have covered so far.

- Chapter 7, **Test-Taking Strategies,** explains what to expect on Part I of the Language Arts, Writing Test. This chapter points out
  1) common grammar errors that will be covered
  2) different kinds of organization errors that will be tested
  3) three formats of questions that will be used on the test

- Part II: the Essay includes a **Writing a GED Essay** practice exercise at the end of each chapter. These exercises lead you through the process of writing a five-paragraph essay.

- A special feature called **Raising Your Score** helps you understand the essay scoring guide and shows you how to use the guide to evaluate and improve your own writing.

- **Additional Essay Topics** are included at the back of the book for extra writing practice.

- The **Answer Key** explains the correct answers for the exercises; if you make a mistake, you can learn from it by reading the explanation that follows the answer and then reviewing the question to analyze the error.

- A **Glossary** and **Index** are included at the back of the book for easy reference.

After you have worked through the book and covered the entire writing process, you should take the Posttest. The Posttest is a simulated GED Test that presents questions in the format, at the level of difficulty, and in the percentages found on the actual GED Test. The Posttest will help you determine whether you are ready for the GED Language Arts, Writing Test and, if not, what areas of the book you need to review. After you have reviewed, you can use the Practice Test as a final indicator of your readiness for the GED Test.

Language Arts, Writing Part I

Before you begin to work with this book, take this pretest. The purpose of the pretest is to help you determine which skills you need to develop to pass the GED Language Arts, Writing Test.

Directions: Choose the <u>one best answer</u> to each question. Some of the sentences may contain errors in organization, sentence structure, usage, or mechanics. A few sentences, however, may be correct as written. Read the sentences carefully and then answer the questions based on them. For each question, choose the answer that would result in the most effective writing of the sentence or sentences.

Pretest Answer Grid

1 ① ② ③ ④ ⑤   10 ① ② ③ ④ ⑤   19 ① ② ③ ④ ⑤

2 ① ② ③ ④ ⑤   11 ① ② ③ ④ ⑤   20 ① ② ③ ④ ⑤

3 ① ② ③ ④ ⑤   12 ① ② ③ ④ ⑤   21 ① ② ③ ④ ⑤

4 ① ② ③ ④ ⑤   13 ① ② ③ ④ ⑤   22 ① ② ③ ④ ⑤

5 ① ② ③ ④ ⑤   14 ① ② ③ ④ ⑤   23 ① ② ③ ④ ⑤

6 ① ② ③ ④ ⑤   15 ① ② ③ ④ ⑤   24 ① ② ③ ④ ⑤

7 ① ② ③ ④ ⑤   16 ① ② ③ ④ ⑤   25 ① ② ③ ④ ⑤

8 ① ② ③ ④ ⑤   17 ① ② ③ ④ ⑤

9 ① ② ③ ④ ⑤   18 ① ② ③ ④ ⑤

When you have completed the test, check your work with the answers and explanations on page 14. Use the evaluation chart on page 15 to determine which areas you need to review most.

Questions 1–7 refer to the following advertisement.

Take Advantage Of Freedom Mutual's Group Insurance Plan

(A)

(1) Many automobile insurance companies promise to save you money, when you look closely at the numbers, they don't add up. (2) Freedom Mutual gives savings you can count on. (3) For a limited time only, we are able to offer you our preferred Group Savings plan. (4) If you sign up now, you will also receive an extra 10 percent discount off our already low Rates.

(B)

(5) With this group plan, you do not have to sacrifice excellent service, or convenience for savings. (6) You may be eligible for the 10 percent discount and you may be eligible for additional savings based on your driving record, age, and auto safety equipment. (7) Furthermore, we guarantee our rates for a full six months from date of contract. (8) Under this plan, they could save up to $300 every year. (9) What benefits do our customers receive with this group plan?

(C)

(10) For starters, policyholders receive round-the-clock claim service. (11) Another great benefit is our 24-hour emergency roadside assistance service.

(D)

(12) You may also choose any one of our convenient payment options with no interest or service fees. (13) Call us any time, day or night, to find out what's covered under your plan.

---

1. Sentence 1: **Many automobile insurance companies promise to save <u>you money, when you look </u>closely at the numbers, they don't add up.**

   Which is the best way to write the underlined portion of the text? If the original is the best way, choose option (1).

   (1) you money, when you look
   (2) you money when you look
   (3) you money, but when you look
   (4) you money, so when you look
   (5) you money, when you looked

2. Sentence 4: **If you sign up now, you will also receive an extra 10 percent discount off our already low Rates.**

   What correction should be made to sentence 4?

   (1) replace *If* with *Because*
   (2) remove the comma after *now*
   (3) replace *will* with *did*
   (4) insert a comma after *discount*
   (5) change *Rates* to *rates*

3. **Sentence 5: With this group plan, you do not have to sacrifice excellent service, or convenience for savings.**

   What correction should be made to sentence 5?

   (1) remove the comma after *plan*
   (2) replace *do* with *did*
   (3) remove the comma after *service*
   (4) insert a comma after *convenience*
   (5) no correction is necessary

4. **Sentence 6: You may be eligible for the 10 percent discount and you may be eligible for additional savings based on your driving record, age, and auto safety equipment.**

   If you rewrote sentence 6 beginning with

   In addition to the 10 percent discount, the next words should be

   (1) eligible savings may be based on
   (2) your eligibility for savings may be based on
   (3) even greater savings for you may be based on
   (4) you may find additional savings you may be eligible for
   (5) you may be eligible for even greater savings

5. **Sentence 8: Under this plan, they could save up to $300 every year.**

   What correction should be made to sentence 8?

   (1) remove the comma after *plan*
   (2) replace *they* with *you*
   (3) replace *they* with *we*
   (4) replace *could save* with *were saving*
   (5) no correction is necessary

6. **Sentence 9: What benefits do our customers receive with this group plan?**

   Which revision should be made to sentence 9?

   (1) move sentence 9 to the end of paragraph A
   (2) move sentence 9 to the beginning of paragraph B
   (3) move sentence 9 to the beginning of paragraph C
   (4) move sentence 9 to follow sentence 5
   (5) remove sentence 9

7. **Sentences 12 and 13: You may also choose any one of our convenient payment options with no interest or service fees. Call us any time, day or night, to find out what's covered under your plan.**

   Which revision should be made to sentences 12 and 13?

   (1) move sentences 12 and 13 to the end of paragraph A
   (2) move sentences 12 and 13 to the beginning of paragraph B
   (3) move sentences 12 and 13 to the beginning of paragraph C
   (4) move sentences 12 and 13 to the end of paragraph C
   (5) remove sentences 12 and 13

Questions 8–14 refer to the following passage.

Depression

(A)

(1) Depression is a disorder that can be marked by sadness, and it can also be marked by hopelessness, and loss of energy and pleasure, or it can be marked by difficulty concentrating. (2) This disease affects three out of ten Americans at some point in they're lives, but it often goes undiagnosed and untreated. (3) Some of the symptoms of depression are described below. (4) Is it possible that you or someone you love are affected by depression?

(B)

(5) People who are depressed often lose interest in things that used to give them pleasure. (6) For example, a person who normally enjoys reading no longer having any interest in picking up a book. (7) Or someone who has always enjoyed her children finds herself wanting to be away from them for long periods of time. (8) This lack of interest alone did not always mean a person is depressed, but it can be a warning sign.

(C)

(9) Changes in sleeping and eating patterns can also signal depression. (10) A person who gains or loses a great deal of weight in a short period of time might be depressed. (11) Gaining a lot of weight can put stress on your heart. (12) Similarly, if a person finds himself sleeping more than usual or being awake a lot during the night, depression might be a factor.

(D)

(13) For a complete list of warning signals of depression, contact a mental health provider or check out the website for the National Depressive and Manic-Depressive Association (http://www.ndmda.org). (14) Depression is a highly treatable disease, but there is absolutely no reason for a person to suffer in silence.

8. **Sentence 1: Depression is a disorder that can be marked by sadness, and it can also be marked by hopelessness, and loss of energy and pleasure, or it can be marked by difficulty concentrating.**

   The most effective revision of sentence 1 would include which group of words?

   (1) that can be marked by sadness, but it can also be marked by hopelessness, and loss of energy and pleasure, or it can be marked by difficulty concentrating.
   (2) that can be marked by sadness and hopelessness and loss of energy and pleasure or difficulty concentrating.
   (3) that can be marked by sadness, hopelessness, loss of energy and pleasure, or difficulty concentrating.
   (4) that can be marked by sadness even though hopelessness, loss of energy and pleasure, or difficulty concentrating.
   (5) no revision is necessary

9. **Sentence 2: This disease affects three out of ten Americans at some point in <u>they're lives, but it often goes</u> undiagnosed and untreated.**

   Which is the best way to write the underlined portion of the text? If the original is the best way, choose option (1).

   (1) they're lives, but it often goes
   (2) they're lives but it often goes
   (3) there lives, but it often goes
   (4) their lives, but it often goes
   (5) they're lives, so it often goes

10. **Sentence 4: Is it possible that you or someone you love are affected by depression?**

    What correction should be made to sentence 4?

    (1) change *love* to *loved*
    (2) replace *are* with *is*
    (3) replace *are* with *were*
    (4) change *affected* to *effected*
    (5) insert a comma after *affected*

11. **Sentence 6: For example, a person who normally enjoys reading no longer <u>having any interest in picking</u> up a book.**

    Which is the best way to write the underlined portion of the text? If the original is the best way, choose option (1).

    (1) having any interest in picking
    (2) have any interest in picking
    (3) has any interest in picking
    (4) having any interest in picked
    (5) are having any interest in picking

12. **Sentence 8: This lack of interest alone did not always mean a person is depressed, but it can be a warning sign.**

    What correction should be made to sentence 8?

    (1) change *did* to *does*
    (2) change *did* to *do*
    (3) remove the comma after *depressed*
    (4) replace *it* with *they*
    (5) no correction is necessary

13. Sentence 11: Gaining a lot of weight can put stress on your heart.

Which revision should be made to sentence 11?

(1) move sentence 11 to the end of paragraph B
(2) move sentence 11 to the beginning of paragraph C
(3) move sentence 11 to follow sentence 9
(4) move sentence 11 to follow sentence 12
(5) remove sentence 11

14. Sentence 14: Depression is a highly treatable <u>disease, but there is</u> absolutely no reason for a person to suffer in silence.

Which is the best way to write the underlined portion of the text? If the original is the best way, choose option (1).

(1) disease, but there is
(2) disease but there is
(3) disease, but they're is
(4) disease, but there was
(5) disease, so there is

Questions 15–20 refer to the following letter.

June 30, 2002

Dear PlayToy Customer:

(A)

(1) In accordance with the procedures specified by the United States Consumer Protection Agency, we are writing to inform you of the recall of two models of trucks manufactured by PlayToy. (2) This letter provides information concerning which models are being recalled, how to identify them, and it also provides information concerning what to do with the defective toy if you possess one. (3) While very few of these trucks were actually delivered to stores, we here at PlayToy is taking every precaution possible to ensure the safety of our customers and their children.

(B)

(4) The defective toys be the Tough Truck II and the Wheel Master. (5) Each of these toys bears a label on their right rear bumper. (6) Unfortunately, the plastic hubcaps on some of these truck wheels are not fastened on adequately, and they can pose a choking risk for young children. (7) Possessing one of these toy trucks, attempting to repair the wheels yourself is NOT advised. (8) Instead, follow the procedures outlined below.

(C)

(9) If you do own a Tough Truck II or a Wheel Master, you have two options for return. (10) You may bring the truck back to the store for a full refund, or, alternatively, you can mail the truck back to our return department, and we will reimburse you for the cost of the shipping and send you a new truck if this is the option you would like in terms of the return of the defective merchandise. (11) The replacement trucks will not have the defective hubcaps.

(12) If you do not choose either of these options, we ask that you please destroy the truck immediately so as not to endanger the welfare of any child.

Sincerely,
Wallace H. Smith
President, PlayToy, Inc.

15. **Sentence 2: This letter provides information concerning which models are being recalled, how to identify them, and it also provides information concerning what to do with the defective toy if you possess one.**

The most effective revision of sentence 2 would include which group of words?

(1) This letter is attempting to provide some type of information
(2) This letter provided information
(3) concerning which models the company would like to recall, how to identify those models, and what to do with those models
(4) concerning models, identification of models, and what to do with the models
(5) which models are being recalled, how to identify them, and what to do with the defective toy

16. **Sentence 3: While very few of these trucks were actually delivered to <u>stores, we here at PlayToy is taking</u> every precaution possible to ensure the safety of our customers and their children.**

Which is the best way to write the underlined portion of the text? If the original is the best way, choose option (1).

(1) stores, we here at PlayToy is taking
(2) stores, we hear at PlayToy is taking
(3) stores, we here at playtoy is taking
(4) stores, we here at PlayToy are taking
(5) stores, we here at PlayToy was taking

17. **Sentence 4: The defective <u>toys be</u> the Tough Truck II and the Wheel Master.**

Which is the best way to write the underlined portion of the text? If the original is the best way, choose option (1).

(1) toys be
(2) toys, be
(3) toys being
(4) toys were
(5) toys are

18. **Sentence 5: Each of these toys bears a label on their right rear bumper.**

What correction should be made to sentence 5?

(1) change *their* to *it's*
(2) change *bears* to *bear*
(3) replace *their* with *they're*
(4) replace *their* with *its*
(5) replace *their* with *there*

19. **Sentence 7: <u>Possessing one of these toy trucks, attempting</u> to repair the wheels yourself is NOT advised.**

Which is the best way to write the underlined portion of the text? If the original is the best way, choose option (1).

(1) Possessing one of these toy trucks, attempting
(2) Possessing one of these toy trucks, attempt
(3) Possessing one of these toy trucks, you are attempting
(4) If you possess one of these toy trucks, attempting
(5) Having possessed one of these toy trucks, attempting

20. Sentence 10: You may bring the truck back to the store for a full refund, <u>or, alternatively, you can mail the truck back to our return department, and we will reimburse you for the cost of the shipping and send you a new truck if this is the option you would like in terms of the return of the defective merchandise.</u>

Which is the best way to write the underlined portion of the text? If the original is the best way, choose option (1).

(1) or, alternatively, you can mail the truck back to our return department, and we will reimburse you for the cost of the shipping and send you a new truck if this is the option you would like in terms of the return of the defective merchandise.

(2) or you can mail the truck back to our return department, and we will reimburse you for the shipping cost and send you a new truck.

(3) or, alternatively, you can mail the truck back to our return department, and we will reimburse you.

(4) or, alternatively, you can mail the truck back to our return department, and we will send you a new truck.

(5) or you can mail the truck back to our return department, if this is the option you would like in terms of the return of the defective merchandise.

Questions 21–25 refer to the following article.

Preparing For Your Move

(A)

(1) Moving residences can be difficult and stressful in a number of ways. (2) Planning ahead and making good use of the months prior to your move can help. (3) Here are a few tips that can make some of the challenges seem less daunting. (4) In general, everything seem more doable if you keep to a schedule. (5) Effective methods of dealing with stress include meditation and exercise.

(B)

(6) First of all, about four weeks before you plan to move, schedule a rental truck or moving company. (7) There are several good national rental truck and moving chains that you can choose from. (8) You may want to call a couple of them, compare their rates. (9) If you have children who will be entering a different school system from your new residence, call the school administration in that new community to enroll. (10) Next, arrange to have your gas, electricity, cable, water, and other services connected in your new home the day before you move in. (11) Have the service at your old address turned off the day after you move. (12) Having received your request well in advance, it is easier for utility companies to ensure continued service.

21. Sentence 2: **Planning ahead and making good use** of the months prior to your move can help.

    Which is the best way to write the underlined portion of the text? If the original is the best way, choose option (1).

    (1) Planning ahead and making good use
    (2) Planning ahead, and making good use
    (3) Plan ahead and make good use
    (4) Planning ahead and make good use
    (5) Planning ahead and you are making
       good use

22. Sentence 4: **In general, everything seem more doable if you keep to a schedule.**

    The most effective revision of sentence 4 would begin with which group of words?

    (1) In general, everything seem more able to
       do if
    (2) In general, everything seemed more
       doable if
    (3) In general, everything seems more
       doable if
    (4) In general, everything seem more
       doable, if
    (5) In general, everything seeming more
       doable if

23. Sentence 5: Effective methods of dealing with stress include meditation and exercise.

Which revision should be made to sentence 5?

(1) move sentence 5 to follow sentence 1
(2) move sentence 5 to follow sentence 3
(3) move sentence 5 to the beginning of paragraph B
(4) remove sentence 5
(5) no revision is necessary

24. Sentence 8: You may want to call a couple of them, compare their rates.

The most effective revision of sentence 8 would include which group of words?

(1) of them, compare them.
(2) of them and compare their rates.
(3) Comparing their rates, you may
(4) to ask about rates and to compare rates.
(5) no revision is necessary

25. Sentence 12: <u>Having received your request well in advance, it is easier for utility companies</u> to ensure continued service.

Which is the best way to write the underlined portion of the text? If the original is the best way, choose option (1).

(1) Having received your request well in advance, it is easier for utility companies
(2) Having received you're request well in advance, it is easier for utility companies
(3) Receiving your request well in advance, it is easier for utility companies
(4) It is easier for utility companies, having received your request well in advance,
(5) To receive your request well in advance, it is easier for utility companies

Answers are on page 000.

Language Arts, Writing Part II

This part of the pretest is designed to find out how well you write.

Essay Directions and Topic:

Look at the box on the following page. In the box is your assigned topic.

You must write on the assigned topic ONLY.

You will have 45 minutes to write on your assigned essay topic. You may return to the multiple-choice section after you complete your essay if you have time remaining in this test period.

Pay attention to these features as you write:

- Well-focused main points
- Clear organization
- Specific development of your ideas
- Control of sentence structure, punctuation, grammar, word choice, and spelling

As you work, be sure to do the following:

- Do not leave pages blank.
- Write legibly **in ink**.
- Write on the assigned topic.
- Write your essay on a separate sheet of paper.

PRETEST

─ TOPIC ─

Nowadays, people read less than they did 15 or 20 years ago. Why do people read less today than in the past?

In your essay, tell why you think people read less than they did 15 or 20 years ago. Give specific reasons to back up your ideas.

Part II is a test to determine how well you can use written language to explain your ideas.

In preparing your essay, you should take the following steps:

* Read the **DIRECTIONS** and the **TOPIC** carefully.

* Plan your essay before you write. Use scratch paper to make any notes.

* After you finish writing your essay, reread what you have written and make any changes that will improve your essay.

Your essay should be long enough to develop the topic adequately.

Evaluation guidelines are on page 16.

PRETEST
Part I Answer Key

1. (3) The original sentence contains a comma splice. This answer adds the conjunction *but* to correctly show contrast between the two clauses.

2. (5) The noun *rates* is not a proper noun and should not be capitalized.

3. (3) A comma does not belong between the two nouns *service* and *convenience*.

4. (5) This answer expresses the same thought more efficiently.

5. (2) The rest of this passage is written using the second person, *you*. The plural pronoun *they* is not consistent.

6. (3) This answer correctly positions sentence 9 as a topic sentence to paragraph C, which deals with customer benefits.

7. (4) This change combines two paragraphs. Sentences 12 and 13 belong under the topic sentence of paragraph C.

8. (3) This answer eliminates the wordiness of the original sentence and correctly separates the items in the series—*sadness, hopelessness, loss of energy and pleasure, or difficulty concentrating*.

9. (4) The original sentence contains the contraction *they're*, meaning *they are*, which makes no sense. The possessive pronoun *their* is correct.

10. (2) When the conjunction *or* is used in a compound subject, the verb should agree with the part of the subject closer to it— *someone*. The correct verb is the singular *is*.

11. (3) The original sentence is actually a fragment. This answer corrects the error by changing the verb from *having* to *has*.

12. (1) The passage is in the present tense, so replace *did*, which is past tense, with *does*, which is present tense and agrees with the singular subject, *lack*, and the present-tense verb *is*.

13. (5) A sentence about weight gain and stress on the heart does not belong in this paragraph about symptoms of depression.

14. (5) The two clauses joined here have a cause-effect relationship. The conjunction *so* is a better choice than *but*, which shows contrast.

15. (5) This answer eliminates the wordiness of the original sentence while maintaining parallel structure.

16. (4) The subject of the sentence is *we*, which agrees with the plural verb *are*, not the singular *is*.

17. (5) The correct verb form is *are*, not *be*.

18. (4) The plural possessive pronoun *their* is not correct. The pronoun *its* correctly agrees with the singular antecedent *each*.

19. (4) The original sentence contains a dangling modifier, *possessing one of these toy trucks*. This answer adds a subject to the dependent clause.

20. (2) The original is very repetitive. This answer removes all the extra words and correctly expresses the same thought.

21. (1) The original sentence is correct as written.

22. (3) The present-tense verb *seems* agrees with the tense of the rest of the passage and with the singular subject, *everything*.

23. (4) The main idea of this article is preparing for a move. A sentence about ways to deal with stress does not belong.

24. (2) The original sentence contains a comma splice. This answer corrects the error by deleting the comma and adding the conjunction *and* to create a compound verb.

25. (4) This answer correctly places the modifier *having received your request well in advance* closer to the noun it describes, *companies*.

PRETEST
Part I Evaluation Chart

On the following chart, circle the number of any item you answered incorrectly. Next to each group of item numbers, you will see the pages you can review to learn how to answer the items correctly. Pay particular attention to reviewing skill areas in which you missed half or more of the questions.

Skill Area	Item Number	Review Pages
ORGANIZATION		
Text divisions	6, 7	120–126
Topic sentences		
Unity/coherence	13, 23	127–133
SENTENCE STRUCTURE		
Complete sentences, fragments, and sentence combining	11	19–24, 83–104
Run-on sentences/ comma splices	1, 24	86–88, 96
Wordiness/repetition	4, 8, 20	97–98, 103–104
Coordination/subordination	14	83–84, 89–98
Modification	19, 25	145–153
Parallelism	15	154–156
USAGE		
Subject-verb agreement	10, 16, 22	51–59, 62–73
Verb tense/form	12, 17	51–61, 101–102
Pronoun reference/ antecedent agreement	5, 18	38–42, 157–165
MECHANICS		
Capitalization	2	29, 34–35, 177–178
Punctuation (commas)	3, 21	31, 87, 93, 96, 183–185
Spelling (possessives, contractions, and homonyms)	9	43, 179–182

PRETEST

Part II Evaluation Guidelines

If at all possible, give your instructor your essay to evaluate. You will find his or her objective opinion helpful in deciding whether you are ready for the actual GED. If this is not possible, have another student evaluate your paper. If you cannot find another student to help you, review your paper yourself. If you do this, it is usually better to let your paper sit for a few days before you evaluate it. This way you will experience your essay much the same way a first-time reader will experience it. No matter which way you review your work, think about the following questions as you reread your essay:

1. After you read your topic, did you plan your answer, jotting down ideas for your essay? Was this process easy or hard? If gathering your ideas seemed hard, pay particular attention to Chapter 9 of this book.

2. Did you take time to organize your ideas before you began writing? Was this process easy or hard? For help with organizing your ideas, pay particular attention to Chapter 10.

3. Were you able to write a clear introduction to your essay? Did the introduction clearly indicate the organization of the rest of the essay? For more information on this aspect of writing, see pages 255–258 in Chapter 11.

4. As you were writing your essay, were you able to compose body paragraphs that stated main ideas and supported them with plenty of details? For more information on this aspect of writing, see pages 259–264 in Chapter 11.

5. Were you able to write a clear concluding paragraph for your essay? For help in this area, see pages 265–266 in Chapter 11.

6. After you finished writing, did you revise your essay to improve its content and organization? If you want help in this area, see pages 276–292 in Chapter 12.

7. After you finished writing, did you revise your essay to improve its control of spelling, punctuation, and so on? If you want help in this area, see pages 293–294 in Chapter 12.

If possible, talk to your instructor, another student, or a friend about your feelings as you wrote. Together, you will be able to identify your current writing strengths as well as any weaknesses. Based on this combined evaluation, review the sections of Chapters 9–12 of this book that will help you most in improving your writing.

Editing

CHAPTER 1

Sentence Basics

Parts of a Sentence

Suppose a friend called you on the phone one day and said, "Won the lottery." What would your question be? Wouldn't you want to know *who* won the lottery?

Similarly, if someone said to you, "My next-door neighbor," wouldn't you want to ask, "*What about* your next-door neighbor? What did he or she do?"

And think about this group of words: "When the project is complete." Aren't you left wondering *what happens* "when the project is complete"?

In all three of these cases, the speaker did not use a complete sentence. Information was missing—information that was necessary to make his or her point clear and understandable.

A **sentence** is a basic building block of clear, effective writing.

A group of words must pass three tests in order to be called a sentence.

1. A sentence must have a **subject.** A subject tells the reader whom or what the sentence is about. The first example above is not a sentence because it does not tell you *who* won the lottery.

    My wife's sister won the lottery.

    This sentence has a subject. It tells *who* won the lottery.

2. A sentence must have a **predicate.** A predicate tells the reader what the subject *is* or *does*. The second example above is not a sentence because it does not tell *what* the next-door neighbor *is* or *does*.

    My next-door neighbor plays softball on Tuesday nights.

    This sentence has a predicate. It tells *what* the next-door neighbor *does*.

3. A sentence must express a **complete thought.** The group of words should not leave the reader with unanswered questions. The third example above is not a complete sentence because it does not express a complete thought.

    When the project is complete, you will get a bonus.

    This sentence expresses a complete thought. It tells *what* will happen when the project is complete.

19

A group of words that does not have the three requirements for a complete sentence is called a **fragment** or **sentence fragment.** A group of words can be very short and still be a complete sentence or very long and still be a fragment. In the writing you do on your own and on the Language Arts, Writing Test, a fragment is an error that needs to be corrected.

Let's look at some examples. See if you can tell which groups of words are sentences and which are fragments. Write *S* or *F* on the line for each.

_____ Leaving the office at noon.

_____ The customer will be helped immediately.

_____ This apartment has been rented.

_____ The old graying dentist.

Did you write an *F* for fragment in the first and last word group? The first group is missing a subject. *Who* is leaving the office at noon? The last group does not have a predicate. It does not tell you what the dentist *did*.

The other two word groups are sentences. They have all three elements of a complete sentence.

EXERCISE 1

Directions: One group of words in each pair is a sentence and one is a fragment. Write *S* or *F* on the appropriate line for each.

Examples: __*S*__ Working six days a week is hard on George.

__*F*__ Working six days a week and getting tired.

1. _____ Time on our hands.

   _____ We have time on our hands.

2. _____ The overtired baseball team finished its practice.

   _____ The overtired baseball team next to the bus.

3. _____ While you were sleeping on the couch.

   _____ While you were sleeping, we took your picture.

4. _____ The mileage on your car.

   _____ The mileage on your car is low.

5. _____ Emmanuel works at the front desk.

   _____ Emmanuel at the front desk of the hotel.

6. _____ The idea you had.

   _____ The idea sounds good.

Answers are on page 365.

Identifying the Subject and Predicate

Learning to identify the subject and the predicate in a sentence is essential in avoiding and correcting sentence fragments. This skill will also help you later on when you work on subject-verb agreement.

What is the subject in the sentence below? What is the predicate?

The assignment was written on the whiteboard.

The subject is *The assignment*. It tells you what the sentence is about. The predicate is *was written on the whiteboard*. It tells you what the subject is or does.

In the sentence below, underline the subject once and the predicate twice.

Olivia is in charge of the grand opening.

Did you underline *Olivia* once and *is in charge of the grand opening* twice? If so, you are correct. Read the examples below to get a better idea of how to identify subjects and predicates.

Delivering the mail	was my least favorite part of the job.
SUBJECT	PREDICATE

The store aisles	will be crowded due to the sale.
SUBJECT	PREDICATE

Marty	reads the newspaper first thing every morning.
SUBJECT	PREDICATE

Now practice writing subjects and predicates. Fill in the blanks as indicated.

_____ is my favorite time of day.
SUBJECT

One of my good friends _____.
PREDICATE

The subject you wrote should tell what your favorite time of day is. Your predicate should tell something about one of your good friends.

EXERCISE 2

Part A   **Directions:** Underline the subject of each sentence once. Underline the predicate twice.

Example: My favorite kind of music is salsa.

1. Daniel and his son usually do the housework.

2. The task has been completed.

3. We plan to visit the cemetery on Saturday.

4. Fruits and vegetables are more healthful than candy.

5. Taxes can take a large chunk out of a paycheck.

Part B   **Directions:** Complete the following sentences by adding either a subject or a predicate. Write an *S* if you've added a subject and *P* if you've added a predicate.

Example: *My cat (S)* likes to climb trees.

1. _____ always will be there.

2. When she graduated, _____ threw her a party.

3. The copying machine out back _____ .

4. Sasha thought we would never _____ .

5. Several copies of the memo _____ .

Part C   **Directions:** Read each group of words below. If it is a complete sentence, write *sentence* on the line below it. If it is a fragment, rewrite it adding a subject and/or predicate to make it a complete sentence.

Example: Elsa's old computer.

Elsa's old computer crashed again.

1. The final pages of the book.

_____

2. The supervisor liked what he saw.

_____

3. Hurrying away from the car.

_____

4. Worries about the future.

_____

Answers are on page 365.

Sentence Fragments in a Paragraph

Sometimes a sentence fragment may be difficult to identify because it is part of a paragraph. With other information around it, a fragment may appear to have all the elements of a sentence. Read the following paragraph from a handbook and see if you can identify the fragment.

> The process for store opening is easy to follow if you read the manual carefully. Most employees have no trouble with the lock system and the cash register start-up. Instructions are clearly posted in both locations. Printed in red ink. When you arrive in the morning, be sure to allow yourself at least fifteen minutes of preparation time before you admit customers.

The fragment is *Printed in red ink.* This group of words does not tell *what* is printed in red ink. There is no subject to make it a sentence. You may infer from the rest of the paragraph that it is the instructions that are printed in red ink. This is why fragments are a greater challenge to find when embedded in a paragraph like this one.

EDITING TIP

Read the paragraph first. Then read each group of words separately and decide if the three elements of a complete sentence are present.

Let's look at another example. Where is the fragment in this paragraph?

> At the end of a business day, it is crucial that all employees follow proper closing procedures. Section Two of the manual outlines the necessary steps. Be sure to turn on the phone answering system. When you have phoned in the last security code. Activating safety lights should be the last action taken.

Here is the fragment in this paragraph:

When you have phoned in the last security code.

Although there is a subject, *you,* and a predicate, *have phoned in the last security code,* a complete thought is not expressed. The conjunction *when* is what creates the fragment here. We are left wondering *what happens* when you have phoned in. Even though the information can be found in the paragraph, this group of words is still a fragment because it cannot stand alone.

To make this fragment a complete sentence, you can connect it to another sentence from the paragraph.

Be sure to turn on the phone answering system when you have phoned in the last security code.

EXERCISE 3

<u>Part A</u> **Directions:** Underline the sentence fragment in each paragraph below.

1.   To get to the stadium from your hotel, take a left out the front entrance and walk three blocks to the subway station marked Elmwood. Take the subway westbound for seven stops. Until you reach Huntington Station. Exit the train and follow signs for Shapleigh Stadium. The entire trip should take fewer than 30 minutes.

2.   The largest source of revenue for the organization. Sales of cold drinks are expected to hit record highs this summer, in part due to record high temperatures in June and July. Although proceeds from sandwiches and snacks have not risen dramatically, close to 70 cases of soft drinks per day have been sold. Organization leaders are very pleased with profit outlooks for the year.

3.   We are pleased to announce that Sam Baker is February's Employee of the Month. Sam has consistently met all company-set goals and is a valuable member of the team. In keeping with company policy, Mr. Baker will receive a $1,000 bonus as well as preferred parking in the company lot. Please join us in congratulating Sam. When you see him around the office. He deserves great praise and recognition.

4.   Getting a great deal on a flight for your vacation is possible. If you are able to plan ahead and do some of your own research. Most important, purchase your ticket as soon as you know the dates you will be traveling. Buying 21 days in advance can save you a great deal of money. In addition, try to fly after 7:00 P.M. These flights are less popular for business travelers and can therefore be cheaper. Finally, shop around. Don't assume all airlines are charging the same rate.

<u>Part B</u> **Directions:** Correct the fragments in the paragraph below by joining each fragment to a sentence in the paragraph. Use the lines provided to rewrite the paragraph.

Finding time for yourself. Is an important part of a healthful life. You may be neglecting your own needs. If you are constantly focused on the needs of other people. Research shows that people who set aside time to do what they enjoy are actually better spouses, friends, and coworkers. Than those who spend all their time accommodating others.

_____

_____

_____

_____

_____

Answers are on page 365.

Simple Subjects and Verbs

Now that you've gotten some practice with subjects and predicates, you can focus on what is often called the skeleton of a sentence—the simple subject and the verb. Knowing the skeleton of a sentence will help you identify errors in writing, and it will make you a more effective writer.

The **simple subject** of a sentence is the key word that tells you *whom* or *what* the sentence is about. The simple subject is one word, without any describing words around it. The sentence below has the subject and predicate labeled. Can you find the simple subject?

The red file folder | was put back on his desk.
        SUBJECT   PREDICATE

The simple subject is *folder*. The words *the red file* tell you what kind of folder it is, and these words are not part of the simple subject.

The **verb** in a sentence is the key word in the predicate that tells what the subject *is* or *does*. The verb is usually one or two words, without any describing words around it. What is the verb in the example above?

The verb is *was put*. The words *back on his desk* tell where the folder was put, and these words are not part of the verb.

In the sentences below, circle the simple subject. Then circle the verb. The subjects and predicates are labeled to help you.

Many people | enjoy outdoor activities in the rainy season.
    SUBJECT   PREDICATE

Last month | several smashed mailboxes | were found on our street.
                        SUBJECT   PREDICATE

The fax machines in the storage area | were claimed by the staff.
                SUBJECT   PREDICATE

You should have circled *people, enjoy, mailboxes, were found, machines,* and *were claimed.*

EDITING TIP

To find the skeleton of a sentence, find the verb first. Ask yourself, "What is happening in this sentence?" Then to find the simple subject, ask yourself, "Who or what is doing or being?"

Action versus Linking Verbs

There are two types of verbs that make up all sentences. One is called an action verb. The other is called a linking verb. Learning to tell the difference between these two types of verbs is an important part of writing and editing.

An **action verb** is as it sounds. It describes the action in a sentence. Examples of action verbs are *run, think, purchase, go,* and *remove*.

A **linking verb** is also a lot like it sounds. It links the subject of the sentence to words that describe or rename it. Examples of linking verbs are *be, is, seem, appear, become,* and *were*.

Above the verb in each sentence below, write *action* or *linking*.

The tall man seems older with his hat on.

The tall man gathered up his coat and hat.

Can you see that in the first sentence, the linking verb *seems* joins the subject *man* with the describing word *older*? In the second sentence, the action verb *gathered* describes the action performed by the subject *man*.

EXERCISE 4

Directions: Circle the simple subject in each sentence below. Then circle the verb. Finally, above the verb, write *action* or *linking*.

Example: The tropical (rainforest) (provides) many valuable resources. *action*

1. The two countries have been strong allies.

2. Despite the weather, we hiked every day last week.

3. One new employee quit immediately after the meeting.

4. Time always seems too short.

5. The tattered banner hung awkwardly in the hallway.

6. January arrived with an angry snowstorm.

7. Each member of the team owned a uniform.

8. On Monday new procedures will be in place at Citico.

Answers are on page 365.

Commands, Questions, and *Here* or *There* Statements

With certain kinds of sentences, finding the subject and verb can be a little tricky. Let's look closely at these sentences to see why.

- A **command** is a sentence that tells someone to do something. The subject of a command is always understood to be *you.*

  Be at the warehouse at noon. = [You] <u>be</u> at the warehouse at noon.

SUBJECT VERB

  Danita, please sign here. = Danita, [you] please <u>sign</u> here.

SUBJECT VERB

The name *Danita* in the sentence above is called a **direct address.** It is <u>not</u> the subject of the sentence! The subject of all commands is always *you.*

- A **question** is a sentence that asks something. The verb in a question comes before the subject. To find the subject and verb, rewrite the question as a statement.

  Are the instructions in the box? = The <u>instructions</u> <u>are</u> in the box.

SUBJECT VERB

In some questions the verb consists of more than one word. In this case, part of the verb comes before the subject and part comes after the subject.

  <u>Does</u> <u>Julio</u> <u>want</u> the job? = <u>Julio</u> <u>does want</u> the job.

VERB SUBJECT VERB   SUBJECT VERB

- A *here* or *there* **statement** is a sentence that starts with the word *here* or *there*. In these sentences, the subject comes after the verb. Don't be tricked into thinking that *here* or *there* is the subject—it never is!

  Here are the order forms. = The order <u>forms</u> <u>are</u> here.

SUBJECT VERB

  There seems to be something wrong. = <u>Something</u> <u>seems</u> to be wrong.

SUBJECT VERB

EDITING TIP

To find the skeleton of the sentence in a command, a question, or a *here* or *there* statement, rewrite the sentence so that the subject comes before the verb.

EXERCISE 5

Directions: Find the skeleton in each sentence. First rewrite each sentence as you learned in this lesson. Then write the subject and verb in the spaces provided.

Example: Turn the monitor off before you leave, Roberto.

[You] turn the monitor off before you leave, Roberto.

<u>*You*</u>   <u>*turn*</u>
SUBJECT   VERB

1. Will you take this phone call, Mary?

_____

_____   _____
SUBJECT   VERB

2. Please obey the rules of the game.

_____

_____   _____
SUBJECT   VERB

3. There were several comments written on the page.

_____

_____   _____
SUBJECT   VERB

4. Here are the pictures of your building.

_____

_____   _____
SUBJECT   VERB

5. Ms. Walton, don't tell me your ideas yet.

_____

_____   _____
SUBJECT   VERB

6. Did the supervisor arrive?

_____

_____   _____
SUBJECT   VERB

7. Think about your plans for the job.

_____

_____   _____
SUBJECT   VERB

8. There should be more effort in this.

_____

_____   _____
SUBJECT   VERB

Answers are on page 365.

Rules of the Sentence

There are two more important rules for writing a sentence correctly.

1. **Every sentence must start with a capital letter.**

   Correct: Checks are payable to the Atlantic Phone Company.

   Incorrect: checks are payable to the Atlantic Phone Company.

2. **Every sentence must end with a punctuation mark.**

   A statement ends with a period. Occasionally an exclamation point is appropriate.

   > Saving receipts is a wise habit to develop.

   > We wish you could be here.

   > The deadline has already passed!

   A question ends with a question mark.

   > Will you be at the meeting?

   > Does your friend want to come along?

   A command ends with a period or occasionally an exclamation point.

   > Please be sure you close the door tightly.

   > Call the police!

   <u>Remember:</u> Even if a group of words ends with a punctuation mark, this does not mean it is a complete sentence. Be sure all three parts of a sentence are present!

EXERCISE 6

Directions: Correct this advertisement by putting capital letters and correct end punctuation where they belong. Correct any sentence fragments.

If you are between the ages of 45 and 75, you may want to buy whole life insurance at an affordable rate? Have you considered the future of your dependents. you probably want them to be covered. If you become ill or incapacitated. Call our toll-free number? Hurry.

Answers are on page 366.

Compound Subjects and Verbs

Sometimes when you look for the skeleton of a simple sentence, you may find more than one subject or more than one verb. These are called compounds. A compound is formed by using conjunctions such as *and* and *or*.

What is the predicate in this sentence?

James signed his timecard and handed it in.

You are correct if you said *signed his timecard and handed it in.*

Notice that this predicate actually has <u>two</u> verbs in it—*signed* and *handed*. This is a **compound verb.**

What is the subject in this sentence?

The manager and her staff went out to lunch.

The subject is *the manager and her staff.* The simple subject, *manager and staff*, is called a **compound subject.**

Recognizing compounds will be important later as you begin to work with subject-verb agreement in Chapter 2.

EXERCISE 7

Directions: Write the skeleton of each sentence below. Be sure to include both parts of compound subjects or verbs.

Example: After your meeting, walk the dog and cut the grass.

<u>*You*</u>   <u>*walk and cut*</u>
SUBJECT   VERB

1. Marika and Leroy joined a book club.

   _____   _____
   SUBJECT   VERB

2. Please find a chair or sit on the couch.

   _____   _____
   SUBJECT   VERB

3. The line forms at the right and exits the back door.

   _____   _____
   SUBJECT   VERB

4. More energy and commitment are needed to make this work.

   _____   _____
   SUBJECT   VERB

Answers are on page 366.

MIND ON MECHANICS

Commas with Compounds

There is a lot of confusion about when to use commas in a sentence—especially with compounds. Basically, don't use a comma unless you are <u>absolutely</u> sure you need one! Here are some guidelines.

- **<u>Do not</u> separate a subject from a predicate with a comma.**

Incorrect:	The woman in the yellow dress, is my boss.
Correct:	The woman in the yellow dress is my boss.

- **<u>Do not</u> put a comma between two parts of a compound subject or verb.**

Incorrect:	The tools, and the wire are on the bench.
Correct:	The tools and the wire are on the bench.

Incorrect:	These boxes have been packed, and labeled.
Correct:	These boxes have been packed and labeled.

- **<u>Do</u> use a comma when a compound has three or more subjects or verbs.**
  The comma always follows each part of the compound.

Incorrect:	Do not fold tape or staple this document.
Incorrect:	Do not, fold, tape or staple this document.
Correct:	Do not fold, tape, or staple this document.

Incorrect:	My brothers my father and I went together.
Correct:	My brothers, my father, and I went together.

EXERCISE 8

Directions: Correct the comma errors in this memo by adding commas where needed and crossing out unnecessary commas.

To: Support Staff

From: Marjorie Santiago

Managers, and salespeople will arrive tomorrow. Please be sure that offices conference rooms and lounges are neat and tidy. The documents for the meeting, should be prepared by the end of today. Everyone will need to, greet our colleagues, attend all meetings, and join us for dinner tomorrow night. This conference promises to be the best ever!

Answers are on page 366.

Nouns

A **noun** is a word that labels a person, place, thing, or idea. Being able to identify nouns is an important building block to effective writing. Read the paragraph from a tourist guide below. The nouns appear in **boldface.**

The **Trolley** in **Washington, D.C.,** is a wonderful **form** of **transportation** on which to see the city. The **tour** highlights many of the important historical **sites** in the **area,** as well as **government buildings** and other **attractions.** The **excitement** of seeing the very **square** where **George Washington** lived and worked is beyond **description. Tourists** from all over the **world** enjoy the **narration** of the **tour guide.**

People: George Washington, tourists, tour guide

Places: Washington, D.C., city, square, world

Things: Trolley, form, transportation, tour, sites, area, government buildings, attractions, narration

Ideas: excitement, description

A noun that labels an idea, such as *excitement* or *description* above, is sometimes more difficult to identify than a person, place, or thing. Other examples of idea nouns are *sorrow, bravery, anger, delight,* and *intelligence.*

Can you underline the nouns in the newspaper editorial below?

The time has come to cast a vote for mayor. Although the candidates may not be exactly what we would like to see, there are differences among them that will have an impact on how we live our lives for the next several years. The decision of whom to vote for is less important than the actual act of voting. Please come down to Warner Hall and put a ballot in the box. You will be doing something good for this city.

You should have underlined *time, vote, mayor, candidates, differences, impact, lives, years, decision, act, Warner Hall, ballot, box, something,* and *city.*

When there is more than one of something, a noun often ends in *s.* In the example above, there is more than one candidate, so we write *candidates.* There is more than one difference, so we write *differences.* A noun that names more than one person, place, thing, or idea is called a **plural noun.**

You may also have noticed that a noun can sometimes begin with a capital letter even when it does not begin a sentence. Such nouns are called **proper nouns.** In general, a noun is capitalized if it names a <u>specific</u> person, place, or thing. *Warner Hall* in the paragraph above is the specific name of the hall. You will learn more about capitalizing nouns in the Mind on Mechanics lesson on page 34.

EXERCISE 9

Directions: Underline the nouns in the body of the business letter below.

January 10, 2001
Ms. Tasha Williams
14 Oakwood Street
Apartment 101

Easton, MD 21601

Dear Ms. Williams:

Thank you for your letter, which we received on Monday. We appreciate it when our customers let us know their thoughts about our products.

As you know, we here at The Dairy Company work hard to make excellent dairy products. We believe our yogurt, butter, cheese, and salad dressings are of excellent quality. Each employee here does his or her best work to ensure top quality.

Unfortunately, we do make mistakes. The yogurt you purchased at your local grocery store was mislabeled. The label should have read "Raspberry/Banana" instead of simply "Raspberry." We are sorry that you had to throw away all six cups of yogurt because of this problem.

As an apology to you, Ms. Williams, we have enclosed a coupon with this letter. Take this coupon to a store near your home and you will receive twelve cups of your favorite flavors.

Again, we are sorry for the trouble. Please have a good day.

Sincerely,

Lynette Samuelson
Customer Manager, The Dairy Company

Answers are on page 366.

Proper Nouns

You learned that a proper noun is a noun that names a <u>specific</u> person, place, thing, or idea. All proper nouns should begin with a capital letter.

These rules should help you keep track of when to use a capital letter.

1. **Capitalize specific names.**

   You should turn left on the next **street**.

   You should turn left on **Grove Street**.

   What **day** do you have off next week?

   I have **Monday** off next week, which is **Labor Day**.

   Can you see that in the first sentence of each pair, the boldface word does not name anything specific? In the second sentence of each pair, a *specific* street and day are mentioned.

2. **Capitalize titles.**

   Who is the best **doctor** to see for my eyes?

   I think **Doctor Chen** is the best eye **doctor** in the area.

   The noun *doctor* in *Doctor Chen* is capitalized because it is part of the person's title. The other examples of the noun *doctor* are not part of a specific title.

   I read the newspaper **daily**.

   Our local newspaper is called The **Daily** Journal.

   The noun *Daily* is capitalized in the second sentence because it is part of the newspaper title.

3. **Capitalize the names of places.**

   The sales meeting will be held in **New York City** this year.

   What **city** was it held in last year?

   Last year, the winner of the sales competition went to **North Carolina**.

   The best way to get there is to head **north** on the interstate.

   Can you see that the first sentence in each pair names a specific place, whereas the second sentence in each pair uses a general (also called common) noun?

4. **Capitalize holidays, months, and days of the week, but not seasons.**

    This **May** has been very hot, especially **Memorial Day**.

    Please make an appointment for next **Friday**.

    Mr. Murphy reported that **spring** of 2000 was a successful season.

Remember: There are two kinds of capitalization errors on the Language Arts, Writing Test. One is not capitalizing a proper noun. The other is putting a capital letter on a common noun. Both errors occur often.

EXERCISE 10

Part A   **Directions:** Correct any capitalization errors that appear in the boldfaced words below. Cross out the incorrect letter and write the correct one above it. Not all boldfaced words are incorrect.

Example: **Wendy** plans to move to ~~o~~hio in the ~~S~~pring.

1. Several **Months** ago **John's** supervisor asked him to take on a new **task**.

2. Did you fax the analysis to **senator Jones** before he left for the **Office**?

3. The **Building** on your left is called the **Graymore building**.

4. My **coworkers** prefer to eat at the **japanese** restaurant next **Door**.

5. Both **Hanukkah** and **Christmas** are **Winter holidays**.

Part B   **Directions:** Correct the errors in capitalization in these instructions.

Shopping Wisely

Shopping for Groceries can be a quick errand to grab some Milk. Or it can be an exhausting Day in the aisles of saveway grocery store, in which you do hundreds of math calculations in order to save a few Dollars. writing the week's grocery list before you leave Home can help you buy only what you need. Without a list, you may end up buying on impulse—an extra pint of Ice cream that you really don't need, for example. In addition, the sunday newspaper usually carries lots of valuable coupons that will help you save money. fifty cents off a bottle of clorox bleach can go a long way toward a lower grocery bill, especially if you are not choosy about what kind of Laundry Bleach you use.

Answers are on page 366.

Possessive Nouns

What is an easier, shorter way to write the expression below?

> **the chair that belongs to Kareem**

To show that Kareem owns the chair, we can use this phrase:

> **Kareem's chair**

In this case the noun *Kareem's* is called a **possessive noun.** It means that Kareem *possesses,* or owns, the chair. An apostrophe *(')* and an *s* are used to show possession. Here are some more examples:

> **the dinner that belongs to the guest = the guest's dinner**

> **the report belonging to our group = our group's report**

If the possessive noun is plural (meaning there are more than one), and it ends in *s* as many plurals do, simply add an apostrophe after the final *s* as in this example:

> **the house of the Browns = the Browns' house**

Some plural nouns do not end in an *s.* To form a possessive from these nouns, add an apostrophe and *s.*

> **the clothes of the children = the children's clothes**

Look at how two short sentences can be combined with a possessive noun.

> **The employees have a union. The union voted to strike last Monday.**

> **The employees' union voted to strike last Monday.**

Try combining these two sentences using a possessive noun:

> **James owns a Porsche. The Porsche was stolen from in front of his apartment.**

You should have written *James's Porsche was stolen from in front of his apartment.*

A common writing error is to confuse possessive nouns with plural nouns. Watch out for this mistake! In the sentence below, *flowers* is a plural noun. It does not need an apostrophe.

> **The flowers gave off a wonderful fragrance.**

How is that sentence different from the next one?

One **flower's** fragrance filled the room.

In the sentence above, *flower's* is a possessive, singular noun. The fragrance belongs to one flower. Therefore, an apostrophe is used to show this possession. If there were more than one fragrant flower, the apostrophe would go after the *s*.

EXERCISE 11

Part A **Directions:** Rewrite each pair of sentences using a possessive noun. Be sure to place the apostrophe correctly using the rules you learned on page 36.

Example: Katrina has a bicycle. The bicycle has a flat tire.

Katrina's bicycle has a flat tire.

1. The newspaper has a weather report. The report says it will rain.

    _____

2. The girls had an argument. The argument ended when their mother called.

    _____

3. The town has a pool. The pool is closed for cleaning.

    _____

4. Marcus has a dog. The dog is a Labrador retriever.

    _____

5. The Binders have an apartment. The apartment is down the street.

    _____

6. Women have clothing. The clothing is often impractical.

    _____

Part B **Directions:** Insert apostrophes wherever they are needed in the memo below. Also, cross out or move any incorrect apostrophes.

To: All Night-Shift Employees'

This shifts performance this past week has not been of high quality. The managers office was not vacuumed last night, and the hall's have not been vacuumed all week. Our contracts' clearly state that this shifts responsibilities include vacuuming. Please do better on next weeks shift.

Answers are on page 366.

Pronouns

Compare these two sentences:

Yolanda saw the book and immediately bought the book.

Yolanda saw the book and immediately bought **it**.

The word *it* in the sentence above is called a **pronoun.** It takes the place of a noun that came before it—*book.* Can you see that the second sentence is less repetitive than the first one? Pronouns are used to make writing more interesting and less cumbersome.

Here are some more examples of pronouns at work. Notice that pronouns can replace all kinds of nouns.

Please fill out the form and leave **it** at the front desk.

THE FORM

David met Margaret, and **he** married **her**.

DAVID   MARGARET

The parents dropped **their** children off at the playground.

THE PARENTS'

The noun that a pronoun replaces is called the **antecedent.** Different pronouns are used to refer to singular antecedents and plural antecedents, as well as to males and females. In the next few lessons you'll get lots of practice working with pronouns of all kinds.

EXERCISE 12

Directions: For each boldfaced pronoun below, write the antecedent—the noun that the pronoun refers to.

Example: When Gerard works the night shift, **he** sometimes gets bored.

Gerard

When Gerard works the night shift, **it** sometimes gets boring.

shift

1. When Les buys cookies, she eats **them** all right away. _____

2. When Les buys cookies, **she** eats them all right away. _____

3. Susan and Rob took **his** car to work today. _____

4. Susan and Rob took **their** car to work today. _____

5. The clerk stocked the shelves, then **he** went home. _____

6. The clerk stocked the shelves, then he labeled **them**. _____

Answers are on page 366.

Pronoun Forms

Read the sentences below and see how the same noun can be replaced by different pronouns, depending on how the noun is used in the sentence.

Noun as Subject:	**The man** grasped my hand firmly.
Pronoun as Subject:	**He** grasped my hand firmly.
Noun as Object:	I thanked **the man** for helping me.
Pronoun as Object:	I thanked **him** for helping me.
Possessive Noun:	**The man's** voice silenced the crowd.
Possessive Pronoun:	**His** voice silenced the crowd.

This chart summarizes how some pronouns change in form depending on their use in a sentence.

Subject	Object	Possessive with a Noun	Possessive without a Noun
I	me	my	mine
you	you	your	yours
he	him	his	his
she	her	her	hers
it	it	its	---
we	us	our	ours
they	them	their	theirs
who	whom	whose	whose

To decide which pronoun to use, follow these guidelines:

• When a pronoun is the subject of a sentence, use a pronoun from the first column.

   She will make a great president.   **not**   **Her** will make a great president.

• When a pronoun is not a subject or a possessive, use an object pronoun from the second column.

   Give the food to **them**.   **not**   Give the food to **they**.

• When a pronoun shows possession with a noun after it, use a pronoun from the third column.

   The people took **their** seats.   **not**   The people took **they** seats.

• When a pronoun shows possession without a noun after it, use a pronoun from the last column.

   Those documents are **mine**.   **not**   Those documents are **my**.

EXERCISE 13

Part A **Directions:** Use the chart on page 39 to help you choose the correct pronoun for each sentence below. Underline the correct choice.

Example: Drop (*my*, *mine*) book off at the library, please.

1. (*Us*, *We*) heard the news on the radio this morning.

2. The song they played was (*their*, *theirs*) favorite tune.

3. The computer fell off (*it*, *its*) stand during the move.

4. The instructions say to bring (*you*, *your*) files with you Saturday.

5. Please offer (*she*, *her*) the hamburger and fries.

6. Is that hotel across the street (*our*, *ours*)?

Part B **Directions:** Replace the boldfaced nouns below with the correct pronoun. Think about whether you need a subject, object, or possessive pronoun.

Example: The decision to take ~~Joe and Lisa's~~ *their* complaint to the store manager was ~~Joe and Lisa's~~ *theirs*.

1. **Christine** is a lawyer and a power weightlifting champion.

2. The Russians challenged **President Kennedy** by sending missiles to Cuba.

3. Chun insisted, "**Chun's** favorite vegetables really are rutabagas."

4. Dick assembled the scooter within an hour after buying **the scooter**.

5. Who told **the senators** that we would support **the senators'** decision?

6. My friends, please give me **my friends'** trust.

7. Why do weddings make **that woman** sad?

8. **Doug and Hannah** were delighted with the news.

Answers are on page 367.

Pronouns in Compounds

Sometimes it is difficult to figure out which pronoun to use in a sentence. Which sentence below sounds correct?

Angela processed the report for Paulo and **I**.

Angela processed the report for Paulo and **me**.

To help you decide, cross out one part of the compound—*Paulo and*. Would you say *Angela processed the report for I*? Or *Angela processed the report for me*?

You are correct if you chose the object pronoun *me*. Try the crossing-out technique with the example below. Which pronoun is correct?

Jim or **(I, me)** will be in charge of this year's event.

If you ignore *Jim or* in this sentence, you can probably see that the subject pronoun *I* is correct here. *Jim or I will be in charge of this year's event.*

EXERCISE 14

Directions: Underline the correct pronoun in each sentence.

Example: You and (I, me) were chosen to present the sales award at the company banquet.

1. Keep an eye on Young-Soo and *(she, her)* until we get back.

2. Where did Jessica and *(he, him)* go after work yesterday?

3. The flu hit *(he, him)* and *(I, me)* hard this winter.

4. *(They, them)* and their supervisors will be at the conference this week.

5. When Scott and *(him, he)* spoke, the audience was silent.

6. They met the Johnsons and *(we, us)* at the theater.

7. Give the check to Renata or *(I, me)*, please.

8. A new apartment would give Joe and *(they, them)* more space.

Answers are on page 367.

EXERCISE 15

Directions: Correct the pronoun errors in the letter below.

Dear Mr. Howe:

My wife and me would like to complain about the poor condition of the apartment complex. Yours superintendent here, Mrs. Mitchell, is not doing she job very well at all.

The hallways are never swept, and we can see dust and dirt all over they. We have told Mrs. Mitchell about the hallways, but when will her clean them? Both her and her son seem lazy.

In addition the garbage sits in it bin for more than a week, smelling up the building incredibly. The stench really bothers my wife and I. Mrs. Mitchell and her son should take theirs job more seriously.

You or her must take care of this problem, Mr. Howe. Otherwise, us will have to start looking for a new apartment. Please be considerate of yours tenants. We do not want to move.

Sincerely,

Kenneth and Rawanda Jones
Apartment 125A

Answers are on page 367.

Contractions, Possessives, and Plurals

Many writers get confused about when to use apostrophes. Much of this confusion is caused because of "soundalike words," called **homonyms.** Let's look at some examples of homonyms.

> The disk should be put back in **its** sleeve.

> I believe **it's** time for our lunch break.

In the first sentence *its* is a possessive pronoun that refers back to *the disk*. In the second sentence *it's* is a contraction meaning *it is*. A **contraction** is two words, shortened and joined together with the use of an apostrophe.

Possessives and contractions get confusing because we think of all possessives as needing an apostrophe. Remembering one simple fact should help:

Possessive nouns need apostrophes; possessive pronouns <u>do not</u> use apostrophes.

Here are some confusing homonyms—possessive pronouns and contractions. Notice how they follow the simple rule above.

Possessive Pronouns	**Contractions**
its	it's (it is, it has)
theirs	there's (there is)
your	you're (you are)
whose	who's (who is)

Another common writing error is using an apostrophe to form a plural noun. This error is also made because a plural noun can sound just like a possessive noun.

Incorrect:	The neighbor's are getting loud.
Correct:	The neighbors are getting loud.
Correct:	The neighbors' voices are getting loud.

The first sentence is incorrect because it uses an apostrophe in a plural noun that is not intended to show possession. The next two sentences are correct. One shows a simple plural; the other shows a possessive plural with an apostrophe.

EXERCISE 16

Directions: Correct the pronoun, possessive, and plural errors in this excerpt from a health pamphlet.

Healthful Sleeping

Its a common problem, say doctor's. People are not getting enough healthful sleep. "There's growing concern," reports Dr. John Santiago of North Medical Center, "that stress and unhealthful habit's are preventing many people from getting the sleep they need to function well." The good news, however, is that theirs a lot you can do about it.

First of all, doctors advise, pay attention to you're sleep patterns. Do you stay up late reading in bed, then have difficulty falling asleep? Or do you fall asleep quickly, only to awaken several time's a night? The person whose aware of his or her sleeping patterns is already on the track to a better night's sleep.

Surprisingly enough, what you eat can affect how you sleep. If your the kind of person who eats a large, spicy dinner accompanied by beer or wine, there's evidence that you're sleep may be affected. "Its simple," states Dr. Santiago. "Your body is like a machine. One system affects another." His advice is to eat smaller meal's throughout the day rather than one huge one shortly before bed. In addition, he says, alcohol creates sleep disturbances. "It's sedative qualities induce sleep unnaturally," says the doctor.

What about people who sleep too much? "There's is sometimes a more serious problem," states Dr. Santiago. "A person who sleeps a lot during the day may have some kind of physical illness that he's unaware of. Or perhaps depression is the cause. Either way, its a problem that a doctors appointment will help solve."

Answers are on page 367.

Sentence Basics: Editing Practice

Directions: The following passage contains errors in sentence basics. Find and correct these errors using this checklist as your editing guide:

☐ Are all sentences complete or are there fragments?

☐ Do sentences end with a period, question mark, or exclamation point?

☐ Do any unnecessary commas separate the subject from the predicate?

☐ Are commas in compounds placed correctly?

☐ Are proper nouns capitalized and common nouns not capitalized?

☐ Are all pronouns correct in form?

☐ Are apostrophes used correctly?

PROTECT YOUR FUTURE
Get a MajorBank Rollover IRA Now!

Are you planning on retirement soon? Or are you changing jobs? If so, think about you're financial needs. You might consider a lump-sum distribution from your Employer. This is a popular course of action. Taken by many people. But is it a wise move.

Financial experts across the country, believe there is a better way. With a rollover IRA you can avoid taxes IRS penalties and unnecessary paperwork. Here's what Arthur C. Evans of chicago, illinois, says about his MajorBank rollover IRA: "I received, personalized attention from a retirement specialist. Him turned out to be a real help to my wife and I. When we needed investment advice."

Without a rollover IRA, your risking up to 35 percent of you're savings to federal, and state taxes. In addition, they're might be early withdrawal penalties. Call MajorBank now? To get your free brochure.

Answers are on page 367.

Chapter Review

Directions: Choose the <u>one best answer</u> to each question. Some of the sentences may contain errors. A few sentences, however, may be correct as written. Read the sentences carefully and then answer the questions based on them. For each question, choose the answer that would result in the most effective writing of the sentence or sentences.

Questions 1–8 refer to the following newspaper article.

Rowe Fund Awards Grant to EEG

(A)

(1) In June the Environment Education Group was awarded a grant of $50,000 by the Harriet S. Rowe Fund to continue it's work building public support for better labeling on food products purchased in the United States. (2) The Rowe Fund has been in existence for 35 years, with a focus on meeting consumer needs in an increasingly complex world. (3) Mary Davidson is the founder, director, and spokesperson for EEG. (4) Both the assistant director and her were present to receive the award.

(B)

(5) "We are delighted to be the recipients of this award," stated Ms. Davidson. (6) "EEG is committed to informing consumers of they're rights concerning the foods they and their families consume every day. (7) Food is so essential to us. (8) That without it, we die. (9) However, what do we know about the synthetic hormones chemicals and pesticides that are ingested by humans each day? (10) We believe consumers would be shocked. (11) To learn how impure some of their daily foods really are. (12) More detailed food labeling is a basic consumer right."

(C)

(13) At the Rowe Fund annual meeting held this year in detroit, Michigan, several other awards were granted. (14) Among the largest of the grants was a $100,000 gift to researcher Dr. Harold Kim. (15) Dr. Kim has been involved in exploring the effects of ozone layer depletion in Countries close to the equator.

1. **Sentence 1: In June the Environment Education Group was awarded a grant of $50,000 by the Harriet S. Rowe Fund to continue it's work building public support for better labeling on food products purchased in the United States.**

   What correction should be made to sentence 1?

   (1) change *June* to *june*
   (2) change *it's* to *its*
   (3) change *it's* to *its'*
   (4) change *products* to *product's*
   (5) change *States* to *states*

2. **Sentence 4: Both the assistant director and her were present to receive the award.**

   What correction should be made to sentence 4?

   (1) replace *assistant* with *Assistant*
   (2) change *director* to *director's*
   (3) replace *her* with *hers*
   (4) replace *her* with *she*
   (5) no correction is necessary

3. Sentence 6: **EEG is committed to informing <u>consumers of they're rights</u> concerning the foods they and their families consume every day.**

   Which is the best way to write the underlined portion of the text? If the original is the best way, choose option (1).

   (1) consumers of they're rights
   (2) consumer's of they're rights
   (3) consumers of their rights
   (4) consumers of they are rights
   (5) consumers of they're right's

4. Sentences 7 and 8: **Food is so essential <u>to us. That without it,</u> we die.**

   Which is the best way to write the underlined portion of the text? If the original is the best way, choose option (1).

   (1) to we. That without it
   (2) to us that without them
   (3) to we, that without it
   (4) to us that without it
   (5) to you that without it

5. Sentence 9: **However, what do we know about <u>the synthetic hormones chemicals and pesticides</u> that are ingested by humans each day?**

   Which is the best way to write the underlined portion of the text? If the original is the best way, choose option (1).

   (1) the synthetic hormones chemicals and pesticides
   (2) the synthetic hormones, chemicals, and pesticides
   (3) the, synthetic hormones, chemicals, and pesticides
   (4) the synthetic hormone's chemical's and pesticide's
   (5) the synthetic hormones chemicals and pesticides,

6. Sentences 10 and 11: **We believe consumers would be <u>shocked. To learn</u> how impure some of their daily foods really are.**

   Which is the best way to write the underlined portion of the text? If the original is the best way, choose option (1).

   (1) shocked. To learn
   (2) shocked, to learn
   (3) shocked to learn
   (4) Shocked to learn
   (5) shocked, To learn

7. Sentence 13: **At the Rowe Fund annual meeting held this year in detroit, Michigan, several other awards were granted.**

   What correction should be made to sentence 13?

   (1) change *detroit* to *Detroit*
   (2) change *Michigan* to *michigan*
   (3) change *awards* to *award's*
   (4) insert a comma after *awards*
   (5) no correction is necessary

8. Sentence 15: **Dr. Kim has been involved in exploring the effects of ozone layer depletion in Countries close to the equator.**

   What correction should be made to sentence 15?

   (1) change *Dr.* to *dr.*
   (2) insert a comma after *Dr. Kim*
   (3) change *effects* to *effect's*
   (4) change *Countries* to *countries*
   (5) change *Countries* to *Country's*

Questions 9–15 refer to the following application letter.

Kristin Smith, Human Resources Manager
Hartford Electrical Services
4815 W. Allen Street
Hartford, CT 06150

Dear Ms. Smith:

(A)

(1) I am writing to apply for the job you advertised in the *hartford daily news*. (2) My résumé is enclosed, and I think you will see that my experience is perfect for you're company. (3) In this letter I will highlight my reasons for believing we are a good match.

(B)

(4) I have been employed at Johnson Electric for seven years now. (5) Thinking I have been here long enough. (6) My boss is a good person. (7) Me and him get along well, and we work well together. (8) However, the job just does not have the same excitement for me that it used to. (9) When I first started at Johnson, I was learning new things every day, and each day was different. (10) Now I feel I am just going through the same boring motions. (11) And one is starting to think that I am ready for a change.

(C)

(12) I am looking for a position that will interest challenge and excite me. (13) Its a question of my priorities. (14) I would actually accept a smaller paycheck if it meant I would be happy going to work each day. (15) This is, where your company comes in. (16) Please read over my résumé and give me a call at your earliest possible convenience.

Sincerely,
Charles Cruz

9. **Sentence 1: I am writing to apply for the job you advertised in the *hartford daily news*.**

   What correction should be made to sentence 1?

   (1) insert a comma after *writing*
   (2) insert a comma after *job*
   (3) change *hartford daily news* to *Hartford Daily News*
   (4) change *news* to *new's*
   (5) no correction is necessary

10. **Sentence 2: My résumé is enclosed, and I think you will see that my experience is perfect for you're company.**

    What correction should be made to sentence 2?

    (1) replace *I* with *me*
    (2) replace *you* with *your*
    (3) replace *my* with *mine*
    (4) change *you're* to *your*
    (5) no correction is necessary

11. Sentence 5: <u>Thinking I</u> have been here long enough.

Which is the best way to write the underlined portion of the text? If the original is the best way, choose option (1).

(1) Thinking I
(2) Thinking my
(3) thinking I
(4) Think I
(5) I think I

12. Sentence 7: <u>Me and him</u> get along well, and we work well together.

Which is the best way to write the underlined portion of the text? If the original is the best way, choose option (1).

(1) Me and him
(2) him and me
(3) I and him
(4) He and I
(5) He and me

13. Sentence 11: **And one is starting to think that I am ready for a change.**

The most effective revision of sentence 11 would begin with which group of words?

(1) One is ready for
(2) We are starting
(3) Starting to think,
(4) I am starting to think
(5) no correction is necessary

14. Sentence 13: **Its a question of my priorities.**

Which is the best way to write the sentence? If the original is the best way, choose option (1).

(1) Its a question of my priorities.
(2) It's a question of my priorities.
(3) Its a question of mine priorities.
(4) Its a question of my priority's.
(5) Its a question, of my priorities.

15. Sentence 15: **This is, where your company comes in.**

What correction should be made to sentence 15?

(1) remove the comma after *is*
(2) change *your* to *you're*
(3) change *company* to *Company*
(4) insert a *comma* after *company*
(5) no correction is necessary

Answers are on page 368.

Evaluate Your Progress

On the following chart, circle the number of any item you answered incorrectly in the Chapter 1 Review on pages 46–49. Next to each group of item numbers, you will see the pages you can review to learn how to answer the items correctly. Pay particular attention to reviewing skill areas in which you missed half or more of the questions.

Skill Area	Chapter 1 Review Item Number	Review Pages
SENTENCE STRUCTURE		
Complete sentences, fragments, and sentence combining	4, 6, 11	19–24
USAGE		
Pronoun reference/ antecedent agreement	2, 12, 13	38–42
MECHANICS		
Capitalization	7, 8, 9	29, 34–35
Punctuation (commas)	5, 15	31
Spelling (possessives, contractions, and homonyms)	1, 3, 10, 14	43

EXERCISE 1

Part A   **Directions:** Underline the correct verb for each sentence below. Circle any clue words you find in the sentence.

Example: (Later) today, Jean (*filed, file, <u>will file</u>*) the final paperwork.

1. I (*mailed, mail, will mail*) the letter tomorrow.

2. James (*satisfied, satisfies, will satisfy*) the course requirement in 1990.

3. Every day Harriet takes the #152 bus downtown and (*arrived, arrives, will arrive*) at nine o'clock.

4. Several times last month our bank balance (*dipped, dips, will dip*) below the $200 minimum.

5. My wife usually (*skipped, skips, will skip*) breakfast and makes up for it at lunch.

6. Each day the sun (*dipped, dips, will dip*) below the horizon while we watch.

7. The meeting (*began, begins, will begin*) later this morning.

8. The boy always (*liked, likes, will like*) what he sees.

Part B   **Directions:** Complete each sentence below, being careful to use the correct verb tense.

Example: Yesterday *we cleaned the apartment.*

1. During 1999 _____

_____.

2. Next month _____

_____.

3. When my friend was younger, _____

_____.

4. Every day I _____

_____.

5. When I think about myself, I _____

_____.

6. Before I die, _____.

Answers are on page 368.

Continuing Tenses

The continuing tenses are used to show action in progress or action that is ongoing—in the past, present, or future.

The **present continuing tense** shows action happening now.

John **is staring** at me.

The **past continuing tense** shows past action that continued for some time.

We **were planning** a meeting that addressed those issues.

The **future continuing tense** shows ongoing action in the future.

The staff **will be staying** several hours late tonight.

Continuing tenses are formed with a helping verb (a form of *have, do,* or *be*) plus the base verb ending in *ing*. The chart below will help you understand this.

Present Continuing	I	am	looking
	he, she, it, and all singular nouns	is	looking
	we, you, they, and all plural nouns	are	looking
Past Continuing	I, he, she, it, and all singular nouns	was	looking
	we, you, they, and all plural nouns	were	looking
Future Continuing	I, he, she, it, we, you, they, and all nouns	will be	looking

EXERCISE 2

Directions: Underline the correct continuing tense in each sentence below.

Example: I (*am starting, was starting, will be starting*) to relax last weekend.

1. Tomorrow you (*are flying, were flying, will be flying*) to Puerto Rico.

2. Right now I (*am thinking, was thinking, will be thinking*) about you.

3. The visitors (*are leaving, were leaving, will be leaving*) next Wednesday.

4. Ron (*is doing, was doing, will be doing*) some research last week.

Answers are on page 368.

Perfect Tenses

The **perfect tenses** are used to show action completed before or continuing to a specific time.

The Present Perfect Tense

The **present perfect tense** shows action that started in the past and continues into the present or has just been completed.

> Sam **has worked** here since 1998.
> *(Sam worked here in the past and is still working here.)*

> I **have finished** my book.
> *(I finished the book in the recent past.)*

To form the present perfect tense of regular verbs, use either *has* or *have* and the base form of the verb plus *ed*.

he, she, it, and all singular nouns	has	looked
I, you, we, they, and all plural nouns	have	looked

Complete this sentence using a present perfect verb:

I think that newspapers _____ .

The Past Perfect Tense

The **past perfect tense** is used to show action that took place before a specified time in the past.

> By the afternoon, the meeting **had ended.**

To form the past perfect tense of regular verbs, combine *had* with the base form of the verb plus *ed*.

I, you, he, she, it, we, they, and all nouns	had looked

Complete this sentence using a past perfect verb:

By last month, _____ .

The Future Perfect Tense

The **future perfect tense** shows action that will be completed by a specified time in the future.

> By next year I **will have finished** this project.

To form the future perfect tense of regular verbs, combine *will have* with the base form of the verb plus *ed*.

I, you, he, she, it, we, they, and all nouns	will have looked

Complete this sentence using a future perfect verb:

> By the end of next year _____.

Time Clues to Perfect Tenses

Phrases beginning with the word *by* often signal a perfect tense.

> By the end of the day the recycling crew **had picked** up the trash.

Sometimes a phrase like *for the past. . .* or *for the last. . .* can signal a perfect tense.

> For the last nine months they **have waited** for this baby.

EXERCISE 3

Directions: Underline the correct verb tense in each sentence below.

Example: For the past year, Sonya (*lived*, *has lived*, *will have lived*) on Long Road.

1. By six o'clock last night we (*cleaned*, *have cleaned*, *had cleaned*) the car.

2. Raoul (*worked*, *has worked*, *will have worked*) for me for the last five years.

3. Jane (*talked*, *will talk*, *will have talked*) to her mother last night.

4. By this time next week you (*are passing*, *pass*, *will have passed*) this test.

5. Before last week's race, I (*have*, *had*, *will have*) run over 200 miles.

6. The mayor (*makes*, *had made*, *will make*) his decision next Sunday.

Answers are on page 368.

Irregular Verbs

So far you have worked with **regular verbs,** which follow a familiar pattern, such as adding *ed* to form a past tense. Most verbs in the English language follow these regular rules.

However, there are many important verbs that do not follow these rules. What is wrong with the sentences below?

Last week we seed the new movie at the Cineplex.

The jury finded the defendant not guilty.

Verbs such as *see* and *find* are called **irregular verbs.** Their past tense is not formed by adding *ed* to the base. Here are the corrected sentences:

Last week we saw the new movie at the Cineplex.

The jury found the defendant not guilty.

When you are studying irregular verbs, the three parts of each verb that you must learn are the present form, the simple past tense, and the **past participle,** which is used in all perfect tenses. Regular verbs all simply add *ed* or *d* to form the past tense and past participle. Irregular verbs do not follow this pattern for the past tense and the past participle.

Some irregular verbs are used so frequently that learning them is essential to effective writing. The chart below shows some of these important verbs and how to form their tenses. Consider memorizing these words before the GED Test.

Essential Irregular Verbs

Base Verb	Present Tense	Past Tense	Perfect Tense*
be	am, is, are	was, were	(have, has, had) been
do	do, does	did	(have, has, had) done
have	has, have	had	(have, has, had) had
go	go, goes	went	(have, has, had) gone
come	come, comes	came	(have, has, had) come
run	run, runs	ran	(have, has, had) run
see	see, sees	saw	(have, has, had) seen
bring	bring, brings	brought	(have, has, had) brought

*If you use a perfect-tense verb, be sure to add the correct helping verb in front, as shown on the chart.

Complete each sentence using one of the irregular verbs from the chart.

The last movie I saw _____ .

From the grocery store I _____ .

Troublesome Verb Pairs

Because they sound so much alike, yet have slightly different meanings, three verb pairs are tricky to use correctly: *lie–lay, sit–set,* and *rise–raise*.

The first verb in each pair *(lie, sit,* and *rise)* is used when the subject of the sentence is moving (or resting).

Our dog **lies** in the shade of the bushes on hot days.

We like to **sit** on the edge of the pier and dangle our feet into the lake.

I **rise** reluctantly from my warm bed on cold winter mornings.

The second verb in each pair *(lay, set,* and *raise)* is used when the subject of the sentence moves an object.

Before I go to bed each night, I **lay** my clothing out for the next day.

Sofia usually **sets** her briefcase under her desk.

Jennifer **raises** her shades to let the morning sun into her room.

The charts below summarize the forms of these pairs of verbs.

Subject is Moving

Present Tense	Past Tense	Perfect Tense*
lie(s)	lay	(have, has, had) lain
sit(s)	sat	(have, has, had) sat
rise(s)	rose	(have, has, had) risen

Subject Moves an Object

Present Tense	Past Tense	Perfect Tense*
lay(s)	laid	(have, has, had) laid
set(s)	set	(have, has, had) set
raise(s)	raised	(have, has, had) raised

*If you use a perfect-tense verb, be sure to add the correct helping verb in front, as shown on the chart.

E D I T I N G   T I P

The same spelling is used for the past tense of *lie* and the present tense of *lay*. You must use the context of the sentence to reveal the difference in meaning.

EXERCISE 4

Part A   **Directions:** Underline the correct verb to complete each sentence. If you choose the perfect tense, circle its helping verb. Some helping verbs may be part of a contraction, such as *I've (I have)* or *it's (it has)*.

Example: Jackie (has) (do, <u>done</u>, did) a good job on the report.

1. The management hopes your visit has *(went, gone)* well.

2. Last night we *(seen, saw)* a show about humpback whales.

3. Have we *(run, runned, ran)* out of brown sugar?

4. Jamaal *(bringed, brought, brung)* his new girlfriend over to meet his folks.

5. Who *(lay, laid)* this money on my desk?

6. The dog just *(comed, came, come)* in with burrs on his coat.

7. We *(were, been)* expecting your call sooner.

8. Lisa's *(ran, run, runned)* the Boston Marathon before.

9. Don't *(sit, set)* on that chair with the broken leg.

10. The truth is that I *(is, am, are)* proud of your achievements.

Part B   **Directions:** Correct the verb errors in the memo below.

To: All Employees

From: Ms. Dasio

We have came to the end of our fiscal year, and it was now my pleasure to announce our budget results. Although we runned over on some expenses, I am happy to report that we done well. We have reached our sales goals for the year! With that happy news it is clear that by next September we had become leaders in the company. Congratulations on a job well done.

Last year at this time, as you may recall, things will not look so rosy. We was in debt, and the president of our division have predicted disaster. So we should be proud of what we done and rise our expectations even higher for next year.

Answers are on page 368.

Using Consistent Verb Tenses

You have seen how time clues can tell you what verb tense is correct in a sentence. But you also know that these clues do not appear in every sentence. In a paragraph or longer piece of writing it is very important not to switch verb tenses unnecessarily. Inconsistent verb tense confuses the reader.

What verb tense seems out of place in this memo?

> This report serves as a summary of what I learned on the recent Jameston Factory tour. I arrived last Friday, March 3, at 9:00 A.M. The production process had already begun, and Ms. Gordon will be my tour guide. She began the tour by taking me to the refinery area, where raw materials are collected and stored. She then proceeded to the molding area, where the actual forms are made.

Did you find that the use of the future tense *will be* in the third sentence is incorrect? The other verbs are in the past tense to describe the tour that took place in the past. In addition, some present-tense verbs are used to describe something that is always true. The use of a future-tense verb to describe a past action is incorrect.

Some of the questions on Part I of the GED Language Arts, Writing Test will ask you to make sure that verb tense is consistent in a piece of writing. In addition, you will want to pay attention to verb tense in your own writing.

Of course, sometimes a switch in verb tense is appropriate. Just because a verb tense is not exactly the same as the others in a paragraph does not mean it is incorrect. Which tense is not consistent with those in the rest of this memo?

> During the tour, factory workers were attentive and engaged in the tasks before them. They operated the machinery safely and accurately. The supervisors walked around the floor, assisting anyone who needed help. They will have cleaned up any excess trash in the area. I will be happy to give more details of this tour if anyone would like.

The future perfect tense *will have cleaned* is not necessary in this paragraph. The simple past *cleaned* would be correct. However, the future tense *will be happy* in the last sentence is correct even though the other verbs in this paragraph are past tense. The writer is talking about an event that will happen in the future.

EXERCISE 5

Directions: Find and correct the verb errors in this letter of request. Pay particular attention to inconsistent verb tenses.

April 5, 2001

Mr. Robert Enright
334A Bloom Avenue
San Francisco, CA 94160

Dear Mr. Enright:

I be writing to you to request a letter of recommendation for a manager's job for which I am applying at the Downtown Sports Arena. I believe I was a perfect candidate for this position, and I think you will be able to say something positive about my qualifications.

As you know, I was a basketball instructor in your program from January 1999 until January 2000. I will have been a great member of your team. The kids in my class and my fellow instructors liked me and admired me. If you check my employment record, you will find that I was taking only one sick day that year and was never late for work. In fact, on many occasions, I will work overtime when the other instructors didn't show up for work.

I hope to become a manager for the Downtown Sports Arena, and I think I did a good job as a manager there. If you are willing to write a recommendation for me, I will be very grateful. I seen that you are a good person, and I enjoyed working for you.

Sincerely,

Joe Robinson

Answers are on page 369.

Basic Subject-Verb Agreement

Now that you have learned how to choose and write the correct verb tense, you're halfway to achieving proper verb form. Your final step is to learn how to make verbs agree with their subjects.

Choosing a present-tense verb to match a singular or plural subject is called **subject-verb agreement.**

Look at the two pairs of sentences below. Why is the first sentence in each pair correct and the second sentence incorrect?

The employees **think** the manager is unreasonable.

The employees **thinks** the manager is unreasonable.

The manager **wants** to open the office at 6:00 A.M.

The manager **want** to open the office at 6:00 A.M.

The verb *think* is correct in the first sentence because the subject *employees* is plural, so you do not include an *s* at the end of the verb. The verb *wants* is correct because the subject *manager* is singular and an *s* is needed at the end of the verb. (Review this basic rule on page 51.)

Notice the subject-verb agreement patterns below:

I

You

We   **hate** to get up in the morning.

They

(and any plural noun)

He

She   **hates** to get up in the morning.

It

(and any singular noun)

Basic Rules for Subject-Verb Agreement

1. The present-tense verbs of singular subjects (except *I* and *you*) end in *s*.

2. The present-tense verbs of plural subjects (and *I* and *you*) do not end in *s*.

Some verbs may end in *es*, as you learned on page 51. Here are some examples:

I, You, We, They, The dogs   **lurch** into the kitchen.

He, She, It, The dog   **lurch<u>es</u>** into the kitchen.

In general, verbs ending in a "hissing" sound (*s*, *sh*, *ch*, *x*, and *z*) take an *es* ending.

EDITING TIP

Remember the rules of subject-verb agreement when you use contractions such as *doesn't* and *don't* or *isn't* and *aren't*.

He **doesn't** do the dishes.
They **don't** do the dishes.

As with many skills in the conventions of English, the more you practice, the easier the rules will be to understand and remember.

EXERCISE 6

Directions: Underline the verb form that is correct in each sentence. Remember the subject-verb agreement rules for singular and plural subjects.

Example: George *(take, <u>takes</u>)* the bus to work.

1. She *(doesn't, don't)* work here anymore.

2. We *(was, were)* just getting ready to leave.

3. They *(live, lives)* on less than one hundred dollars per week.

4. It *(don't, doesn't)* make sense anymore.

5. Every morning Jim *(jog, jogs)* to work.

6. Even thunderstorms *(doesn't, don't)* stop him.

7. The votes *(has, have)* been counted for every precinct.

8. Harriet's job *(is, are)* challenging but rewarding.

9. Each person in my office *(look, looks)* tired.

10. You *(think, thinks)* that's too good to be true.

Answers are on page 369.

Compound Subjects

The subjects in the sentences below are almost exactly the same, but the verb forms are not. Why? Circle the words that are different in the two sentences below.

Samantha and Luigi eat out every night.

Samantha or Luigi eats out every night.

Did you circle the connecting words *and* and *or* as well as the verbs? The connecting words form **compound subjects,** and they let you know whether the subject is singular or plural.

Samantha <u>and</u> Luigi = two people, so this subject is plural. Therefore, use the verb form that agrees with a plural subject: *eat.*

Samantha <u>or</u> Luigi = one person, not both. In this case, the verb should agree with the subject closer to it. Luigi is a singular subject, so the verb is *eats.*

Which verb is correct in the sentence below?

Either Rashad or the twins *(walk, walks)* the dog hourly.

A good way to determine the correct verb with an *or* or *nor* compound is to cover up the subject farther from the verb. Then work with the sentence that remains.

~~Either Rashad or~~ the twins **walk** the dog hourly.

See what happens when the compound elements are switched. Now which is correct?

Either the twins or Rashad *(walk, walks)* the dog hourly.

Can you see that now the verb must agree with *Rashad*, a singular subject?

Either the twins or Rashad **walks** the dog hourly.

Subject-Verb Agreement with Compound Subjects

1. When a compound subject is formed using *and*, the subject is plural. The present-tense verb does not end in *s*.

2. When a compound subject is formed using *or* or *nor*, the verb should agree with the subject closer to it.

EXERCISE 7

Part A   **Directions:** Use the rules on page 64 and underline the correct verb in each sentence below.

Example: The administrative assistant or the salespeople (*answer*, *answers*) the phone.

1. Neither Juanita nor Damaris (*want*, *wants*) to work here forever.
2. Both the subway and the bus (*stops*, *stop*) near the post office.
3. Either George or his coworkers (*check*, *checks*) the mail each day.
4. Locks or an alarm (*provide*, *provides*) some security against break-ins.
5. Both the carrots and the sweet potato (*provides*, *provide*) vitamin A.
6. Neither here nor the western states (*is*, *are*) known for mild winters.
7. Both Boston and San Francisco (*offers*, *offer*) opportunities for walking.
8. Poor spelling and handwriting (*interferes*, *interfere*) with the message.

Part B   **Directions:** Find and correct the verb errors in the article below.

Do I Have an Ulcer, and How Did I Get It?

An ulcer are a sore on the lining of your stomach or small intestine. Stress and spicy food does not cause an ulcer, but they do irritate it. Actually, either an infection or some medicines causes ulcers. Recognizing the symptoms of an ulcer and knowing what to do if you have one is important steps toward feeling better.

We doesn't know how people acquire the bacteria that can cause ulcers. However, research show that long-term use of nonsteroidal anti-inflammatory medicines can cause ulcers. Also, older men is at higher risk of developing intestinal ulcers, while older women develop more stomach ulcers. Both cigarettes and alcohol is also contributing factors.

Answers are on page 369.

Inverted Word Order

Subject-verb agreement can also be tricky in commands, questions, and *here* or *there* statements. Just as you learned in Chapter 1, changing the order of the words in the sentence will help you remember which verb is correct to use. Which verb is correct in the sentence below?

(Do, Does) the supervisor have the information she needs?

If you put the subject of the sentence first, you will quickly see which verb is correct.

The supervisor **does** have the information she needs.

The subject is singular, so the present tense verb ends in *s*. What verb is correct in this next sentence?

Here **(is, are)** the copies I made of your drawings.

Again, change the word order so that the subject comes first:

The copies I made of your drawings **are** here.

Since the subject is plural *(copies)*, the correct verb is *are*. Is the following sentence written correctly?

Trevon, brings me today's newspaper, please.

Remember that in a command, the understood subject is always *you*. Do not be confused by the direct address, *Trevon*. The verb in the command above should be *bring*, as in *you bring*.

Trevon, **bring** me today's newspaper, please.

Some sentences begin with an introductory phrase, not with the subject. Watch out for subject-verb agreement errors here.

On the bookshelves **(are, is)** an old photograph.

The subject of the sentence is *photograph*, not *bookshelves*. Therefore, the verb *is* is the correct choice.

On the bookshelves **is** an old photograph.

Practice choosing the correct verb in the inverted sentences below. Change the order of the words if that helps you.

Why *(is, are)* disaster films so popular?

There *(sit, sits)* my unfinished project.

(Tell, Tells) us another story about your past.

You should have underlined *are*, *sits*, and *Tell*.

EXERCISE 8

<u>Part A</u>   **Directions:** Circle the subject and underline the verb that agrees with it in each sentence below.

1. Where *(is, are)* my glasses?

2. Here *(is, are)* the test result you ordered from the lab.

3. *(Do, Does)* we really need to review this now?

4. Angela, please *(takes, take)* notes on this presentation.

5. There *(is, are)* some things we need to work out between us.

6. Why *(don't, doesn't)* the government devise a fair tax system?

7. There *(isn't, aren't)* many doctors at this conference.

8. Paul, *(put, puts)* the lumber in the larger lot, please.

<u>Part B</u>   **Directions:** Find and correct the errors in subject-verb agreement in the article below.

Is Americans becoming more interested in physical fitness? There is many indications that they are. There have been an increase in the popularity of biking, swimming, and hiking. There is many companies that offer free use of gyms for their employees. They finds that it saves more money on health insurance than it costs them to provide wellness programs. Does you do anything special to keep in shape? What fitness activities is you interested in?

Answers are on page 369.

Prepositional Phrases and Other Interrupters

Sometimes a simple subject may be hard to find in a sentence because it is separated from the verb by a prepositional phrase or other interrupter. If you can recognize this phrase, it will be easier to make sure that the subject and verb agree. What is the simple subject in this sentence?

The price of electricity never goes down.

If you are not sure whether the subject is *price* or *electricity*, find the verb *(goes)* and ask yourself, "Who or what never goes down?" The answer is the simple subject, *price*. The words *of electricity* are a prepositional phrase that describes *price*.

A **prepositional phrase** is a word group that starts with a preposition and ends with a noun or pronoun. It describes another word in the sentence.

Prepositional phrases are important to recognize because they <u>never</u> contain the subject of a sentence. The chart shows some common prepositions to look for, with sample phrases that they might introduce.

Prepositions	Prepositional Phrases
of	of the three women, of December
in	in the entire universe, in a long line
for	for the team, for a new plan
to	to the company, to them
from	from the president, from New York
with	with the beard, with several comments
on	on the third floor, on television

Other common prepositions include *above, across, at, before, between, down, into, near, through, under,* and *up.* Insert a prepositional phrase between each subject and predicate below.

The woman_____crossed the street.

The letter_____ arrived yesterday.

My office_____ is a total mess.

You might have written prepositional phrases such as *near the bus stop, from my uncle,* and *on the fifth floor.*

Use the following three-step process to make sure subjects and verbs agree in sentences with prepositional phrases. Try the sample sentence below.

The cars on the showroom floor *(is, are)* new.

1. Cross out the prepositional phrase.

   The cars ~~on the showroom floor~~ *(is, are)* new.

2. Circle the simple subject of the sentence. With the phrase crossed out, it is easy to see that *cars* is the subject.

   The (cars) ~~on the showroom floor~~ *(is, are)* new.

3. Choose the verb that agrees with the subject.

   The (cars) ~~on the showroom floor~~ *(is, __are__)* new.

Try the three-step process with the sentence below. First, cross out the prepositional phrase or phrases. Second, circle the simple subject. Third, underline the verb that agrees with the subject.

A vase of wildflowers *(stand, stands)* on the kitchen table.

The correct sentence would look like this:

A (vase) ~~of wildflowers~~ *(stand, __stands__)* on the kitchen table.

Watch out for the words in the box below. Sometimes they seem to make the subject plural, but they actually introduce interrupting phrases.

as well as	along with	besides
in addition to	together with	

These phrases are usually easy to spot because they are set off by commas.

Gabriela, **as well as three friends,** lives in a tiny one-bedroom apartment in Manhattan.

The verb *lives* agrees with the singular subject *Gabriela*. Subject-verb agreement is not influenced by the interrupting phrase. Contrast this pattern to a sentence using a compound subject.

Gabriela and three friends live in a tiny one-bedroom apartment in Manhattan.

In this case, the verb *live* agrees with the compound subject *Gabriela and three friends*. Although the two sentences have essentially the same meaning, the subject-verb agreement patterns are different.

EXERCISE 9

Directions: Use the three-step process to find the correct verb in each sentence below.

1. The people on the telephone (*seem, seems*) incredibly busy.

2. The reasons for my call (*is, are*) difficult to explain quickly.

3. I heard that two men from my building (*has, have*) decided to move.

4. The days between Friday and Monday (*is, are*) called the weekend.

5. The space between the two posts (*appear, appears*) empty.

6. Kristi, as well as five other candidates, (*has, have*) applied for the position.

7. The ability to communicate, together with a positive attitude, (*help, helps*) a person become successful in life.

8. The man and woman across the aisle (*look, looks*) unhappy.

9. The babies in the hospital ward (*was, were*) born yesterday.

10. Colleen, in addition to her two cousins, (*start, starts*) college in August.

Answers are on page 369.

Indefinite Pronouns

Sometimes it is difficult to decide if a subject is singular or plural. For example, is the subject *everyone* singular or plural?

Everyone *(know, knows)* you are an excellent cook.

Although you might think of *everyone* as more than one person and therefore plural, it is actually a singular indefinite pronoun. An **indefinite pronoun** is a pronoun that does not name a specific person or thing.

Some indefinite pronouns are always considered singular in standard written English. You'll learn these more easily if you concentrate on the word *one, body,* or *thing* at the end of each. Here is a list of singular indefinite pronouns.

Singular Indefinite Pronouns		
each (one)	no one	everyone
either (one)	nothing	everything
neither (one)	nobody	everybody
one	anyone	
someone	anything	
something	anybody	
somebody		

Note the singular verbs in each sentence below:

Nobody **understands** him.

Does anyone agree with me?

Neither of the radios **works.**

Each of the survivors **gets** an equal share.

EDITING TIP

Remember to cross out any prepositional or interrupting phrases as you work with indefinite pronouns. Add the word *one* after *each, either,* or *neither* to remind yourself that these words are singular.

Neither of the companies *(employ, employs)* part-time workers.

Neither (one) ~~of the companies~~ *(employ, **employs**)* part-time workers.

Not all indefinite pronouns are singular. Here are some that are always plural:

Plural Indefinite Pronouns
both few many several

Many **are** called. Few **are** chosen.

Both **write** extremely well.

Some indefinite pronouns can be either singular or plural depending on their antecedent, the noun to which the pronoun refers. (See page 38 for a review.)

Singular or Plural Indefinite Pronouns
some most any none all

Look at the two sentences below. The indefinite pronoun *all* is the subject in each. Why is one considered singular and one considered plural?

All of the **snow** <u>has</u> melted.

All of the candy **bars** <u>have</u> disappeared.

In the first sentence *all* is considered singular because the antecedent *snow* is a singular noun. Therefore, the singular verb *has* is correct. In the second sentence *bars* is plural, so *have* is the correct verb form. Which verb is correct below?

All of my money **(have, has)** been stolen.

Since *all* refers to the singular noun *money*, the verb *has* is correct.

Sometimes you may have to look in an earlier sentence for a pronoun's antecedent. Is *some* singular or plural in the sentence below?

The construction workers came to the site. Some were on their lunch break.

The antecedent of *some* is *workers*, a plural noun. Therefore, *were* is the correct verb. Find the correct verb below:

The lunch was laid out on the table. Some **(was, were)** already eaten.

Because the antecedent of *some* is *lunch*, a singular noun, the verb *was* is correct.

EXERCISE 10

Part A **Directions:** Circle the indefinite pronoun and underline the correct verb in each sentence below.

Example: (All) of the soup (*taste*, *tastes*) salty.

1. Everyone in the club (*want*, *wants*) a more diverse membership.

2. None of the memos (*was*, *were*) written by Mary's team.

3. Some of the ice (*melts*, *melt*) each year.

4. Most of the listeners (*understands*, *understand*) the speaker's message.

5. Few of the children (*arrives*, *arrive*) at the child-care center before we do.

6. Someone in the audience (*has*, *have*) a question.

7. Only one of these dogs (*bites*, *bite*) without provocation.

8. Neither of my coworkers (*attends*, *attend*) night classes.

Part B **Directions:** Find and correct the errors in subject-verb agreement with indefinite pronouns in the letter below.

Dear Ms. Howard:

Our communications class would like to invite you to speak to our department this spring. Many has spoken of your valuable experience and excellent skills. It would be an honor to have you share your expertise. Everyone hopes you can fit us into your busy schedule.

Our class is studying media influences on popular culture. Anything related to this topic are a good idea for your talk. Since no one has spoken about the upcoming local elections, you may be interested in addressing this topic. Or perhaps you'd rather speak about the more general topic of the Internet. Either are fine with us.

Please call me at 555-1313 to discuss this matter further, Ms. Howard. Someone is always in the office. Thank you.

Sincerely,
Celia Perez

Answers are on page 370.

Using Verbs: Editing Practice

Directions: Find and correct the verb errors in the instructions below. Use this checklist as your editing guide:

- ☐ Do present-tense verbs agree in number with their subjects?

- ☐ Is the correct verb tense used for each sentence and for the passage as a whole?

- ☐ Are irregular verb forms used correctly?

- ☐ Are regular verb forms spelled correctly?

Steps to Create Job Satisfaction for Your Employees

Job satisfaction for all employees are possible when you work at it. As a manager you are responsible for making sure employees stay on the job and perform well. Here is some steps you can take to ensure job satisfaction in your department.

Step 1: Be clear about what the job is. Everyone wants to know exactly what he or she is expected to do each day. Don't add or take away new tasks unless you discusses it with the employee first.

Step 2: Recognize excellent performance. You can do this in writing or speech. Either are acceptable as long as the employee gets the message clearly. Praise and support makes an employee feel that you value the work he or she does.

Step 3: Include all employees in the decision-making process as much as possible. Why doesn't workers always follow the rules you've set? Often it is because they does not feel any ownership of those rules. Allowing them to help establish guidelines can go a long way toward job satisfaction.

Answers are on page 370.

Chapter Review

Directions: Choose the <u>one best answer</u> to each question. Some of the sentences may contain verb errors. A few sentences, however, may be correct as written. Read the sentences carefully and then answer the questions based on them. For each question, choose the answer that would result in the most effective writing of the sentence or sentences.

Questions 1–8 refer to the following essay.

Get Involved in Your Community!

(A)

   (1) Does you want to feel more connected to your community? (2) If so, you are like millions of other Americans. (3) It seemed that during the 1990s people will be too busy focusing on their careers and their families to do much in their communities. (4) In this new millennium, however, people are feeling a need to reach out. (5) They are redefining what it means to be a citizen.

(B)

   (6) To get involved in your community, start locally. (7) Picks up a newspaper and check out the "volunteer help needed" section. (8) Often there is people in your own neighborhood who could use your help. (9) Maybe you could serve dinner at a veteran's shelter or teach a recent immigrant to read. (10) In this way your time and effort is well spent.

(C)

   (11) Here's another idea. (12) Think about the little boys' and girls' soccer coach you see practicing with the kids every afternoon.
(13) Don't he deserve a helping hand? (14) You might get a great feeling of connection to your community by getting involved in youth sports. (15) The joy of working with children are indescribable. (16) Nothing compares to it.

1. Sentence 1: **Does you want to feel more connected to your community?**

   What correction should be made to sentence 1?

   (1) change *Does* to *Doesn't*
   (2) change *Does* to *Do*
   (3) replace *you* with *he*
   (4) insert a comma after *feel*
   (5) no correction is necessary

2. Sentence 3: **It seemed that during the 1990s <u>people will be too busy focusing</u> on their careers and their families to do much in their communities.**

   Which is the best way to write the underlined portion of the text? If the original is the best way, choose option (1).

   (1) people will be too busy focusing
   (2) people will have been too busy focusing
   (3) people were too busy focusing
   (4) people been too busy focusing
   (5) people will be too busy focused

3. Sentence 5: **They are redefining what it means to be a citizen.**

   What correction should be made to sentence 5?

   (1) replace *are* with *were*
   (2) change *redefining* to *redefined*
   (3) replace *means* with had *meaned*
   (4) change *means* to *mean*
   (5) no correction is necessary

4. Sentence 7: **<u>Picks up</u> a newspaper and check out the "volunteer help needed" section.**

   Which is the best way to write the underlined portion of the text? If the original is the best way, choose option (1).

   (1) Picks up
   (2) Pick up
   (3) He picks up
   (4) He picked up
   (5) Pickes up

5. Sentence 8: **Often there is people in your own neighborhood who could use your help.**

   What correction should be made to sentence 8?

   (1) change *is* to *are*
   (2) change *is* to *was*
   (3) change *is* to *will have been*
   (4) change *use* to *used*
   (5) no correction is necessary

6. Sentence 10: **In this way your time and effort is well spent.**

   What correction should be made to sentence 10?

   (1) change *is* to *has been*
   (2) change *is* to *was*
   (3) change *is* to *were*
   (4) change *is* to *are*
   (5) no correction is necessary

7. Sentence 13: **<u>Don't he deserve</u> a helping hand?**

   Which is the best way to write the underlined portion of the text? If the original is the best way, choose option (1).

   (1) Don't he deserve
   (2) Doesn't he deserve
   (3) Didn't he deserve
   (4) Don't they deserve
   (5) Don't we deserve

8. Sentence 15: **The joy of working with children are indescribable.**

   What correction should be made to sentence 15?

   (1) change *working* to *worked*
   (2) change *working* to *was working*
   (3) change *are* to *were*
   (4) change *are* to *is*
   (5) no correction is necessary

Questions 9–15 refer to the following memo.

TO: Production Crew

FROM: Will Montrose

(A)

(1) As you knows, we will soon be switching our lines over to the new high-speed A700 drivers. (2) The speed and accuracy of this line is a great opportunity for us all to increase productivity. (3) Before the change, those of us in management wants to give you some important background information.

(B)

(4) To provide this information, we will divide the production crew into several smaller groups. (5) Each group met during normal working hours, and a schedule will be posted in the cafeteria. (6) Everybody have a group leader who is a member of our management team. (7) Anyone who is absent on meeting day are asked to see Jorge Sanchez for more information.

(C)

(8) By the end of next month we had completed 25 straight shifts with the new A700 belt driver. (9) We certainly hope we will be satisfied with the results.

9. **Sentence 1: <u>As you knows, we will soon be</u> switching our lines over to the new high-speed A700 drivers.**

    Which is the best way to write the underlined portion of the text? If the original is the best way, choose option (1).

    (1) As you knows, we will soon be
    (2) As you knowed, we will soon be
    (3) As you was knowing, we will soon be
    (4) As you knows, we were soon being
    (5) As you know, we will soon be

10. **Sentence 2: The speed and accuracy of this line is a great opportunity for us all to increase productivity.**

    What correction should be made to sentence 2?

    (1) change *is* to *are*
    (2) change *is* to *was*
    (3) change *is* to *be*
    (4) change *is* to *has been*
    (5) no correction is necessary

11. **Sentence 3: Before the change, those of us in management <u>wants to give</u> you some important background information.**

    Which is the best way to write the underlined portion of the text? If the original is the best way, choose option (1).

    (1) wants to give
    (2) was wanting to give
    (3) has given
    (4) want to give
    (5) wanting to give

12. Sentence 5: <u>**Each group met**</u> **during normal working hours, and a schedule will be posted in the cafeteria.**

Which is the best way to write the underlined portion of the text? If the original is the best way, choose option (1).

(1) Each group met
(2) Each group will meet
(3) Each group will have met
(4) Each group had met
(5) Each group hasn't met

13. Sentence 6: Everybody have a group leader who is a member of our management team.

What correction should be made to sentence 6?

(1) change *have* to *had*
(2) change *have* to *has*
(3) change *is* to *was*
(4) change *is* to *were*
(5) no correction is necessary

14. Sentence 7: Anyone who is absent on meeting day are asked to see Jorge Sanchez for more information.

What correction should be made to sentence 7?

(1) change *is* to *are*
(2) change *is* to *were*
(3) change *are* to *were*
(4) change *are* to *is*
(5) no correction is necessary

15. Sentence 8: By the end of next month we <u>**had completed**</u> **25 straight shifts with the new A700 belt driver.**

Which is the best way to write the underlined portion of the text? If the original is the best way, choose option (1).

(1) had completed
(2) has completed
(3) will have completed
(4) were completing
(5) was completing

Answers are on page 370.

Cumulative Review

Directions: Choose the <u>one best answer</u> to each question. Some of the sentences may contain errors in organization, sentence structure, usage, and mechanics. A few sentences, however, may be correct as written. Read the sentences carefully and then answer the questions based on them. For each question, choose the answer that would result in the most effective writing of the sentence or sentences.

Questions 1–8 refer to the following informative article.

Man's Best Friend

(A)

(1) Why is dogs such popular pets worldwide? (2) They are messier than cats and less intelligent than pigs. (3) They can't be kept in cages. (4) Like hamsters and parakeets. (5) Yet not one of these other animals has been referred to as "man's best friend." (6) There has to be some good reasons.

(B)

(7) One reason for the popularity of dogs are their loyalty. (8) By nature following the leader of the pack just like wolves and coyotes. (9) In a dog's case the leader of the pack had been a human being. (10) A properly trained dog obeys it's master's commands, just as wild animals obey their leader.

(C)

(11) Another reason there are so many dogs kept as pets is they're variety. (12) One person might want a large, exuberant pet. (13) Another might prefer a small, docile pet. (14) Both of these preferences can be satisfied by buying a dog.

1. Sentence 1: **Why <u>is dogs</u> such popular pets worldwide?**

   Which is the best way to write the underlined portion of the text? If the original is the best way, choose option (1).

   (1) is dogs
   (2) was dogs
   (3) are dogs
   (4) is dogs being
   (5) has dogs been

2. Sentences 3 and 4: **They can't be <u>kept in cages. Like</u> hamsters and parakeets.**

   Which is the best way to write the underlined portion of the text? If the original is the best way, choose option (1).

   (1) kept in cages. Like
   (2) kept in cages like
   (3) kept in cage's. Like
   (4) kept, in cages. Like
   (5) kept in cages' like

3. Sentence 6: **There has to be some good reasons.**

   What correction should be made to sentence 6?

   (1) change *has* to *was*
   (2) change *has* to *have*
   (3) insert a comma after *be*
   (4) change *reasons* to *reason's*
   (5) no correction is necessary

4. Sentence 7: **One reason for the popularity of dogs are their loyalty.**

   What correction should be made to sentence 7?

   (1) change *dogs* to *dog's*
   (2) insert a comma after *dogs*
   (3) change *are* to *is*
   (4) change *their* to *they're*
   (5) no correction is necessary

5. Sentence 8: **By nature following the leader of the pack just like wolves and coyotes.**

   The most effective revision of this sentence would include which group of words?

   (1) By nature following the leader of the pack. Just
   (2) By nature they follow the leader of the pack just
   (3) Following the leader of the pack, by nature just like
   (4) Just like wolves and coyotes, by nature following
   (5) Just like wolves and coyote's packs

6. Sentence 9: **In a dog's case the leader of the pack <u>had been</u> a human being.**

   Which is the best way to write the underlined portion of the text? If the original is the best way, choose option (1).

   (1) had been
   (2) have been
   (3) was
   (4) is
   (5) are

7. Sentence 10: **A properly trained dog obeys it's master's commands, just as wild animals obey their leader.**

   What correction should be made to sentence 10?

   (1) change *obeys* to *obeyed*
   (2) change *it's* to *its'*
   (3) change *it's* to *its*
   (4) change *master's* to *masters*
   (5) change *animals* to *animal's*

8. Sentence 11: **Another reason there are so many dogs kept as pets is they're variety.**

   What correction should be made to sentence 11?

   (1) change *are* to *is*
   (2) change *dogs* to *dog's*
   (3) change *pets* to *pet's*
   (4) change *is* to *are*
   (5) change *they're* to *their*

Questions 9–16 refer to the following excerpt from a memo.

TO: All Night Shift Drivers

FROM: Shift Safety Manager

(A)

(1) As we do every month, we are sending this memo to remind you of critical safety issues that you must keep in mind. (2) This month we would like to turn you attention to the hazards of driving at night. (3) Next week you headed off on a four-day haul to Detroit, and we would like you to focus on making the trip safe.

(B)

(4) Before we get to specific rules and policies, we would be remiss if we did not mention the accident that occurred in Toledo, ohio, just last week. (5) A trucker from another company was driving recklessly and struck a car from behind. (6) No one were badly injured, but both drivers have been hospitalized. (7) Neither the company president nor I wants this sort of thing to happen to you.

(C)

(8) Here is some pointers to keep in mind as you drive at night. (9) Get enough sleep the night before. (10) Even if that means you take an afternoon off. (11) The monthly schedule manager will be able to help you do this.

9. Sentence 2: **This month we would like to turn you attention to the hazards of driving at night.**

   What correction should be made to sentence 2?

   (1) change *month* to *Month*
   (2) change *you* to *his*
   (3) change *you* to *you're*
   (4) change *you* to *your*
   (5) no correction is necessary

10. Sentence 3: **Next week you headed off on a four-day haul to Detroit, and we would like you to focus on making the trip safe.**

    What correction should be made to sentence 3?

    (1) replace *headed* with *will head*
    (2) replace *headed* with *had headed*
    (3) change *Detroit* to *detroit*
    (4) replace *we* with *us*
    (5) change *making* to *made*

11. **Sentence 4: Before we get to specific rules and policies, we would be remiss if we did not mention the accident that <u>occurred in Toledo, ohio, just</u> last week.**

Which is the best way to write the underlined portion of the text? If the original is the best way, choose option (1).

(1) occurred in Toledo, ohio, just
(2) will occur in Toledo, ohio, just
(3) had occurred in Toledo, ohio, just
(4) occurred in Toledo, Ohio, just
(5) occurred in toledo, ohio, just

12. **Sentence 6: No one were badly injured, but both drivers have been hospitalized.**

What correction should be made to sentence 6?

(1) change *were* to *been*
(2) change *were* to *was*
(3) add a comma after *one*
(4) replace *have* with *has*
(5) replace *have been* with *will have been*

13. **Sentence 7: Neither the company <u>president nor I wants</u> this sort of thing to happen to you.**

Which is the best way to write the underlined portion of the text? If the original is the best way, choose option (1).

(1) president nor I wants
(2) President nor I wants
(3) president nor I want
(4) president nor I has wanted
(5) president nor I was wanting

14. **Sentence 8: Here is some pointers to keep in mind as you drive at night.**

What correction should be made to sentence 8?

(1) change *is* to *are*
(2) insert a comma after *pointers*
(3) change *pointers* to *pointer's*
(4) change *drive* to *drives*
(5) no correction is necessary

15. **Sentences 9 and 10: Get enough sleep the night <u>before. Even if that means</u> you take an afternoon off.**

Which is the best way to write the underlined portion of the text? If the original is the best way, choose option (1).

(1) before. Even if that means
(2) before. Even if that mean
(3) before. Even if that will mean
(4) before. Even if that was meaning
(5) before even if that means

Answers are on page 370.

CHAPTER 3

Combining Sentences

Compound Sentences

How could the following two short sentences be combined to create one longer one?

> I filled out an application. I got the job.

Although there are several possibilities, the simplest is to use the coordinating conjunction *and*:

> I filled out an application, **and** I got the job.

The sentence above is called a **compound sentence** because it contains two complete clauses joined by the coordinating conjunction *and*. A **clause** is a group of words containing a subject and a verb.

Underline each subject-verb pair in the example sentence above. You are correct if you found *I filled* and *I got*.

The two clauses in the example sentence are considered **independent clauses** because they can stand alone as complete sentences.

The chart below shows the most common **coordinating conjunctions** used to connect independent clauses.

Coordinating Conjunction	Use	Example
and	to add related information	My boss dictates the memo, **and** Marlene types it.
but, yet	to show contrast	We filled out the correct forms, **but** the office misplaced them.
or	to present a choice	The customers can wait in line, **or** they can order over the phone.
nor	to show rejection of two choices	He hasn't called, **nor** has he written.
for	to link effect to cause	She left work early, **for** she was not feeling well.
so	to link cause to effect	She was not feeling well, **so** she left work early.

Notice in the example sentences that a comma precedes each coordinating conjunction.

Here is a breakdown of a compound sentence:

Compound Sentence		
Mr. Thomasina is not in the office now,	so	you should call him back tomorrow.
INDEPENDENT CLAUSE	COORDINATING CONJUNCTION	INDEPENDENT CLAUSE

Not all clauses work well together in a compound sentence. What's wrong with the sentence below?

The Yankees played the Red Sox, but the customer order was filled at the warehouse.

The conjunction *but* is used to show contrast, but the two clauses are not related at all. The combined sentence does not make sense. Compare it to this compound sentence:

The Yankees played the Red Sox, but the game was not televised.

Can you see that the two clauses make sense together? The conjunction *but* correctly shows the contrast between two related ideas.

Does the coordinating conjunction used in the sentence below make sense?

Our sales department did not meet its goal, but our supervisor was disappointed.

The writer of the sentence above uses a conjunction that indicates contrast. But do the two ideas really contrast each other? No. Instead the writer should choose a conjunction that links an effect to a cause:

Our sales department did not meet its goal, so our supervisor was disappointed.

When clauses are combined with coordinating conjunctions, the wording of both clauses is unchanged except when *nor* is used. Then the subject and verb in the second clause are reversed.

He doesn't like anchovies. He doesn't like pizza

He doesn't like anchovies, nor does he like pizza.

A correctly written compound sentence . . .

- joins two independent clauses.
- uses a coordinating conjunction that makes sense.
- has a comma before the conjunction.

On the Language Arts, Writing Test you will be expected to know all three of these features. Paying attention to the *meaning* of conjunctions as well as how they are used is an important skill for success on the GED Test.

EXERCISE 1

<u>Part A</u>   **Directions:** Combine the sentences in each pair below using one of the coordinating conjunctions from the chart on page 83. Pay close attention to the meaning of the conjunction you choose. There is often more than one way to join the two sentences. Be sure to place a comma before the conjunction.

Example: I can pay my rent by mail. I can pay at the manager's office.

I can pay my rent by mail, or I can pay at the manager's office.

1. The phone was ringing. The assistant answered it.

2. It was time for us to go. The waitress got our coats.

3. Your résumé looks impressive. We have no job openings at the moment.

4. I did not like the computer class. I did not like the keyboard class.

5. Please bring a pen. You will have nothing with which to write.

6. The staff always reads the memo board carefully. It contains important information.

<u>Part B</u>   **Directions:** Create a compound sentence by using the conjunction given and adding a related independent clause. Remember to place the comma correctly.

Example: *(for)* I was tired last weekend, *for I worked overtime several days last week.*

1. *(but)* The Amadeos wanted a new car _____.
2. *(yet)* He wanted to be respected _____.
3. *(for)* Tua is studying computer science _____.
4. *(so)* We enjoy your company _____.
5. *(nor)* The supervisor did not like the girl's attitude _____.
6. *(and)* The painters arrived early _____.
7. *(so)* The club needs new members _____.
8. *(yet)* The Internet is a useful tool _____.

Run-on Sentences

Do you think the two sentences below are examples of good writing?

> The bills your company keeps sending are incorrect I paid them months ago.

> My daughter will not be in school today, so I would like her homework sent home with her brother, and she will probably be in tomorrow, but if she isn't that means she is still sick so please give her homework to her brother again, and I thank you very much.

Both of these sentences are called **run-on sentences.** They need to be broken up to become correct compound sentences.

The first example is actually two independent clauses joined together *without* a coordinating conjunction. Here is the corrected sentence:

> The bills your company keeps sending are incorrect, **for** I paid them months ago.

The second sentence uses conjunctions, but too many clauses are joined into one sentence. Two, or sometimes three, clauses can be joined to form a compound, but more than two or three create an awkward run-on that is hard to follow. Look at how this sentence can be broken up so that it is easier to read:

> My daughter will not be in school today, so I would like her homework sent home with her brother. **She** will probably be in tomorrow, but if she isn't that means she is still sick. **Please** give her homework to her brother again. I thank you very much.

To turn a run-on sentence into a compound sentence, join two (or sometimes three) independent clauses using a comma and a coordinating conjunction.

EXERCISE 2

Directions: Correct the run-on sentences below by using conjunctions correctly.

Example: The roads were covered with ice,ᵇᵘᵗ I managed to control the car.

1. The weather has been terrible the hotel parties have all been indoors.

2. We expect your company to investigate these complaints, and we want to hear from you before Friday so we can finally resolve this matter, and if we do not hear from you, we will have to call a lawyer.

3. The manager told us he would be here early he arrived close to midnight.

4. We do not plan to come to the meeting we will not be at the conference.

Answers are on page 371.

Commas with *And*

Do you use a comma with *and*, or don't you? Unfortunately this is a question that does not have a simple yes or no answer. However, these three basic rules will help.

1. **Use a comma before *and* if it connects two independent clauses.**

   John washed the dinner dishes, **and** Marian dried them.
   INDEPENDENT CLAUSE   INDEPENDENT CLAUSE

2. **Use a comma before *and* in a series of three or more compound elements.**

   Honesty, integrity, **and** dedication are the qualities we look for in an employee.

3. **Do not use a comma with *and* if it connects only two compound elements.**

   The welder is an important part of the production team **and** a key part of our success.

Why is a comma used in the first sentence below and not the second sentence? To help you decide, think about which of the two is a compound sentence (a sentence made up of two independent clauses joined with a conjunction).

   LaTasha found the number in the phone book, and she dialed it immediately.

   LaTasha found the number in the phone book and dialed it immediately.

The first sentence is a compound sentence, so a comma is needed. The second sentence has a compound predicate, *found and dialed*; however, it lacks two independent clauses, or two sentences that can each stand on their own. Thus, the second sentence is not a compound sentence, and no comma is needed.

EXERCISE 3

<u>Part A</u>   **Directions:**   Using the rules on page 87, add commas where necessary. If the sentence is correct, write the word *correct* after it.

Example: The computer class will be interesting‸ and it will fit into my schedule.

1. A cup of coffee and a piece of toast were all she ate today.

2. A cup of coffee a piece of toast and an orange were all she ate today.

3. Tuan asked for an application and he sat down to fill it out.

4. Tuan asked for an application and sat down to fill it out.

5. Julio plans to become a mechanic and Michael wants to be a teacher.

6. Julio plans to become a mechanic and a father.

7. Job openings are available in shipping accounting and filing.

8. The employee looked for a solution to the problem and found one.

9. The employee looked for a solution to the problem and she found one.

10. This letter should be typed up and sent to all customers on our mailing list.

<u>Part B</u>   **Directions:**   Correct the comma errors in the letter below. Add commas where needed and cross out the commas that are not needed.

January 10, 2001

Mr. George Mitropolous
75 Earth Boulevard
South Plainfield, NJ 07080
Dear Mr. Mitropolous:

Thank you for your letter, and your résumé. We are happy to hear of your interest enthusiasm and excitement.

The officers here at GenerCo, Inc., have looked over your file and we have decided we are unable to offer you a job at this time. We are impressed by your résumé and qualifications but there is not a position here that matches your skills. We need a clerk, and an accountant, and your experience is not in these areas.

We hope that you will continue your job search and we'd like to hear from you again when you have gained more experience. Again, thank you for your interest enthusiasm and good effort.

Sincerely,
John Dario, President

Answers are on page 371.

Complex Sentences

Look at how the following two sentences are joined:

The client rang the bell at the desk. She wanted faster service.

The client rang the bell at the desk **because** she wanted faster service.

The second sentence, *She wanted faster service*, provides a cause for the sentence before it, *The client rang the bell at the desk*. The conjunction *because* is used to join the two clauses. In this lesson, you will learn about subordinating conjunctions like *because*. These conjunctions are different from the coordinating conjunctions you have learned so far, and they are used to form complex sentences.

A **complex sentence** contains a dependent clause connected to an independent clause.

In the complex sentence above, the clause *because she wanted faster service* depends on the first clause, *The client rang the bell at the desk*, in order to make any sense. This is why it is called a **dependent clause.**

A complex sentence can begin with either the independent clause or the dependent clause. Here is the complex sentence from above, this time with the dependent clause first:

Because she wanted faster service, the client rang the bell at the desk.

Notice that when the dependent clause comes before the independent clause, a comma is used to separate the two clauses. Here are some examples:

While you are waiting,	you might want to look over our company's brochure.
DEPENDENT CLAUSE	INDEPENDENT CLAUSE

You might want to look over our company's brochure	**while** you are waiting.
INDEPENDENT CLAUSE	DEPENDENT CLAUSE

Although the tasks seem boring,	the project really is exciting.
DEPENDENT CLAUSE	INDEPENDENT CLAUSE

The project really is exciting	**although** the tasks seem boring.
INDEPENDENT CLAUSE	DEPENDENT CLAUSE

Here is a breakdown of a complex sentence:

Complex Sentence
The production schedule has been changed ⌐ since ⌐ so many workers are on strike.
INDEPENDENT CLAUSE   SUBORDINATING CONJUNCTION   DEPENDENT CLAUSE

Words that join a dependent clause to an independent clause are called **subordinating conjunctions.** A list of them is provided below. Pay particular attention to their use.

Subordinating Conjunction	Use	Example
before after while when whenever until as soon as as long as	to show time	**As soon as** the mail arrives, I'll see if the check is there. My boss gets angry **whenever** I am late. **Until** I get a raise, I plan to work hard. Things got very dull **after** you left.
because since so that in order that	to show cause and effect or purpose	We chose this product **because** it is a great bargain. **So that** the job gets finished on time, they hired extra workers.
if unless whether	to show a condition	The payment cannot be sent **unless** he authorizes it. **If** you can come, call me.
though although even though whereas	to show contrast	**Although** he was early, the show had already started. Jim wore white **whereas** his friends wore black.
as though as if	to show similarity	He looked **as if** he had not slept in a week!
where wherever	to show place	The sales representative travels **wherever** she is needed.

To succeed on the GED Language Arts, Writing Test, you will need to know two things about subordinating conjunctions. First, you will need to be able to choose the subordinating conjunction that shows the correct relationship between the two clauses. For example, you will need to know when to use a conjunction that shows cause and when to use one that shows similarity. Second, you will have to know whether to use a comma in the sentence and where to put it. You will learn more about using a comma with subordinating conjunctions in the Mind on Mechanics lesson on page 93.

What subordinating conjunction would work in the space below? To decide, first read the two clauses and think about the relationship between them.

I decided to call my father _____ I didn't want to talk to him.

What relationship is expressed here? Does a person call someone *because* he doesn't want to talk? Does he call *if* he doesn't want to talk? Probably not. Those conjunctions would not make sense here.

The two clauses actually seem to contrast each other, don't they? Therefore, a subordinating conjunction such as *even though* or *although* makes sense.

I decided to call my father **even though** I didn't want to talk to him.

What subordinating conjunction would make sense in the sentence below?

Our electricity was shut off_____ we have not paid our bill in three months.

The relationship here shows cause and effect. You could use either *since* or *because* to correctly show this relationship.

Our electricity was shut off **since** we have not paid our bill in three months.

Think about the possible relationships between the two clauses in the sentence below. How would the meaning change depending on what subordinating conjunction you put in the blank?

The foreman will turn off the assembly belt _____ our shift is over.

Try using several different conjunctions, such as *when, since, as if,* and *although.* Can you see how the meaning of the sentence changes?

EXERCISE 4

<u>Part A</u> **Directions:** Use the chart on page 90 to choose an effective subordinating conjunction for each blank below. More than one conjunction will be correct.

Example: *If* you finish the report before 3:00, come to my office.

1. Please plan to fill out some forms _____ you see the doctor.

2. _____ we can serve you better, we have a toll-free number.

3. _____ it was raining, the picnic was held outside.

4. _____ it was raining, the picnic was held inside.

5. The contract has expired _____ it is past December 31.

6. With that résumé, you will find a job _____ you want to live.

7. I am planning to come _____ you do not want me to.

8. _____ you do not want me to, I am planning to come.

<u>Part B</u> **Directions:** Create a complex sentence by adding a dependent clause to each independent clause below. Use the subordinating conjunction given. If you place the dependent clause first, be sure to follow it with a comma.

1. I planned to go back to school.

   (although)

   _____

2. The office is empty.

   (while)

   _____

3. The man signed the papers.

   (so that)

   _____

4. We will refund your money.

   (since)

   _____

Answers are on page 372.

MIND ON MECHANICS

Commas in Complex Sentences

As you saw in the last lesson, you decide whether to use a comma in a complex sentence by looking at where the dependent clause is placed in the sentence.

- **If the <u>dependent</u> clause precedes (comes before) the independent clause, place a comma before the independent clause.**

    When the time comes, we will be ready.

- **If the <u>independent</u> clause precedes the dependent clause, <u>do not</u> use a comma.**

    We will be ready when the time comes.

EXERCISE 5

<u>Part A</u> **Directions:** Place a comma where needed in the sentences below. If no comma is needed, write the word *correct* after the sentence.

Example: Since the forecast calls for rain, I will take an umbrella to work today.

1. The senator was met with hostility wherever he traveled that day.

2. After he gave this speech for the tenth time he finally knew it by heart.

3. We want new offices even though these are closer to home.

4. Because her prices are lower the vendor will supply the food.

<u>Part B</u> **Directions:** Correct the complex sentence comma errors in the memo below. Some sentences may be correct as written.

To: Benefits Committee

From: Ms. Dowd

Although many of you already have this information I need to clarify a policy. When an employee takes a vacation his or her supervisor must fill out a #20A form. We have fewer problems with payroll, when everyone follows this procedure. You can let me know, if you have any concerns or questions about this form. Thank you.

Answers are on page 372.

Dependent Clauses in a Paragraph

In Chapter 1 you learned about sentence fragments that are difficult to detect when they are part of a paragraph. Many of these fragments are actually dependent clauses that are not connected to an independent clause. In the following paragraph, what are the three fragments?

> Although they used to be just science fiction toys. Robots are now a reality in the business world. These computerized creatures have revolutionized the manufacturing industry. Because they can perform repetitive tasks with relatively few mistakes. You can expect to see more and more robots in the years ahead. As companies take on the challenges of being productive in the twenty-first century.

You may have understood the writing perfectly, but the three groups of words that begin with subordinating conjunctions (*although, because,* and *as*) are fragments. These fragments need to be connected to the sentences around them. Here is the corrected paragraph:

> **Although** they used to be just science fiction toys, robots are now a reality in the business world. These computerized creatures have revolutionized the manufacturing industry **because** they can perform repetitive tasks with relatively few mistakes. You can expect to see more and more robots in the years ahead **as** companies take on the challenges of being productive in the twenty-first century.

Again notice that when the dependent clause begins the sentence, a comma is used. When the dependent clause comes after the independent clause, no comma is used.

All sentences on the Language Arts, Writing Test will appear embedded in paragraphs. Therefore, you will need to be skilled at detecting dependent clauses that are standing alone—that is, not attached to an independent clause.

E D I T I N G   T I P

Look carefully at all subordinating conjunctions! A clause that begins with a subordinating conjunction <u>must</u> be attached to an independent clause.

EXERCISE 6

Directions: Correct each dependent-clause fragment in the paragraphs below by joining it to an independent clause nearby. To help you identify fragments, underline all subordinating conjunctions and see if they are connected to a complete sentence.

1.　This memo serves as a reminder that your rent has not been paid for the past six months. We will give your name to a collection agency. If you do not provide full payment by May 1. Also, whenever you realize that you will be late with your payment. It is a good idea to notify us at once.

2.　I have not paid my rent for six months. Because the landlord has not repaired the leaky roof yet. Although I have not paid. I have been keeping the rent in escrow for later. When you have finally taken care of the roof. I'll release the funds. If you need further information, please call me.

3.　No repairs will be made on the roof. Until you have paid your back rent. If you had put your complaint in writing sooner. We could have solved this problem long ago. Please send a check now for $1,234 to my attention.

4.　I will agree to send the money I owe. When I have an agreement in writing that the roof will be repaired. Water from last night's rainstorm is dripping onto my living room floor. As I sit writing this letter to you. If I hear from you. I will proceed with the payments.

5.　This document outlines the schedule for roof repair. The project will begin. As soon as you sign this letter and mail it back to me. I understand your concern in this matter. Although I wish you had alerted me earlier to the problem. You have acted unprofessionally. As if you expected me to read your mind.

Answers are on page 372.

Comma Splices

You have seen how commas are used with conjunctions to join two clauses together. Remember, however, that a comma by itself cannot join two clauses. What is wrong with the example below?

> The meeting ended at five o'clock, the staff left at six o'clock.

Can you see that there is no conjunction working with the comma? This kind of error is called a comma splice. A **comma splice** is two clauses incorrectly joined by a comma without a conjunction. To fix this error, add a conjunction or break the sentence into two sentences:

> The meeting ended at five o'clock, **and** the staff left at six o'clock.

> The meeting ended at five o'clock, **so** the staff left at six o'clock.

> The meeting ended at five o'clock. The staff left at six o'clock.

Here is another common comma splice error:

> The package arrived on Thursday, however the mailroom attendant misplaced it.

The word *however* is <u>not</u> a conjunction! Use a coordinating conjunction from the chart on page 83 or a subordinating conjunction from page 90 instead.

> The package arrived on Thursday, **but** the mailroom attendant misplaced it.

> The package arrived on Thursday **although** the mailroom attendant misplaced it.

EXERCISE 7

Directions: Some of the sentences below contain comma splice errors. Correct the errors by using a conjunction. Write the word *correct* after the sentence if no changes are necessary.

Example: *Unless*
⌃ You are busy, I would like to ask your advice about something.

1. We would like to order, however, the store is out of stock.

2. The music sounded lovely, she turned up the volume.

3. When you are ready, please let me know.

4. Mr. Enright blew the whistle, the team stood still.

5. Sondra wanted a job, instead she got a vacation.

6. The meeting was called to order, we were asked to sit down.

Rewriting Sentences

You now know the following guidelines for writing sentences with more than one clause:

1. They can be less choppy and more interesting than short, one-clause sentences.

2. They must contain a conjunction (either subordinating or coordinating) to join the two clauses.

3. A comma is sometimes used with a conjunction, but it is never used alone to join two clauses.

4. The meaning of the conjunction used must accurately represent the relationship between the two clauses.

Once you know these four guidelines, you can rewrite sentences correctly in different ways. Look at these examples:

Since the sale is over, you cannot get this television at the lower price.

You cannot get this television at a lower price because the sale is over.

You cannot get this television at a lower price, for the sale is over.

Can you see that all three of these sentences have the same meaning? Take some time and look carefully at each one. Note how and why a comma is used in some sentences but not others.

The chart on the next page summarizes some conjunctions and how they can be used in rewriting sentences. This chart does not list *all* conjunctions, only those most commonly used in rewriting.

Common Conjunctions

Coordinating Conjunction (a comma precedes the conjunction)	Subordinating Conjunction (a comma is used if the dependent clause precedes the independent clause)	Meaning
but, yet	though, although, even though, whereas	contrast
for, so	because, since, so that, in order that	cause/effect

When joining two clauses together, use one of the conjunctions above, but not more than one.

Correct: Although we are late registering, we plan to attend the event.

Correct: We are late registering, but we plan to attend the event.

Incorrect: Even though we are late registering, yet we plan to attend the event.

EXERCISE 8

Directions: Rewrite each of the sentences below using a different conjunction. Be sure to use a comma when and where necessary.

Example: Since Yoshi lives three miles from the plant, he takes the bus to work.

Yoshi lives three miles from the plant, so he takes the bus to work.

1. The computers are down, so the data-entry clerks will be unable to work.

   _____

2. Since you need a letter of recommendation, you should call Mr. Chun.

   _____

3. Though I have little experience, I learn quickly on the job.

   _____

4. All of those lawns need to be mowed, but we are understaffed today.

   _____

5. People should exercise their right to vote because citizenship is a responsibility.

   _____

6. Our prices are at an all-time low, so buy now!

   _____

Answers are on page 373.

Sentence Construction on the GED Test

One kind of question on Part I of the GED Language Arts, Writing Test will require you to change the pattern of a sentence or combine two sentences without changing the meaning of the original. The original sentence or sentences may contain no error at all. Your job will be to figure out what the writer is trying to say and then choose a pattern that expresses the same idea clearly. If you can recognize which conjunctions in compound and complex sentences have similar meanings, as you did in Exercise 8, you'll be able to answer many of these questions correctly.

Look carefully at the following examples of sentence construction questions that will appear on the Language Arts, Writing Test.

Sentence 1: Although the fire was extinguished immediately, there was considerable smoke damage.

If you rewrote the sentence beginning with

The fire was extinguished immediately,

the next word should be

(1) so
(2) then
(3) but
(4) and
(5) if

Answer choice (3) *but* is correct; it shows the contrast between the two clauses just as *although* does in the original sentence.

Sentence 2: I would like to work for your company. I am enclosing my résumé.

The most effective combination of these sentences would include which group of words?

(1) Then I would like to work for your company, so I am
(2) Although I would like to work for your company, I am
(3) I would like to work for your company unless I am
(4) Until I would like to work for your company, I am
(5) I would like to work for your company, so I am

Answer choice (5) is correct. It shows the cause-effect relationship between the two clauses.

EXERCISE 9

Directions: Choose the best answer to each question below.

1. Sentence 1: **Winnie packed up the last crate. She could ship it out.**

   The most effective combination of these sentences would include which group of words?

   (1) Although Winnie packed up the last crate, she could
   (2) Winnie packed up the last crate unless she could
   (3) For Winnie packed up the last crate, she could
   (4) Winnie packed up the last crate so that she could
   (5) Winnie packed up the last crate, but she could

2. Sentence 2: **Even though it had a good growth plan, Exio Company lost business.**

   If you rewrote the sentence beginning with

   Exio Company lost business,

   the next word(s) should be

   (1) but
   (2) so
   (3) however
   (4) unless
   (5) so that

3. Sentence 3: **The vandals kicked in the door. They didn't steal anything.**

   The most effective combination of these sentences would include which group of words?

   (1) The vandals kicked in the door, so they
   (2) The vandals kicked in the door, but they
   (3) Because the vandals kicked in the door, they
   (4) The vandals kicked in the door until they
   (5) The vandals kicked in the door, or they

4. Sentence 4: **The clock struck twelve, and the guests began to leave.**

   If you rewrote the sentence beginning with

   When the clock struck twelve,

   the next words should be

   (1) even though the guests
   (2) but the guests
   (3) the guests
   (4) however the guests
   (5) since the guests

Answers are on page 373.

Sequence of Tenses

You may remember from Chapter 2 that a verb shows time with its tense. For example, *will walk, walk, walked, have walked, had walked, are walking,* and *were walking* each indicate a different aspect of present, past, and future. To review these tenses, go back to pages 51–56.

When there are two clauses in a sentence, the tense of each verb must work logically with the tense of the other verb. This logical relationship between verbs in a sentence is called **sequence of tenses.**

Which of the following sentences is correct?

When George passes the last test, he received his GED diploma.

When George passes the last test, he will receive his GED diploma.

In the first sentence the verbs are not logically related. The present tense *passes* with the conjunction *when* indicates that the action has not taken place yet. Therefore, the past tense *received* does not make sense.

In the second sentence the verb tenses make sense together. George *will receive* his GED diploma; he has not received it yet.

Here are some sequence-of-tense patterns that make sense. Read each of them and decide why each tense is used.

If George passes the test,	he will celebrate for a week.
PRESENT	FUTURE

When a student passes a test,	he is relieved.
PRESENT	PRESENT

While George was taking the test,	his wife kept her fingers crossed.
PAST CONTINUOUS	PAST

While George was taking the test,	his wife was keeping her fingers crossed.
PAST CONTINUOUS	PAST CONTINUOUS

After George had studied for a month,	he took the last test.
PAST PERFECT	PAST

EXERCISE 10

Directions: Choose the best answer to each question.

1. Sentence 1: **When the electrician finished the job, she will get paid.**

   Which is the best way to write the underlined portion of the text? If the original is the best way, choose option 1.

   (1) will get paid
   (2) was paid
   (3) is paid
   (4) has been paid
   (5) will have been paid

2. Sentence 2: **Whenever the President holds a press conference, all the networks are carrying it live.**

   Which is the best way to write the underlined portion of the text? If the original is the best way, choose option 1.

   (1) are carrying
   (2) carried
   (3) carry
   (4) were carrying
   (5) had been carrying

3. Sentence 3: **I sleep while you were talking.**

   Which is the best way to write the underlined portion of the text? If the original is the best way, choose option 1.

   (1) sleep
   (2) will sleep
   (3) will have slept
   (4) slept
   (5) am sleeping

4. Sentence 4: **After Tom had finished his report, he circulated it among the staff.**

   Which is the best way to write the underlined portion of the text? If the original is the best way, choose option 1.

   (1) had finished
   (2) will finish
   (3) was finishing
   (4) finishes
   (5) will have finished

Answers are on page 373.

Effective Revisions

Can you find an error in this sentence?

> Reminders for safety and guidelines for safety are the things that are posted on the employee bulletin board to remind employees of safety issues.

Although there is not a specific error in grammar or usage in this sentence, you probably agree the repetition and awkward phrasing make it difficult to understand. Here is a good revision of the sentence:

> Reminders and guidelines for safety are posted on the employee bulletin board.

Can you see that this sentence is less wordy yet has all of the same ideas as the original?

Some items on the Language Arts, Writing Test will require you to choose an effective revision of a wordy sentence. Here are some tips to reduce wordage:

1. **Change verbs from passive to active.** With an **active verb,** the subject is doing the acting. A **passive verb** is one in which the subject is acted upon.

   Passive: The report was written by Angela.

   The subject *report* is not doing the action.

   Active: Angela wrote the report.

   The subject *Angela* does the action.

   To easily identify a verb in the passive voice, look for a phrase beginning with *by*. It tells who performs the action in the sentence.

   Passive: Hector was nominated by the committee.

   The subject *Hector* does not perform the action of the sentence.

   Active: The committee nominated Hector.

   The subject *committee* performs the action.

2. **Look for repeated words or phrases and try to combine ideas**.

   Having a cookout is an idea thought of by me, and inviting the new employees is another idea that I had.

   The sentence above can be simplified in the following manner:

   I had the idea of having a cookout and inviting the new employees.

3. **Remember that run-on sentences are too wordy.** Even if a sentence is grammatically correct, it is not necessarily effective.

> Dressing for a job interview is an important part of the whole job search process because first impressions count, and you want to look as if you could fit right into the workplace even if you're not really sure you want the job, so wear something simple and clean and appropriate.

This sentence should be broken up into two or three shorter sentences.

> Dressing for a job interview is an important part of the whole job search process, because first impressions count. You want to look as if you could fit right into the workplace even if you're not really sure you want the job, so wear something simple, clean, and appropriate.

EXERCISE 11

Directions: Rewrite each sentence below to make it shorter and more effective. Create two sentences if you need to. Each revised sentence is started for you.

1. One skill I have is using computers, and another skill I have is getting along well with people, and I also am skilled in working with numbers.

   Using computers, getting along well with people, and _____

   _____ .

2. The room was decorated by Parties & Company, and Parties & Company provided entertainment, and they also prepared the food.

   Parties & Company _____

   _____ .

3. When my supervisor arrives at work, she first reads the newspaper, then she makes a pot of coffee, and after that she gets on the phone to talk to her sister, and if we do not interrupt her, she then does the crossword puzzle.

   When my supervisor arrives at work, _____

   _____ .

4. To keep your finances in good order, you need to write down every penny you spend, and to keep your finances in good order, you need to anticipate future expenses.

   To keep your finances in good order, _____

   _____ .

Combining Sentences: Editing Practice

Directions: Find and correct the errors in sentence combining in the instructions below. Use this checklist as your editing guide:

- ☐ Are clauses linked logically by conjunctions?
- ☐ Are compound and complex sentences punctuated correctly?
- ☐ Have comma splices and run-ons been avoided?
- ☐ Have dependent-clause fragments been avoided?
- ☐ Do verbs follow a logical sequence of tenses?

How to Deal with Insomnia

Do you have trouble falling asleep at night or do you wake up several times during the night? Insomnia, or unsatisfying sleep patterns, can affect all aspects of your life. Here are some tips to help you get relief. If you are suffering from this malady.

1. Try to go to bed at the same time every night. Most adults find that somewhere between 9 P.M. and 11 P.M. is a healthy bedtime, but people can vary quite a bit.

2. Limit your use of alcohol and caffeine, before you go to sleep. These substances throw off your natural body rhythms. In addition, eating fatty or spicy foods shortly before bedtime is unwise although these foods require extra work on the part of your body.

3. Exercise regularly. Exercise gets your body ready for sleep, and exercise releases natural relaxation chemicals in your body, and exercise also helps relieve insomnia.

4. Use your bedroom for sleeping purposes only. Eating, reading, or watching TV in bed "teaches" your body that it is not time to rest. Even though you might be tired.

Answers are on page 373.

Chapter Review

Directions: Choose the <u>one best answer</u> to each question. Some of the sentences may contain sentence errors. A few sentences, however, may be correct as written. Read the sentences carefully and then answer the questions based on them. For each question, choose the answer that would result in the most effective writing of the sentence or sentences.

Questions 1–8 refer to the following letter.

June 1, 2001

Dear Store Manager:

(A)

(1) I decided to write to you. (2) Because I had a very unpleasant experience in your store this week. (3) When I tell you the details of what happened you will be as disappointed as I was.

(B)

(4) Last Thursday my husband and I needed some home improvement supplies, so we took the bus to your store on Wentworth and Madison. (5) We began filling our cart with mops, hooks, cleaning products, and paint. (6) When we were ready to pay, we will get in line at cashier desk #6. (7) Even though we did not have cash, we knew our credit card would be accepted from reading the sign in your window.

(C)

(8) The cashier was friendly, and she spoke kindly, and the cashier smiled a lot, too, toward all the customers ahead of us in line. (9) We smiled and said hello when we got to the head of the line, however, she was so rude to us. (10) She slammed our purchases on the counter, so she grumbled something about not knowing how to use the credit card machine.

(D)

(11) We were upset by the service we received from this young lady. (12) Don't accept credit cards. (13) If your employees can't handle them. (14) Otherwise you will lose customers.

Sincerely,
Maria Lopez

1. **Sentences 1 and 2: I decided to write to <u>you. Because</u> I had a very unpleasant experience in your store this week.**

   Which is the best way to write the underlined portion of the text? If the original is the best way, choose option (1).

   (1) you. Because
   (2) you because
   (3) you, because
   (4) you, although
   (5) you, so

2. **Sentence 3: When I tell you the details of what happened you will be as disappointed as I was.**

   What correction should be made to sentence 3?

   (1) replace *When* with *Although*
   (2) insert a comma after *when*
   (3) insert a comma after *happened*
   (4) replace *will be* with *were*
   (5) replace *will be* with *was*

3. **Sentence 4: Last Thursday my husband and I needed some home improvement supplies, so we took the bus to your store on Wentworth and Madison.**

   What correction should be made to sentence 4?

   (1) change *needed* to *will need*
   (2) change *needed* to *will be needing*
   (3) replace the comma after *supplies* with a period
   (4) replace *so* with *but*
   (5) no correction is necessary

4. **Sentence 6: When we were ready to pay, we will get in line at cashier desk #6.**

   What correction should be made to sentence 6?

   (1) change *were* to *been*
   (2) remove the comma after *pay*
   (3) change *will get* to *will have gotten*
   (4) change *will get* to *got*
   (5) no correction is necessary

5. **Sentence 8: The cashier was friendly, and she spoke kindly, and the cashier smiled a lot, too, toward all the customers ahead of us in line.**

   The most effective revision of sentence 8 would begin with which group of words?

   (1) The cashier was friendly, spoke kindly, and smiled
   (2) The cashier was friendly, the cashier spoke kindly, and the cashier smiled
   (3) Friendly was the cashier, she also spoke kindly and smiled
   (4) Although the cashier was friendly, she spoke kindly and smiled
   (5) Because she was friendly and she spoke kindly and she smiled,

6. **Sentence 9: We smiled and said hello when we got to the head of the <u>line, however, she was</u> so rude to us.**

   Which is the best way to write the underlined portion of the text? If the original is the best way, choose option (1).

   (1) line, however, she was
   (2) line, but she was
   (3) line however she was
   (4) line, but she will be
   (5) line, however, she is

7. **Sentence 10: She slammed our purchases on the counter, so she grumbled something about not knowing how to use the credit card machine.**

   What correction should be made to sentence 10?

   (1) change *slammed* to *slams*
   (2) change *slammed* to *was slamming*
   (3) replace *so* with *and*
   (4) replace *so* with *but*
   (5) change *grumbled* to *grumbles*

8. **Sentences 12 and 13: Don't accept credit cards. If your employees can't handle them.**

   Which is the best way to write the underlined portion of the text? If the original is the best way, choose option (1).

   (1) cards. If your employees can't handle
   (2) cards so your employees can't handle
   (3) cards if your employees can't handle
   (4) cards, if your employees can't handle
   (5) cards if your employees did not handle

Questions 9–15 refer to the following brochure.

Add a DVD Component to Your Home Entertainment System

(A)

(1) There's good news for you, if you are in the market for clear sound and vivid pictures on your movie night at home. (2) The technology of digital video disks (DVDs) has arrived, and is more affordable than ever before. (3) If you have been waiting to find out whether DVDs were really going to catch on, your wait is over. (4) DVDs are one of the hottest consumer electronics products ever.

(B)

(5) What are some features that make DVDs so popular? (6) One advantage is that you can play a DVD on your home computer as well as your television. (7) Although you take your laptop on the road, you can bring along a DVD to watch when your work is finished! (8) In addition, your CDs can be played on your DVD player, there is no need to hang on to your CD player.

(C)

(9) Another advantage of a DVD is its capacity. (10) It holds more than 20 times what a CD holds. (11) Meaning more audio, video, and PC data. (12) Better resolution is a feature that a DVD has in terms of being superior to a VHS tape, and more realistic sound is another improved feature, and a DVD is more durable than a VHS tape. (13) Customers who watched only VHS in the past are amazed at the superior quality of a DVD.

9. **Sentence 1: There's good news for <u>you, if you are</u> in the market for clear sound and vivid pictures on your movie night at home.**

    Which is the best way to write the underlined portion of the text? If the original is the best way, choose option (1).

    (1) you, if you are
    (2) you, although you are
    (3) you if you are
    (4) you, if you were
    (5) you so if you are

10. **Sentence 2: The technology of digital video disks (DVDs) has arrived, and is more affordable than ever before.**

    What correction should be made to sentence 2?

    (1) remove the comma after *arrived*
    (2) change *and* to *but*
    (3) change *and* to *so*
    (4) add a comma after *is*
    (5) no correction is necessary

11. Sentence 3: If you have been waiting to find out whether DVDs were really going to catch on, your wait is over.

What correction should be made to sentence 3?

(1) replace *If* with *Although*
(2) replace *If* with *Whenever*
(3) replace *If* with *But*
(4) remove the comma after *on*
(5) no correction is necessary

12. Sentence 7: Although you take your laptop on the road, you can bring along a DVD to watch when your work is finished!

What correction should be made to sentence 7?

(1) replace *Although* with *When*
(2) replace *Although* with *Because*
(3) remove the comma after *road*
(4) insert *but* after the comma
(5) insert *and* after the comma

13. Sentence 8: In addition, your CDs can be played on your DVD player, there is no need to hang on to your CD player.

Which is the best way to write the underlined portion of the text? If the original is the best way, choose option (1).

(1) player, there is
(2) player, since there is
(3) player, but there is
(4) player, so there is
(5) player, although there is

14. Sentences 10 and 11: It holds more than 20 times what a CD holds. Meaning more audio, video, and PC data.

Which is the best way to write the underlined portion of the text? If the original is the best way, choose option (1).

(1) holds. Meaning
(2) holds, and meaning
(3) holds, and that means
(4) holds, but that means
(5) holds, and meaning

15. Sentence 12: Better resolution is a feature that a DVD has in terms of being superior to a VHS tape, and more realistic sound is another improved feature, and a DVD is more durable than a VHS tape.

The most effective revision of sentence 12 would begin with which group of words?

(1) In terms of better resolution, a DVD has features
(2) DVD features such as better resolution and the feature of
(3) Features such as better resolution, more realistic sound, and durability are
(4) DVDs have many features that are better, one such feature being
(5) A feature such as better resolution and a feature of more realistic sound, and a feature

Answers are on page 374.

Cumulative Review

Directions: Choose the <u>one best answer</u> to each question. Some of the sentences may contain errors in organization, sentence structure, usage, and mechanics. A few sentences, however, may be correct as written. Read the sentences carefully and then answer the questions based on them. For each question, choose the answer that would result in the most effective writing of the sentence or sentences.

Questions 1–8 refer to the following document.

Tobacco Settlement

(A)

(1) This document serves as the agreement between Triton Tobacco Company and the United States Government concerning all tobacco products sold in this Country. (2) Government officials and the TTC chief executive officer have spent countless hours developing this plan, we hope it is a plan with which we can all live.

(B)

(3) The transit and billboard advertising of tobacco products are banned. (4) This ban includes privately owned vehicles. (5) As well as public vehicles. (6) In addition, the parties agree that there had been no distribution of merchandise with tobacco brand names or logos. (7) This ban includes caps, T-shirts, and backpacks.

(C)

(8) This agreement specifically prohibits TTC sponsorship of concerts and events with a significant youth audience. (9) Although there is no ban against the use of tobacco products in movies and television shows, payment for this use is not allowed. (10) There is no free samples of tobacco products allowed at any time to any person. (11) Finally, over the next 25 years, billions of dollars have been paid to the states.

1. Sentence 1: **This document serves as the agreement between Triton Tobacco Company and the United States Government concerning all tobacco products sold in this Country.**

   What correction should be made to sentence 1?

   (1) change *Triton Tobacco Company* to *triton tobacco company*
   (2) change *United States* to *united states*
   (3) change *tobacco* to *Tobacco*
   (4) change *Country* to *country*
   (5) no correction is necessary

2. Sentence 2: **Government officials and the TTC chief executive officer have spent countless hours developing this <u>plan, we hope</u> it is a plan with which we can all live.**

   Which is the best way to write the underlined portion of the text? If the original is the best way, choose option (1).

   (1) plan, we hope
   (2) plan. We hope
   (3) plan, we will hope
   (4) plan, we hoped
   (5) plan, unless

3. **Sentence 3: The transit and billboard advertising of tobacco products are banned.**

   Which is the best way to write the underlined portion of the text? If the original is the best way, choose option (1).

   (1) products are
   (2) product's are
   (3) products is
   (4) products were
   (5) products been

4. **Sentences 4 and 5: This ban includes privately owned vehicles. As well as public vehicles.**

   Which is the best way to write the underlined portion of the text? If the original is the best way, choose option (1).

   (1) vehicles. As well
   (2) vehicles. But as well
   (3) vehicles although as well
   (4) vehicles since as well
   (5) vehicles as well

5. **Sentence 6: In addition, the parties agree that there had been no distribution of merchandise with tobacco brand names or logos.**

   What correction should be made to sentence 6?

   (1) change *agree* to *has agreed*
   (2) change *agree* to *have agreed*
   (3) replace *there* with *they're*
   (4) change *had been* to *has been*
   (5) change *had been* to *will be*

6. **Sentence 9: Although there is no ban against the use of tobacco products in movies and television shows, payment for this use is not allowed.**

   What correction should be made to sentence 9?

   (1) replace *Although* with *However*
   (2) replace *there* with *they're*
   (3) change *is* to *are*
   (4) remove the comma after *shows*
   (5) no correction is necessary

7. **Sentence 10: There is no free samples of tobacco products allowed at any time to any person.**

   Which is the best way to write the underlined portion of the text? If the original is the best way, choose option (1).

   (1) There is
   (2) Their is
   (3) They're is
   (4) There are
   (5) There were

8. **Sentence 11: Finally, over the next 25 years, billions of dollars have been paid to the states.**

   What correction should be made to sentence 11?

   (1) change *dollars* to *Dollars*
   (2) change *have* to *has*
   (3) change *have been* to *will be*
   (4) change *states* to *States*
   (5) change *states* to *state's*

Questions 9–15 refer to the following letter.

August 20, 2001

Ms. Eva Molnich
Vice President, Human Resources
Cushing & Co.
100 North Avenue
New York, NY 10001

Dear Ms. Molnich:

(A)

(1) José Wilton has asked me to write a letter recommending him for the job of office clerk at your company. (2) In this recommendation is some things about José that you may not already know. (3) You're interest in this job applicant will increase once you have heard what I have to say.

(B)

(4) José worked for me when we will both be at TelCo in 1995. (5) He was a hardworking employee, José was a responsible employee, and he was a smart person in terms of being an employee. (6) The managers at TelCo were disappointed although José took another job at Cinecorp in 1996. (7) The truth is that no one ever want a person like José to leave.

(C)

(8) The other thing you should know about José is how much people enjoy working with him. (9) He is friendly, kind, funny, and compassionate. (10) Office morale and productivity improves dramatically when José is in the building. (11) If you don't hire him, Ms. Molnich, someone else will.

Sincerely,
Greta Tompkins

9. **Sentence 2: In this recommendation is some things about José that you may not already know.**

   What correction should be made to sentence 2?

   (1) change *is* to *was*
   (2) change *is* to *are*
   (3) change *you* to *your*
   (4) change *know* to *knew*
   (5) change *know* to *will know*

10. **Sentence 3: You're interest in this job applicant will increase once you have heard what I have to say.**

    What correction should be made to sentence 3?

    (1) change *You're* to *Your*
    (2) insert a comma after *applicant*
    (3) change *will increase* to *has increased*
    (4) change *you have* to *you has*
    (5) change *I have* to *I had*

11. **Sentence 4: José worked for me <u>when we will both be</u> at TelCo in 1995.**

    Which is the best way to write the underlined portion of the text? If the original is the best way, choose option (1).

    (1) when we will both be
    (2) although we will both be
    (3) when we are both
    (4) when we were both
    (5) when you will both be

12. **Sentence 5: He was a hardworking employee, José was a responsible employee, and he was a smart person in terms of being an employee.**

    The most effective revision of sentence 12 would begin with which group of words?

    (1) He worked hard and was a responsible employee,
    (2) In terms of being an employee and a smart person,
    (3) José was a hardworking, responsible, and smart
    (4) José was hardworking, he was smart, but he was
    (5) He was a hardworking employee, he was responsible

13. **Sentence 6: The managers at TelCo were disappointed <u>although José took</u> another job at Cinecorp in 1996.**

    Which is the best way to write the underlined portion of the text? If the original is the best way, choose option (1).

    (1) although José took
    (2) when José took
    (3) but José took
    (4) although José will take
    (5) although José was taking

14. **Sentence 7: The truth is that no one ever want a person like José to leave.**

    What correction should be made to sentence 7?

    (1) change *is* to *will be*
    (2) insert a comma after *is*
    (3) change *want* to *wants*
    (4) insert a comma after *want*
    (5) no correction is necessary

15. **Sentence 10: Office morale and productivity improves dramatically when José is in the building.**

    What correction should be made to sentence 10?

    (1) change *improves* to *improved*
    (2) change *improves* to *improve*
    (3) replace *when* with *although*
    (4) replace *when* with *for*
    (5) change *is* to *will be*

    Answers are on page 374.

CHAPTER 4

Organization

Effective Paragraphs

A **paragraph** is a group of sentences that communicates one idea. All of the writing you will see on Part I of the GED Language Arts, Writing Test will be in paragraph form. To succeed on this test, you will need to recognize the parts of a paragraph and determine if they are effective. If the parts of a paragraph are not effective, you will need to know how to revise them.

The **topic sentence** of a paragraph, which is often the first sentence, tells what the rest of the paragraph will be about. What kind of sentences would come after the topic sentence below?

There are many reasons that I left my job at the bank.

You are correct if you thought that the next few sentences would probably list some reasons that the writer left her job at the bank.

There are many reasons that I left my job at the bank. First of all, I had been working there for many years, and I was burned out. Second, my boss and I did not get along. Finally, I found a better-paying job that suits my lifestyle much more than the bank job.

The group of sentences above is an effective paragraph because it states a clear main idea in the first sentence and then gives more information with **supporting sentences.**

Is the next paragraph an example of effective writing?

There have been several problems with following our safety guidelines over the last month. It is Mary's birthday tomorrow, so please stop by the front desk to donate toward her celebration lunch. Progress reports are due in Mr. Blandini's office by noon today. Whenever I see a customer at the warehouse, I try to be friendly and helpful.

Although there are no errors in grammar or usage, this paragraph is <u>not</u> effective writing! The first sentence tells you that you will be reading about safety problems. However, the following sentences do not support this main idea.

Your first step in understanding organization questions on the Language Arts, Writing Test is to be able to tell the difference between an effective paragraph and an ineffective one.

EXERCISE 1

Directions: Read each paragraph below and decide if it is well written. If it is, write *effective* in the space provided. If it is not, write *ineffective*.

1. Next Wednesday is the company annual meeting, and we hope you all can attend. The meeting will begin promptly at 2:00 P.M. in the Underwood Room of Building A. Please plan to be on time, as important matters will be discussed. Following the meeting, we will adjourn to the cafeteria for a catered dinner. _____

2. Your son has been very disruptive during the past several days, Mrs. Renfro. Next week we'll be focusing on fractions, and the week after that will be the standardized test session. There are two new children in the school who recently moved to town from Korea. We hope that they will feel welcome here. _____

3. Thank you for your interest in learning more about ProtoCorp. We do not currently have any job openings here, but we will keep your résumé on file. If a position opens up that requires skills such as yours, we will call you to set up an interview. Again, we appreciate your interest in ProtoCorp. _____

4. To apply for a new credit card, follow these simple steps. I use my credit card to purchase only those items I know I can afford. The new restaurant in town does not accept credit cards. A credit card can make life easier, or it can complicate life with unacceptable debt. _____

5. Planning is the single most important ingredient in effective home management in this era of households with two working parents. If you don't have children, things are not quite so complicated. In the year 2000, more than 30 percent of the people in Jackson County were living at or below the poverty level. Most of these people were children. _____

6. Once again, Mr. Andrews, I write to tell you that your storage rental payment is past due. StowZone Company owns many storage sites, and all are located in New England. Storage units are used for everything from temporary furniture holdings to permanent carports. These storage units can be expensive. _____

Answers are on page 374.

Inserting a Topic Sentence

Some questions on the Language Arts, Writing Test will ask you to choose a sentence to put at the beginning of a paragraph. Essentially, you are being asked to choose the most effective topic sentence—the sentence that best states the main idea of the other sentences in the paragraph.

Look at the following example:

(A)

(1) First, we plan to discuss changes in department personnel. (2) Next, we'll hear a presentation from our benefits manager about the new retirement plan the company is offering. (3) Finally, if time permits, we'll end the meeting with a general discussion of employee morale and our upcoming holiday party.

Which sentence below would be most effective at the beginning of paragraph A?

(1) Now is the time to make plans for the company's social activities.
(2) Our department does not have enough people to do all the work we have.
(3) Here is the agenda for today's departmental meeting.
(4) Working in this department is challenging yet rewarding.
(5) There was a lot to discuss at yesterday's company luncheon.

To answer this type of organization question, you need to read the paragraph and understand what the main idea is. In this paragraph, each sentence describes one thing that will happen at a meeting. You are correct if you chose (3) as your answer. Now try another example:

(B)

(1) You can use them to line pet cages. (2) You can use them in your garden to cut down on weeds and conserve water. (3) You can use old newspapers instead of new paper towels to wash windows. (4) The main goal is not to throw them in the trash!

Which sentence below would be most effective at the beginning of paragraph B?

(1) Cleaning is one of our staff's least favorite responsibilities.
(2) Don't throw away old newspapers; recycle them!
(3) There has been interesting information in this week's newspapers.
(4) Newspapers are often made from other recycled papers.
(5) Newspapers, bottles, and cans should be recycled.

What is the main idea expressed in the example above? Each of the first three sentences gives a use for newspapers, and the last sentence gives a summary. The choice that best describes the main idea is (2).

Remember that a sentence is not necessarily an effective topic sentence just because it relates to the other sentences. For example, why is choice (3) not correct? It relates to newspapers, just as the rest of the paragraph does. But *newspapers* is not the main idea of the other sentences. Instead, *the many uses of used newspapers* is the main idea. Be careful to look at all answer choices closely to see which is the best match.

EXERCISE 2

Directions: Choose the best answer for each question below.

1. (1) Choose a quiet place in your home where you can work undisturbed. (2) Be sure to have plenty of pencils, pens, necessary books, and paper within easy reach so that you do not have to get up and waste time locating them. (3) Remember to ask family members to respect your needs to be alone and to concentrate. (4) Try to stick to studying one subject at a time, and allow plenty of time for each. (5) Finally, take breaks when you need to because studying is hard work.

    Which sentence below would be most effective at the beginning of this paragraph?

    (1) It is important to do well in school.
    (2) There are several things you can do to make study time more productive.
    (3) Peace and quiet are luxuries that can be difficult to find.
    (4) It is time to review what we know about effective writing.
    (5) Children can be taught to work hard.

2. (1) First of all, the water that comes from your kitchen faucet may not be the best thing to drink. (2) The taste may be off because of chemicals present in your town's water source, and there is always the danger of harmful bacteria. (3) Second, bottled water can get very expensive. (4) The average cost for a half-gallon of bottled spring water is now $1.40 in many areas. (5) For these reasons, a PureH$_2$O water filtration system is the best water source for your family. (6) Call 1-800-555-1111 now for more information!

    Which sentence below would be most effective at the beginning of this paragraph?

    (1) Don't drink the water!
    (2) Your water may be too dangerous to drink.
    (3) A PureH$_2$O water filtration system is your family's best source of drinking water.
    (4) Filtering your water at home is expensive and difficult.
    (5) Our town's water supply should be evaluated every few months.

3.   (1) Before doing anything else, push the emergency button located at every work station. (2) Immediately apply an ice pack to the burned area on the victim. (3) DO NOT apply any cream, oil, or lotion. (4) If the victim is unconscious, try to determine whether he or she is breathing. (5) By this time, emergency workers should have arrived. (6) Quickly give them the details of the accident and fill out the necessary accident report forms.

Which sentence below would be most effective at the beginning of this paragraph?

(1) The number of burn victims in the workplace continues to increase.
(2) Burns should be treated with care.
(3) Yesterday, an employee had an unfortunate accident involving fire.
(4) Emergencies are going to occur regardless of how careful we are.
(5) Here are our procedures for helping a coworker who has been burned.

4.   (1) The customer has asked for pressure-treated lumber and pine lattice for the sides. (2) The entire deck area should be stained with our honey-maple stain and then sealed with polyurethane. (3) The size of the deck will be 20 feet by 25 feet. (4) The estimated start-up date for this Johnson deck project is June 1, and the expected completion date is July 1. (5) Please let me know if there are any problems with these work orders.

Which sentence below would be most effective at the beginning of this paragraph?

(1) The following information provides the details for the Johnson deck.
(2) There are lots of ways to build a high-quality deck.
(3) A customer recently built a deck on his new home.
(4) Building a deck for any customer is challenging work.
(5) Every deck you build is different depending on customer preferences.

5.   (1) Our pay has not risen in the past 20 months even though our workday increased by 20 minutes. (2) Some of our older employees have been forced out of the company without adequate benefits. (3) Although we have been asking for several years, the safety hazards on the circuit assembly line have not been fixed. (4) Furthermore, our concerns about minority hiring have not been addressed.

Which sentence below would be most effective at the beginning of this paragraph?

(1) This company's safety record is poor.
(2) Yesterday, workers met with management to discuss several issues.
(3) We are requesting a meeting to discuss these important problems in the company.
(4) Our company is great to work at, but the pay is only average.
(5) After a long day of work, we expect certain compensation.

Answers are on page 375.

Dividing Paragraphs

What improvement can be made to the paragraph below?

(A)

(1) The management team would like to call your attention to some changes in our department. (2) We believe that these changes will make our team more productive and better prepared for the future. (3) First of all, we are pleased to announce that Dawn Kim has been promoted to Staff Supervisor. (4) As you know, Dawn has been working hard to update our employee handbook, and her experience with staff policy-making has been invaluable as we grow as a company. (5) She has worked here at Elton Enterprises for almost 10 years, having started as an administrative assistant in the Human Resources Department. (6) Please join us in congratulating her on her new position. (7) We look forward to the many great ideas she will bring to our staff. (8) The second change we would like to announce is our planned move to Building C across the parkway. (9) You have probably noticed how crowded our offices have become over the past year. (10) To accommodate our expanding needs, the Buildings and Grounds Department has determined that we will need an additional 10,000 square feet of space. (11) The only building available to us at this time is Building C; therefore, all of our operations will move to that location by the first of the year. (12) Renovations to the building are going on now, and we anticipate occupying beautiful offices as soon as they are complete. (13) As plans develop, you will be asked for your preferences in terms of office layout, colors, and furniture.

You probably noticed that this paragraph is very long and contains two important main ideas. The best way to improve this paragraph is to divide it into two paragraphs.

Some questions on the GED Language Arts, Writing Test will ask you to decide where a new paragraph should begin. Here is an example using the paragraph above. How would you answer this question?

Which revision would make paragraph A more effective?

Begin a new paragraph

(1) with sentence 5
(2) with sentence 7
(3) with sentence 8
(4) with sentence 9
(5) with sentence 11

Can you see that there are two main ideas discussed in the original paragraph? One is the promotion of Dawn Kim. The other is the move to a new building. The best place to start a new paragraph is with the first sentence of the second main idea. That would be sentence 8.

Sometimes, dividing a paragraph is only one of the possible answer choices in a Language Arts, Writing item. Here's an example:

(B)

(1) As a resident who lives near Darton Park, I am writing to express my appreciation for the work of our Parks Improvement Committee. (2) I have lived in this neighborhood for 17 years, and I have never seen a more well-kept park. (3) When I first moved here, Darton Park was full of run-down pathways, broken glass and trash, and dead trees and shrubs. (4) No one spent time there because it was ugly and dangerous. (5) There were no playground, no basketball court, and no benches. (6) Now the park is just amazing in all it has to offer. (7) It is beautifully landscaped, with plenty of green grass and trees and flowers. (8) There are a playground filled with happy children and a basketball court constantly used by our neighborhood teens. (9) People can safely walk their pets or just sit on one of the many new benches to enjoy the park. (10) My thanks and congratulations go to the Parks Improvement Committee for their hard work. (11) We love what you have done.

Which revision should be made to sentence 6 to make paragraph B more effective?

(1) move sentence 6 to follow sentence 1
(2) move sentence 6 to follow sentence 8
(3) remove sentence 6
(4) begin a new paragraph with sentence 6
(5) no revision is necessary

The writer of this paragraph is comparing the old Darton Park to the new park. It would make sense to divide the paragraph into these two main ideas: old park and new park. Beginning a new paragraph with sentence 6 would be an effective revision to the original paragraph. Choice (4) is correct.

EXERCISE 3

Directions: Choose the best answer for each item below.

1.   (1) What is the best way to get rid of refrigerator odors? (2) Some people say just don't keep any food in the refrigerator! (3) Although that is one option, the solution does not really have to be so drastic. (4) Instead, follow these simple steps for a fresh-smelling fridge that still holds all your favorite foods. (5) Remove all food from drawers and shelves and prepare to clean thoroughly. (6) Create a mixture of water, baking soda, lemon juice, and a drop of ammonia. (7) With a clean sponge dipped in this solution, wipe down all shelves, walls, and drawers of the refrigerator, being careful to get at all the nooks and crannies where food can get stuck. (8) Dry the area thoroughly and replace food. (9) Put a fresh box of baking soda, opened, on the bottom back shelf. (10) Repeat this process at least once a month.

Which revision would make the paragraph more effective?

Begin a new paragraph

(1) with sentence 3
(2) with sentence 5
(3) with sentence 6
(4) with sentence 7
(5) with sentence 8

2.   (1) Summer is a great time to be outdoors and active. (2) But the same precautions we take for ourselves—such as limiting sun exposure, drinking plenty of fluids, and avoiding heavy exertion in extremely hot temperatures—need to be applied to our pets as well. (3) When we're out enjoying a nice day at the beach, we can sometimes forget that our pets aren't able to look out for themselves. (4) These precautions can help you and your pet get the most out of the "dog days" of summer. (5) Keep plenty of cool, fresh drinking water available at all times. (6) Be sure that your pet's doghouse or kennel is located in the shade. (7) Don't go for long walks in the middle of the day and remember that cat and dog paws are sensitive to hot asphalt. (8) Animals with shorter muzzles are more vulnerable to heatstroke, so pay particular attention to these pets.

Which revision would make the paragraph more effective?

Begin a new paragraph

(1) with sentence 2
(2) with sentence 3
(3) with sentence 4
(4) with sentence 6
(5) with sentence 7

3.   (1) Shopping at FreshFarm is the best way to make sure your family gets the healthiest foods available. (2) We buy only from local farmers and wholesalers to ensure that each and every product on our shelves is as fresh as possible. (3) Our produce has been naturally ripened to provide the most nutrients. (4) We stock only organic foods—foods that have not been treated with dangerous pesticides and other chemicals. (5) In addition, we label all of our products according to a useful "health index"—showing fat, cholesterol, and vitamin content. (6) Shopping at FreshFarm will also save you money. (7) Each week we feature "Farmer's Choice" products, which represent a wide variety of discounted fruits, vegetables, and meats that will please the whole family. (8) We also sell many products in bulk quantities at a lower price—another way to stock up and save. (9) Finally, with our frequent-shopper card, you will receive additional discounts on everything you buy. (10) Shop now and save!

Which revision would make the paragraph more effective?

Begin a new paragraph

(1) with sentence 4
(2) with sentence 6
(3) with sentence 7
(4) with sentence 8
(5) with sentence 9

4.   (1) The following items will be discussed at our October 20 meeting at Nellie Patterson's house. (2) First of all, we need to decide who will chair the winter fund-raiser. (3) As we all know, this bake sale is one of our best moneymakers, so it is important to select a capable chairperson. (4) We will also need to plan the children's pageant and figure out the best date for it. (5) The last item on our agenda will be public relations. (6) In other words, how can we let the community know more about our organization? (7) To get to Nellie's home, take I–98 to exit 13 and turn right onto Madison Boulevard. (8) Drive four miles, then take a left at the Sunoco station onto Marsley Way. (9) Nellie lives at 8909 Marsley Way, Apartment 417. (10) You can park anywhere in the lot across the street. (11) If you are taking public transportation, use the Green line and get off at the Rutland stop. (12) Call 555-0001 and we will come and pick you up there, as it is too far to walk.

Which revision would make the paragraph more effective?

Begin a new paragraph

(1) with sentence 4
(2) with sentence 5
(3) with sentence 7
(4) with sentence 9
(5) with sentence 10

5. (1) Do you know of a young person in your community, school, church, temple, or synagogue who has lots of potential in education but limited financial resources? (2) If so, let us know! (3) We are the Braston Youth Foundation, a nonprofit organization looking to reward promising teenagers with the opportunity for scholarships, job training, and paid internships. (4) Students with academic potential, financial need, and strong recommendations can benefit from our program. (5) Here are the details of how we work. (6) First, call us at (800) 555-2222 and tell us the student's name and address. (7) We will send him or her an application, which includes recommendation forms to give to a teacher or counselor. (8) Once the application has been completed and sent in, we will call the student to set up an interview. (9) It's as easy as that. (10) Stop by the Braston booth if you have any questions.

Which revision would make the paragraph more effective?

Begin a new paragraph

(1) with sentence 4
(2) with sentence 5
(3) with sentence 6
(4) with sentence 7
(5) with sentence 8

Answers are on page 375.

Rearranging Sentences and Combining Paragraphs

Sometimes the sentences in a paragraph may need to be rearranged or combined with another paragraph in order to make a piece of writing more effective. Here's an example of how this type of revision might appear on the Language Arts, Writing Test:

Pedestrians Can Help Prevent Traffic Accidents

(A)

(1) We all know how important it is for drivers to use caution on the road. (2) Driving safely requires using appropriate speeds, paying attention to road signs and traffic signals, and staying alert for unexpected events. (3) It is especially important to drive cautiously when there are pedestrians in the area. (4) Too many accidents occur because drivers are not aware of pedestrian traffic.

(B)

(5) What many people forget, however, is that drivers are not the only ones responsible for traffic safety. (6) Pedestrians too must take responsibility for preventing traffic accidents. (7) Like drivers, walkers and bikers must pay careful attention to signs and signals.

(C)

(8) Pedestrians must learn to judge gaps in traffic and cross streets only when and where it is safe and legal to do so.

(D)

(9) Only when both drivers and pedestrians pay attention to traffic safety will we truly prevent accidents on our roads. (10) Let's work together to make our neighborhoods and highways safe places to live and travel.

Which revision would improve this piece of writing?

(1) move sentence 8 to follow sentence 10
(2) remove sentence 7
(3) remove sentence 8
(4) move sentence 8 to the end of paragraph B
(5) no revision is necessary

You are correct if you chose (4) *move sentence 8 to the end of paragraph B.* The main idea of paragraph B is that pedestrians need to observe safety rules. Sentence 8 gives an example of a safety rule, and therefore this sentence is an effective addition to that paragraph.

EXERCISE 4

Directions: Choose the best answer to the question below.

Booth Setup Procedures

(A)

(1) In order to ensure smooth operation of our souvenir sales booth at each game, we are providing this document to each volunteer. (2) Please keep this in a safe place and bring it with you when you work. (3) We will post a copy in the booth as well.

(B)

(4) Before you arrive at the booth, be sure you obtain the key from the previous week's volunteer.

(C)

(5) If you are unable to get into the booth for whatever reason, call Mary Erwin at 555-1010. (6) DO NOT under any circumstances bother either the coaches or the officials. (7) Mary will get you a key, or she will give alternative instructions for getting into the booth.

(D)

(8) Once you are in the booth, your first task is to make sure shelves are well stocked. (9) Potato chips, soda, and hot coffee are the biggest sellers, so be sure you get these items out early. (10) Next, remove the cash drawer from the safe with the key provided. (11) The booth should be open to the public a half-hour before game time.

Which revision would improve this piece of writing?

(1) move sentence 4 to follow sentence 7
(2) move sentence 4 to the beginning of paragraph C
(3) remove sentence 4
(4) move sentence 8 to the end of paragraph B
(5) no revision is necessary

Answers are on page 375.

Deleting Sentences

What improvement can be made to the paragraph below?

Try Word Workshop!

(1) For games to help your child improve vocabulary skills to an easy-to-use built-in dictionary, this website (www.wordshop.com) is the best. (2) The site is packed with lots of information that kids can use in and out of the classroom. (3) For example, with the click of a mouse, a fourth grader can find word definitions that include photographs and diagrams. (4) A preschooler can play an exciting matching game that tests his or her reading and writing skills in a fun and creative way. (5) Fourth graders are usually age nine or ten. (6) If you care about your child's word skills, click on www.wordshop.com and see what this site can do for your whole family.

The main idea of this paragraph is the benefits of a particular website. All of the sentences that follow should support the idea that this is a good website. One sentence, however, does not do this. Which one?

You are correct if you thought that sentence 5 does not support the main idea of the paragraph. Although the sentence is true, and although it is somewhat related to another sentence in the paragraph, it still does not belong. To make this a more effective piece of writing, the sentence should be removed, or deleted.

Some questions on the Language Arts, Writing Test will give you the option of removing a sentence from a paragraph in order to make the writing more effective. Read the example on the next page and answer the question that follows.

Dear Mr. and Mrs. Lynch:

(A)

(1) I am writing to let you know that Matthew has not been turning in his assignments for several weeks now. (2) He is coming to class, but he is not prepared. (3) When I ask him where his written work is, he makes an excuse and says he'll hand it in the next day.
(4) Unfortunately, the next day comes, and I still do not see the work.

(B)

(5) What I am most concerned about, Mr. and Mrs. Lynch, is the huge gap between the homework Matthew is capable of and the work he does. (6) Matthew is one of the brightest students in the class, and his class participation shows this. (7) Matthew's awesome three-pointer in last week's game was a highlight of the basketball tournament. (8) However, if he continues to resist doing the homework, I will be forced to give him a failing grade. (9) Can you help me figure out an effective strategy in working with him? (10) I look forward to hearing your ideas and insights.

Sincerely,
Joanne Riley

Which revision would make paragraph B more effective?

(1) move sentence 10 to the beginning of paragraph B
(2) move sentence 7 to the end of paragraph B
(3) move sentence 7 to the beginning of paragraph B
(4) remove sentence 7
(5) remove sentence 10

You are correct if you chose (4) *remove sentence 7*. Can you see that Matthew's performance in a basketball game is not relevant to the main idea of the paragraph? The rest of the paragraph discusses Matthew's work in the classroom and on homework. Moving this sentence to another place in the paragraph does not help because it still does not support the main idea.

Try some other examples:

(A)

(1) To do a proper job choosing a preschool for your child, you first need to decide what your priorities are. (2) There are many options available, and each school will have its own strengths and weaknesses. (3) Many schools, not just preschools, are strong in the area of literacy. (4) You will want to be sure that your chosen preschool is not weak in an area that you consider your top priority.

(B)

(5) The fact of the matter is that although all parents want a safe, caring place for their children, that is where agreement ends. (6) Some parents value a highly organized environment for their child. (7) Others prefer a less structured, free-form approach. (8) Some parents do not care whether their child is exposed to prereading activities, whereas some expect lots of alphabet and phonics work. (9) Do you want a school in which there are children from all kinds of backgrounds, including socioeconomic, cultural, racial, and religious? (10) These questions should factor into the process of choosing a preschool. (11) Or is diversity of less importance than proximity to your home or workplace?

Which revision would make paragraph A more effective?

(1) move sentence 4 to the beginning of paragraph A
(2) move sentence 3 to the end of paragraph A
(3) move sentence 3 to the beginning of paragraph A
(4) remove sentence 3
(5) remove sentence 2

Which revision would make paragraph B more effective?

(1) move sentence 10 to follow sentence 11
(2) move sentence 10 to the beginning of paragraph B
(3) move sentence 8 to the beginning of paragraph B
(4) remove sentence 10
(5) remove sentence 11

In paragraph A, the sentence that does not belong is sentence 3; therefore, choice (4) is the correct answer. A sentence about literacy does not belong in a paragraph about choosing a preschool. Moving the sentence to another location in the paragraph will not make the paragraph more effective. Only deleting the sentence will help.

In paragraph B, sentence 10 is out of place. It offers a summary of what was discussed in the paragraph and therefore should go at the end. The two sentences about diversity (9 and 11) should be together. Moving sentence 10 to follow sentence 11 makes the paragraph more effective. Choice (1) is the correct answer.

In the next exercise, you'll have a chance to practice rearranging and deleting sentences to make a paragraph more effective.

EXERCISE 5

Directions: Choose the best answer for each question below.

Questions 1–4 refer to the letter below.

September 2, 2001

Dear Valued Customer:

(A)

(1) This letter is sent to inform you of some changes in our billing and delivery policies. (2) We believe these changes are necessary in order to serve you better. (3) As you know, Linden Pharmacy has been providing quality health products to this community for over 40 years. (4) Haverford Hardware has also been on this block for almost that long. (5) We truly believe that the changes we are making will enhance this partnership of business and community.

(B)

(6) We certainly hope you agree. (7) As you know, Linden has long had a policy of mailing a bill each month to cover all costs incurred during the previous 30 days. (8) Beginning in January, we will submit a bill with each purchase, and we will require payment at the time of purchase. (9) We believe that this practice will cut down on overdue payments, which affect our ability to serve all of our customers equally. (10) Most overdue payments are the result of inadequate financial planning. (11) Please be assured that we will continue to work with you regarding all insurance payments.

(C)

(12) For many years, Linden has offered same-day delivery of nonemergency medications and supplies as well as 24-hour delivery of emergency prescriptions sent in by a physician. (13) Due to rapidly escalating health-care costs and Linden's desire to make our products available at as low a price as possible, we find that we are no longer able to offer this service. (14) The second change we will be implementing in January is related to our delivery policy. (15) We regret that starting January 1 we can no longer offer delivery service. (16) Please be assured that our 24-hour prescription service will still be available for your physician, but other arrangements will need to be made for pickup and transport.

Sincerely,

Joseph Jenkins, Manager
Linden Pharmacy

1. **Sentence 4: Haverford Hardware has also been on this block for almost that long.**

   Which revision should be made to sentence 4?

   (1) move sentence 4 to the end of paragraph A
   (2) move sentence 4 to follow sentence 2
   (3) move sentence 4 to follow sentence 6
   (4) remove sentence 4
   (5) no revision is necessary

2. **Sentence 6: We certainly hope you agree.**

   Which revision should be made to sentence 6?

   (1) move sentence 6 to the end of paragraph A
   (2) move sentence 6 to follow sentence 7
   (3) move sentence 6 to follow sentence 9
   (4) move sentence 6 to the end of paragraph B
   (5) remove sentence 6

3. **Which revision would make paragraph B more effective?**

   (1) move sentence 9 to the end of paragraph B
   (2) remove sentence 9
   (3) move sentence 10 to the end of paragraph B
   (4) remove sentence 10
   (5) no revision is necessary

4. **Which revision would make paragraph C more effective?**

   (1) remove sentence 12
   (2) remove sentence 13
   (3) move sentence 14 to the beginning of paragraph C
   (4) move sentence 14 to the end of paragraph C
   (5) remove sentence 14

Answers are on page 375.

Tone and Diction

Which sentence does not belong in the paragraph below?

(1) I'd like to apply for a job at SafeCorp Investments. (2) I read that you have some openings in your customer service department, and the positions sound interesting to me. (3) I am currently employed at WorldBank, and I would welcome a change. (4) Staying in one lousy place for a long time can really start bugging me, know what I mean? (5) I would be appreciative if you would call me for an interview. (6) Thank you for your help in this matter.

You might have noticed right away that one sentence "jumps out" as not belonging. Sentence 4 does not match the rest of the paragraph in its **tone** and **diction.** The tone of the sentence is more casual than the rest of the paragraph. The word choice, or diction, is unlike the word choice in the other sentences. Although the writer might want to include the idea of needing change from his current job, this sentence is not an effective way to do it.

Look at the following example. Which sentence does not belong?

(1) Here's an awesome new soft drink that will knock your socks off! (2) It's called WildWater, and it's brought to you by the same cool folks who brought you SodaSips, the popular cola alternative. (3) If you stock this stuff on your grocery shelves, we guarantee you'll create the next beverage craze. (4) Customers dig WildWater, and they'll dig your store too if you carry all four FANTASTIC flavors—GreatGrape, MellowMelon, SassySour, and LiveLime. (5) This is a product that if marketed efficiently will increase sales by a significant percentage. (6) Just tell your beverage supplier: We want WILD!

You are correct if you decided that sentence 5 does not fit in the paragraph and should be removed. It uses a formal tone and moderate diction, while the rest of the paragraph is more casual and upbeat.

EXERCISE 6

Directions: In each paragraph below, there may be a sentence that does not belong due to its tone and diction. Cross out any sentence that does not belong. If all sentences belong, write *effective* in the space provided.

1. We are interested in coming to visit Redhome Manor to see if it would be a suitable place to live for my 86-year-old mother-in-law. We are moving to the Denver area and need to find a nursing facility close by. From your brochures, Redhome seems to be a lovely and caring place to live. When can we set up an appointment? This old lady is driving me nuts. _____

2. The best way to get a good deal on a used car is to research, research, and research some more. If you simply walk into a dealership and expect to buy what's on the lot, you might end up with a poor deal. Instead, figure out ahead of time the make and model of car you are interested in by reading consumer magazines and newspapers. Next, find out the "blue book" value of the car you want. Any public library can help you find this resource. Just be the dummy you are and ask. Finally, be prepared to negotiate with the car dealer. The consumer has more power than you might imagine when it comes to used cars. _____

3. Here's why you need to vote in favor of the new recreation center. Number one: It's your money. Either your tax dollars can go toward creating a safe environment for people of all ages in this town, or they can go toward cramming more people into a new jail. It's that simple. Number two: This is a one-time offer from one of the best building contractors in this state. If we don't vote this in now, he'll head right over to Westfield and build a rec center there. We need to move on this now. The consequence of remaining immobile and indecisive on the complex decision of whether or not to construct a center in which all of our citizens may have the opportunity to recreate is that our town will no longer be able to entertain the possibility of said center. Let's get down to town hall and vote yes! _____

4. Please join with me in giving a warm welcome to Nancy Resmith, our new comptroller here at Sneed.com. Nancy comes to us with a great deal of financial experience at several different companies. She graduated from the University of Texas in 1995, and she was most recently employed at Davis.com. Nancy will work in the accounting department here at Sneed. She will be part of our benefits analysis team. We are happy to have her working with us. _____

5. To repair a hole in a blacktop driveway, first shovel out all loose rocks and debris from the hole. If the hole is more than four or five inches deep, place a large rock at the bottom. Scoop out a shovelful of prepared blacktop (available in bags of various sizes at any landscape outlet) and begin filling the hole. Repeat until the hole is filled one inch over the top. Use a board or the back of a shovel to tamp down the mixture until it is firm. Drive over the filled hole several times with your car tire to compact the material as much as possible. _____

Answers are on page 375.

Organization: Editing Practice

Directions: The following letter contains errors in organization. Find and correct these errors using this checklist as your editing guide:

- ☐ Do paragraphs begin with an effective topic sentence?
- ☐ Do paragraphs contain only one main idea?
- ☐ Are all sentences placed correctly within the text?
- ☐ Do supporting sentences support the main idea in each paragraph?
- ☐ Do all sentences follow the appropriate tone and diction of the text?

December 7, 2001

Mr. Harold Otis, Manager
Service Systems, Inc.
100 Blake Boulevard
Kansas City, MO 64944

Dear Mr. Otis:

I'd like to set up a meeting to discuss our business relationship with you. We have worked together for two years now, and I think it is time to consider what works and what does not work. Then we can agree on how to proceed with future contracts.

There are three major topics we need to address, as I see it. Of course, if you have other ideas, we can certainly discuss these as well. We have an excellent relationship that is worth taking care of. The first topic that needs to be addressed is maintenance scheduling. Our current contract requires two monthly inspection and maintenance calls; my staff and I believe that one per month would be adequate. It would be beneficial to all of us if we could agree on an effective schedule.

The second subject I'd like to discuss is personnel. Unfortunately, some of your technicians are rude and uncooperative. They have actually threatened several of my tenants in the past. What a huge pain in the neck they are, man! We'd like you to assure us that all of your staff will meet or exceed your own high expectations.

Your services are excellent, but there are other less expensive businesses that might be of equal or better quality. Unless we can get a reduction in price, we may be forced to look elsewhere. Finally, the cost factor of our current agreement needs discussing.

Please call my office, Mr. Otis, at your convenience. We look forward to working out these issues so that we may have a continued business relationship in the future. I call 'em like I see 'em is all I can say! My best to you and your staff.

Sincerely,
Antonia Englewood

Answers are on page 375.

Chapter Review

Directions: Choose the <u>one best answer</u> to each question. Some of the sentences may contain organizational errors. A few, however, may be correct as written. Read the sentences carefully and then answer the questions based on them. For each question, choose the answer that would result in the most effective writing of the sentence or sentences.

Questions 1–5 refer to the following instructions.

How to Select the Right Interior Paint

(A)

(1) Before you head out to the hardware store to buy paint for your latest home improvement project, keep in mind that paint selection is not always a simple matter.
(2) Neither is finding a good lawn mower, for that matter. (3) These detailed instructions will help you avoid expensive and time-consuming mistakes.

(B)

(4) The first decision you'll need to make is whether to purchase a water-based paint or an oil-based one.

(C)

(5) Water-based paints, also called latex paints, dry fast and are nearly odorless. (6) They are easy to use because they clean up with just soap and water. (7) The downside of latex paints is that they are less durable than oil-based paints. (8) Oil-based paints require cleaning with a solvent, which can be messy and smelly, and they are also slower to dry than latex paints. (9) Yuck—who needs to work that hard? (10) The clear advantage of oil-based paint is that it is very durable; therefore, you won't need to repaint as often.

(D)

(11) Paint stores are happy to provide you with paint chips that you can take home and think about. (12) Just remember that color intensity grows with wall size; a pale yellow on a paint chip may look like bright sunshine on a bedroom wall. (13) When you have narrowed your choices down to two or three, buy a small quantity of each and paint a large section of wall in each color. (14) Last but not least, you'll need to decide how much shine you want. (15) Paints come in flat, semigloss, and high-gloss finishes, and each finish is best used for different purposes. (16) In general, the higher the gloss, the more resistant the paint is to wear and tear. (17) Usually people opt for semi- or high-gloss paint for doors, windows, and woodwork and flat paint for walls and ceilings.

1. **Sentence 2: Neither is finding a good lawn mower, for that matter.**

   Which revision should be made to sentence 2?

   (1) move sentence 2 to the beginning of paragraph A
   (2) move sentence 2 to the beginning of paragraph B
   (3) move sentence 2 to the end of paragraph B
   (4) move sentence 2 to the end of paragraph C
   (5) remove sentence 2

2. **Sentence 4: The first decision you'll need to make is whether to purchase a water-based paint or an oil-based one.**

   Which revision should be made to sentence 4?

   (1) move sentence 4 to the end of paragraph A
   (2) move sentence 4 to the beginning of paragraph C
   (3) move sentence 4 to the end of paragraph C
   (4) move sentence 4 to the beginning of paragraph D
   (5) remove sentence 4

3. **Which revision would make paragraph C more effective?**

   (1) move sentence 6 to follow sentence 8
   (2) move sentence 7 to follow sentence 8
   (3) remove sentence 7
   (4) move sentence 9 to follow sentence 10
   (5) remove sentence 9

4. **Which sentence below would be most effective at the beginning of paragraph D?**

   (1) Buying paint is a tricky process.
   (2) The next big decision is what color paint to use.
   (3) Don't buy paint that is too expensive.
   (4) Now is the time to think about how much paint to buy.
   (5) Your next step is to find a good painter.

5. **Which revision would make paragraph D more effective?**

   Begin a new paragraph

   (1) with sentence 13
   (2) with sentence 14
   (3) with sentence 15
   (4) with sentence 16
   (5) with sentence 17

Questions 6–10 refer to the following article.

Three Great Reasons to Support Enviroworld Today

(A)

(1) We know you get phone calls and letters all the time asking you to support worthy causes. (2) And we know you have only so much to give. (3) We think Enviroworld is one of the most important organizations you have the opportunity to help.

(B)

(4) Here are three great reasons to support us now! (5) Supporting other groups such as VoteNow and Peace for Humanity is important too.

(C)

(6) There are over six billion people in the world, and each of us has an opportunity to help save the planet we share. (7) Many organizations seek to help specific cities, regions, and countries, but Enviroworld works to protect all our planet's people. (8) Issues such as global warming affect us all— not just those of us in the United States—and we have an opportunity to protect everyone on earth from the deadly effects of global warming.

(D)

(9) Do we want them to grow up in a world filled with toxins, nuclear waste, and pollution? (10) Our children and our grandchildren will inherit the world that we create for them. (11) If we do not do our part now to stop production of deadly chemicals and weapons, our children and grandchildren will be saddled with an even greater burden. (12) It is time for us to do the work now instead of putting the problem off for future generations. (13) Supporting Enviroworld is not expensive. (14) For just two dollars per month, you will be doing your part to create a better world. (15) Instead of buying that second cup of coffee one day, why not consider making a donation that will last a lifetime? (16) If each of us in this country made this pledge, Enviroworld would be on its way to creating a safer, healthier, and brighter future for all citizens of the earth.

(E)

(17) One way is to call our toll-free number, 1-800-555-1234, and pledge over the phone. (18) The other way is to send a check in the enclosed self-addressed stamped envelope. (19) You, and the world's citizens, will be glad you did.

6. **Sentence 4: Here are three great reasons to support us now!**

   Which revision should be made to sentence 4?

   (1) remove sentence 4
   (2) move sentence 4 to the end of paragraph A
   (3) move sentence 4 to the end of paragraph C
   (4) move sentence 4 to the beginning of paragraph D
   (5) move sentence 4 to the end of paragraph D

7. **Sentence 5: Supporting other groups such as VoteNow and Peace for Humanity is important too.**

   Which revision should be made to sentence 5?

   (1) remove sentence 5
   (2) move sentence 5 to follow sentence 1
   (3) move sentence 5 to follow sentence 2
   (4) move sentence 5 to the end of paragraph D
   (5) move sentence 5 to the end of paragraph E

8. **Sentence 9: Do we want them to grow up in a world filled with toxins, nuclear waste, and pollution?**

   Which revision should be made to sentence 9 to improve paragraph D?

   (1) remove sentence 9
   (2) move sentence 9 to follow sentence 10
   (3) move sentence 9 to follow sentence 12
   (4) move sentence 9 to follow sentence 13
   (5) no revision is necessary

9. **Which revision would make paragraph D more effective?**

   Begin a new paragraph

   (1) with sentence 12
   (2) with sentence 13
   (3) with sentence 14
   (4) with sentence 15
   (5) with sentence 16

10. **Which sentence below would be most effective if inserted at the beginning of paragraph E?**

    (1) Enviroworld is a good organization.
    (2) Enviroworld employs over 50 people across the country.
    (3) There are two ways to donate money to Enviroworld.
    (4) Will you be an Enviroworld volunteer this year?
    (5) How much should you give?

    Answers are on page 376.

Cumulative Review

Directions: Choose the <u>one best answer</u> to each question. Some of the sentences may contain errors in organization, sentence structure, usage, and mechanics. A few sentences, however, may be correct as written. Read the sentences carefully and then answer the questions based on them. For each question, choose the answer that would result in the most effective writing of the sentence or sentences.

Questions 1–8 refer to the following document.

How to Vote by Absentee Ballot

(A)

(1) There are three valid reasons for voting by absentee ballot. (2) One reason is that you will be absent from your city or town on election day. (3) Another is that you have a physical disability that prevents you from voting at your polling place. (4) The last reason is that you cannot vote at the polls due to a Religious belief.

(B)

(5) The instructions for applying for an absentee ballot. (6) All applications must be made in writing and filed no later than noon on the day before the election. (7) Applications must be mailed or hand-delivered to your town or city election commission. (8) You may use any form of written communication, including letter, postcard, or official application form. (9) If you are not able to write, a person assisting you must sign your name and his or her own name, address, and telephone number.

(C)

(10) If you request to vote by mail, a ballot will be sent to any address you specify. (11) When you apply, include your name, address where the ballot should be sent, ward or precinct if you know it, the party ballot you wish to obtain (in a primary election), and you're signature. (12) To be counted, a mailed ballot must be received by the time the polls close on election day. (13) It's a good idea to plan ahead with any activity, including both leisure and work-related tasks.

(D)

(14) If you would like, and if it is your preference, you may ask and request to vote in person prior to election day. (15) Contact your city or town hall. (16) To make an appointment with the clerk. (17) You may apply for an absentee ballot and vote over the counter on the same day. (18) Absentee ballots are usually available three weeks before an election, call ahead to make sure.

1. **Sentence 4: The last reason is that you cannot vote at the polls due to a Religious belief.**

   What correction should be made to sentence 4?

   (1) change *is* to *was*
   (2) change *is* to *will be*
   (3) change *polls* to *poll's*
   (4) change *Religious* to *religious*
   (5) no correction is necessary

2. **Sentence 5: The instructions for applying for an absentee ballot.**

   The most effective revision of sentence 5 would begin with which group of words?

   (1) Here are
   (2) Here is
   (3) And then
   (4) Below,
   (5) Once again,

3. **Sentence 6: All applications must be made in writing and filed no later than noon on the day before the election.**

   Which revision should be made to sentence 6?

   (1) move sentence 6 to the end of paragraph A
   (2) move sentence 6 to the end of paragraph C
   (3) remove sentence 6
   (4) move sentence 6 to follow sentence 12
   (5) no revision is necessary

4. **Sentence 11: When you apply, include your name, address where the ballot should be sent, ward or precinct if you know it, the party ballot you wish to obtain (in a primary <u>election), and you're</u> signature.**

   Which is the best way to write the underlined portion of the text? If the original is the best way, choose option (1).

   (1) election), and you're
   (2) election) and you're
   (3) Election), and you're
   (4) election), and your
   (5) election), and you

5. **Sentence 13: It's a good idea to plan ahead with any activity, including both leisure and work-related tasks.**

   Which revision should be made to sentence 13 to improve paragraph C more?

   (1) move sentence 13 to follow sentence 10
   (2) move sentence 13 to follow sentence 11
   (3) move sentence 13 to the beginning of paragraph D
   (4) remove sentence 13
   (5) no revision is necessary

6. **Sentence 14: If you would like, and if it is your preference, you may ask and request to vote in person prior to election day.**

   The most effective revision of sentence 14 would begin with which group of words?

   (1) If you would like to express a preference, you may ask and request
   (2) If you would like, you may request
   (3) Unless you would like, you can ask
   (4) Even though it is your preference, go ahead and ask
   (5) When you would like, and when it is a preference, you may ask

7. **Sentences 15 and 16: Contact your city or town hall. To make an appointment with the clerk.**

   Which is the best way to write the underlined portion of the text? If the original is the best way, choose option (1).

   (1) town hall. To make
   (2) town Hall. To make
   (3) town hall to make
   (4) town hall, to make
   (5) town hall to makes

8. **Sentence 18: Absentee ballots are usually available three weeks before an election, call ahead to make sure.**

   The most effective revision of sentence 8 would include which group of words?

   (1) Absentee ballots were
   (2) before an election, but call ahead
   (3) before an election call ahead
   (4) before an election, and call ahead
   (5) no revision is necessary

Questions 9–15 refer to the following business letter.

September 1, 2001

Dear District Managers:

(A)

(1) Your stores will soon be receiving a promotion kit similar to the one enclosed. (2) We would like to highlight some of the most important elements of this special sale so that our winter goals will be reached quickly and efficiently. (3) To keep you fully informed and ensure that you can answer any questions your store managers may have, we have put together this informational packet. (4) Please takes the time to look through these materials carefully.

(B)

(5) Winter White Sale posters should be displayed in stores beginning November 1. (6) Please tell store managers that posters should be visible from both the street and the mall entrance. (7) All store employees should wear the "20% off" buttons during december. (8) If you need additional buttons or posters, please call Shelly at extension 230 she will send you what you need.

(C)

(9) To support employee interest in this sales promotion, we have created the Super Salesperson Sweepstakes. (10) You know, it's already so cold out that my car wouldn't start this morning. (11) Basically, a cash bonus will be given to any employee who sells in excess of $1,000 in merchandise during the Winter White Sale. (12) Although we have this kind of incentive, we believe that our sales goals will be reached quickly.

(D)

(13) If you have any questions or concerns regarding this information, please do not hesitate to call me. (14) The last piece of our winter promotion that we want to highlight for you is the radio advertising that will be in effect during the months of November and December. (15) In addition to playing our usual advertisements, WKRO-AM 850 will be airing a contest in which many of our products will be awarded as prizes. (16) We feel that this kind of advertising will bring many new customers into our store's.

Sincerely,
Naomi Goodale
Vice President, Sales Promotion

9. Sentence 4: **Please takes the time to look through these materials carefully.**

   What correction should be made to sentence 4?

   (1) change *takes* to *take*
   (2) insert a comma after *time*
   (3) insert a comma after *look*
   (4) change *materials* to *Materials*
   (5) no correction is necessary

10. Sentence 7: **All store employees should wear the "20% off" buttons during december.**

    What correction should be made to sentence 7?

    (1) change *employees* to *Employees*
    (2) change *should wear* to *were wearing*
    (3) change *buttons* to *Buttons*
    (4) change *december* to *December*
    (5) no correction is necessary

11. Sentence 8: **If you need additional buttons or posters, please call Shelly at <u>extension 230 she will send</u> you what you need.**

    Which is the best way to write the underlined portion of the text? If the original is the best way, choose option (1).

    (1) extension 230 she will send
    (2) extension 230, she will send
    (3) extension 230 she sent
    (4) extension 230, but she will send
    (5) extension 230. She will send

12. Sentence 10: **You know, it's already so cold out that my car wouldn't start this morning.**

    Which revision should be made to sentence 10?

    (1) move sentence 10 to the beginning of paragraph A
    (2) move sentence 10 to the end of paragraph B
    (3) remove sentence 10
    (4) move sentence 10 to follow sentence 11
    (5) move sentence 10 to follow sentence 15

13. Sentence 12: **Although we have this kind of incentive, we believe that our sales goals will be reached quickly.**

    The most effective revision of sentence 12 would include which of the following groups of words?

    (1) Even though we have
    (2) Because we have
    (3) Despite the fact that we have
    (4) So that we have
    (5) Because we had

14. Sentence 13: **If you have any questions or concerns regarding this information, please do not hesitate to call me.**

    Which revision should be made to sentence 13 to improve paragraph D?

    (1) remove sentence 13
    (2) move sentence 13 to follow sentence 14
    (3) move sentence 13 to follow sentence 15
    (4) move sentence 13 to the end of paragraph C
    (5) move sentence 13 to the end of paragraph D

15. Sentence 16: **We feel that this kind of advertising will bring many new customers into our store's.**

    What correction should be made to sentence 16?

    (1) change *feel* to *felt*
    (2) change *feel* to *feels*
    (3) change *customers* to *customer's*
    (4) change *our* to *ours*
    (5) change *store's* to *stores*

    Answers are on page 376.

Evaluate Your Progress

On the following chart, circle the number of any item you answered incorrectly in the Cumulative Reviews for Chapters 2–4. Next to each group of item numbers, you will see the pages you can review to learn how to answer the items correctly. Pay particular attention to reviewing skill areas in which you missed half or more of the questions.

Skill Area	Chapter 2 Item Number (pages 79–82)	Chapter 3 Item Number (pages 111–114)	Chapter 4 Item Number (pages 139—143)	Review Pages
ORGANIZATION				
Unity/Coherence			3, 5, 12, 14	127–133
SENTENCE STRUCTURE				
Complete sentences, fragments, and sentence combining	2, 5, 15	4	2, 7	19–24 83–104
Run-on sentences/ comma splices		2	8, 11	86–88, 96
Wordiness/repetition		12	6	97–98, 103–104
Coordination/subordination		6, 13	13	83–84, 89–98
USAGE				
Subject-verb agreement	1, 3, 4, 12, 13 14	3, 7, 9, 14, 15	9	51–59, 62–73
Verb tense/form	6, 10	5, 8, 11		51–61, 101–102
Pronoun reference/ antecedent agreement	9			38–42
MECHANICS				
Capitalization	11	1	1, 10	29, 34–35
Spelling (possessives, contractions, and homonyms)	7, 8	10	4, 15	43

CHAPTER 5

Using Correct Language

Adjectives and Adverbs

So far you have learned about nouns and verbs, the basic building blocks of a sentence. Other words in our language tell us more about nouns and verbs; they describe the people, things, and actions in a sentence. These words are called **modifiers**—or **adjectives,** which describe nouns and pronouns, and **adverbs**, which describe verbs. Using modifiers correctly is an important skill on the GED Language Arts, Writing Test.

Look at how different adjectives can be used to describe the noun *book*:

What kind of book?	→	the **torn** book
Which book?	→	**that** book
How many books?	→	**one** book

In the phrases above, *torn, that,* and *one* are all adjectives describing the noun *book*.

Now see how an adverb can tell you more about the verb *moved*:

How?	→	moved **quickly**
When?	→	moved **yesterday**
Where?	→	moved **westward**

In the phrases above, *quickly, yesterday,* and *westward* are all adverbs describing the verb *moved*. Many adverbs (like *quickly*) are formed by adding *ly* to an adjective.

An adverb can also be used to modify an adjective or another adverb. Here are some examples:

The lamp is **very** unusual.
(Very is an adverb describing the adjective unusual.)

The building was erected **extremely** quickly.
(Extremely is an adverb describing the adverb quickly.)

When an adjective or adverb appears in a sentence, it usually does not require any special punctuation. Avoid the temptation to add commas around adjectives and adverbs.

Correct:	The report was written sloppily by the student.
Incorrect:	The report was written, sloppily by the student.
Incorrect:	The report was written sloppily, by the student.

When adjectives or adverbs are a part of a series, however, separate them with commas just as you would nouns or verbs. Here are some examples:

She read the speech **clearly, forcefully,** and **persuasively.**

The workplace appeared **cluttered, disorganized,** and **unmanageable.**

A comma is also used when an adverb is placed at the beginning of a sentence:

Gently, the doctor wrapped the wound in clean gauze.

EXERCISE 1

Directions: Insert an adjective or adverb of your choice in each space below. Add a comma if necessary.

Example: Please be sure to return the _stamped_ envelope by next Monday.

1. _____ the carpenter tossed the scrap wood into a corner of the room.

2. Unfortunately, the program is_____ .

3. The workers_____assembled a prototype for the exhibition.

4. Mary reminded me that red felt-tip markers are_____needed at the meeting.

5. Did you make reservations for a_____lunch on Wednesday?

6. _____ the student discovered his mistake.

7. _____the orchestra began its sold-out concert.

8. Several times last year, the committee avoided a_____problem by planning ahead.

9. When will we be able to see the_____video, Mr. Alsbach?

10. _____time is needed to complete the work we've begun together.

Answers are on page 376.

Modifying Phrases

A **modifying phrase** is a group of words that describes another word in a sentence. It can function as an adjective, an adverb, or a noun. A modifier answers a question such as *Who? What? When? Where? How? How much? What kind? How many?* or *Which one?* Using modifying phrases correctly is a skill that is required for the Language Arts, Writing Skills Test.

One kind of modifier is a **prepositional phrase,** which you learned about in Chapter 2. To refresh your memory, a prepositional phrase is a word group that starts with a preposition and ends with a noun or pronoun. It describes another word in the sentence. Underline the prepositional phrase in the sentence below.

The mayor was elected by a narrow margin.

You are correct if you underlined *by a narrow margin.* Now watch what happens when the modifier is placed first in the sentence:

By a narrow margin, the mayor was elected.

Notice that when a prepositional phrase begins the sentence, it is separated from the main clause with a comma. Some items on the Language Arts, Writing Test will require you to know how to place such commas.

Another kind of modifying phrase is a **verbal phrase**, which uses a verbal form to describe a noun. Look at the following example:

The police officer reported a car **swerving in and out of traffic.**

The modifier *swerving* is a form of the verb *swerve*, and it describes the noun *car*. If the modifying phrase comes *before* the noun it describes, a comma is necessary, as shown below:

Swerving in and out of traffic, the car sped out of control.

Here is another example of a modifying verbal phrase:

Stapled and folded, the reports were ready for distribution.

The modifiers *stapled* and *folded* describe the noun *reports*. Because they precede the noun, they are followed by a comma.

Sometimes, a modifying word or phrase comes in the middle of a sentence. In this case, commas should be placed before and after the modifier. Here are some examples:

My manager, **irritated by our laziness,** stormed off the factory floor.

The assembly team, **wanting to work overtime,** asked the supervisor for a meeting.

EXERCISE 2

Part A   **Directions:** Combine the following pairs of sentences by turning one sentence into a modifying phrase. Be sure to insert commas after introductory phrases.

        Example: Something happened in the middle of the night. The bed collapsed.

              In the middle of the night, the bed collapsed.

1. The governor wanted to prevent looting after the shopping-mall fire. The governor called out the National Guard.

     _____

2. The campers were awakened by a bear. It was rummaging through their backpacks.

     _____

3. The crowd was shouting and whistling its approval. The crowd gave Slime Green a standing ovation.

     _____

4. The trucker drove an alternate route. The trucker avoided the weigh station.

     _____

Part B   **Directions:** Add a modifier to each sentence below. You may use a prepositional phrase or a verbal phrase. Be sure to use commas if necessary.

        Example: *Speaking confidently before the group,*
              Mr. Riccardo emphasized teamwork.

1. The child _____ crossed the street.

2. The package arrived _____ .

3. _____ the package arrived.

4. Chris stared in horror at the tarantula _____ .

Answers are on page 377.

Misplaced Modifiers

All of the modifiers you have seen in this chapter so far have been placed as closely as possible to the noun or verb they describe. Look at what happens when this is not the case:

> Ruined by a broken assembly machine, the worker had to discard the product.

In this sentence, what is ruined? The way the sentence is written, it appears that the *worker* was ruined. However, you probably realized that it is actually the *product* that was ruined. To fix the sentence, move the modifier closer to the noun it describes, *product.*

> The worker had to discard the product ruined by a broken assembly machine.

Another way to fix the sentence is to turn the modifying phrase into a dependent clause, using a subordinating conjunction (see Chapter 3, page 90).

> Because the product was ruined by a broken assembly machine, the worker had to discard it.

Underline the misplaced modifier in the sentence below.

> Determined to complete the race, the spectators saw hundreds of runners.

Who is *determined to complete the race*? You are correct if you understood that it is the *runners,* not the *spectators,* who are determined. Use the lines below to correct the sentence:

_____

_____

Did you write something like the following?

> The spectators saw hundreds of runners determined to complete the race.

EXERCISE 3

Directions: Rewrite each sentence below, correcting the misplaced modifier. Be sure to use commas when necessary.

Example: Wandering aimlessly, we watched the disoriented animal leave its cage.

We watched the disoriented animal, wandering aimlessly, leave its cage.

1. The workers were delighted to get the news of a holiday feeling totally overworked.

   _____

2. Stuck under his chair, Paul felt a large blob of bubble gum.

   _____

3. Destroyed by hail, Larry stared gloomily at his wheat field.

   _____

4. The outraged prisoner was led to his cell by a guard screaming for freedom.

   _____

5. Hidden under a pile of newspapers, Harry found his glasses.

   _____

6. The traffic officer handed me a ticket with a stern warning.

   _____

7. Eager to hire top technicians, many people are being given large bonuses by Internet companies.

   _____

8. The beautiful woman walked with her husband wearing her newest dress.

   _____

Answers are on page 377.

Dangling Modifiers

Read the sentence below. Ask yourself who is typing.

Typing the last document, the computers crashed.

You can't answer the question *who is typing?* because the sentence does not provide that information. The structure of the sentence tells us that the noun closest to the modifying phrase *typing the last document* must be performing the action. However, we know that computers do not type by themselves!

The modifier above "dangles." In other words, the sentence does not contain a word for it to describe, or modify.

A **dangling modifier** is a word or phrase that has no word to describe in a sentence. To fix it, you need to add a noun that makes sense and change the wording of the sentence slightly.

As I typed the last document, the computers crashed.

Underline the dangling modifier in the sentence below.

Exhausted after driving, a hot meal and a bath sounded good.

The verbal phrase *exhausted after driving* is the dangling modifier. Use the lines below to rewrite the sentence correctly.

_____

_____

Did you write something like *Because she was exhausted after driving, a hot meal and a bath sounded good?*

Here is another example of a dangling modifier. How would you rewrite this sentence?

Taking a test is not difficult when well rested and prepared.

Turning the two adjectives into a clause will work, as shown below:

Taking a test is not difficult when you are well rested and prepared.

EXERCISE 4

Directions: Rewrite each sentence below, correcting the dangling modifier. Be sure to use commas when necessary.

Example: Walking around the corner, my apartment building seemed like heaven.

As I walked around the corner, my apartment building seemed like heaven.

1. Threading the machine, the spool slipped to the floor.

   _____

2. Departing on track 12, the commuter anxiously rushed ahead.

   _____

3. The bill will be $90.40 when buying a new calculator.

   _____

4. Crossing over the hedge, a wheel fell off.

   _____

5. Having received your check, a new bill will be sent out.

   _____

6. Crying inconsolably, the tears kept flowing long after the movie ended.

   _____

Answers are on page 377.

Renaming Phrases

Another type of modifying phrase is a **renaming phrase,** also called an **appositive.** These modifiers supply additional information about a noun or pronoun in the sentence. Look at the following example:

> The presentation, a project developed by our marketing team, has been successful.

In this sentence, the phrase *a project developed by our marketing team* renames the subject of the sentence, *presentation.*

Like all modifying phrases, a renaming phrase must come as close as possible to the noun it renames. This type of modifying phrase must be set off with commas. Here are two examples:

> I'll give this book to Neilita, the second-grade teacher.

> The railroad station in Greensburg, a town in Pennsylvania, was recently renovated.

In the first example, the renaming phrase, or appositive, *the second-grade teacher*, describes the noun *Neilita*. In the second example, *a town in Pennsylvania* gives more information about *Greensburg*.

EXERCISE 5

Directions: Put commas where needed in the sentences below. Each sentence contains a renaming phrase.

Example: The manager‸ a woman from Denver‸ works part time.

1. The winner of our customer contest a teenage boy will get the grand prize.

2. The program a new documentary about Africa was shown last night.

3. Renew.com an Internet company has been purchased by a larger company.

4. Howard our neighbor across the street sells life insurance.

5. This office the site of our monthly meetings has inspired us all.

6. Time the healer of all wounds has been passing very slowly.

Answers are on page 377.

Using Parallel Structure

In Chapter 1, you learned that a sentence may contain a series of nouns or verbs joined by a conjunction such as *and* or *or*. Here is an example:

The job requires keyboarding, filing, and answering phones.

Notice that the three elements that are connected by *and* have the same form: each one ends in *ing*. Compound elements that are all in the same form have **parallel structure.** Using parallel structure makes a sentence easier to read. On the Language Arts, Writing Test, you will be asked to make sure that compound elements have parallel structure.

Compare the sentence above to the following one:

The job requires keyboarding, to file, and answer phones.

Notice how in this sentence each compound element has a different form. A sentence like this would be incorrect on the Language Arts, Writing Test.

Always use parallel structure with compound elements, whether they are single words, phrases, or clauses. Look at some more examples below:

Parallel: **Confidence and enthusiasm** are qualities we look for in an employee.

Not Parallel: **Confidence and being enthusiastic** are qualities we look for in an employee.

In the first sentence above, two nouns are correctly joined by *and*. In the second sentence, the verb form *being enthusiastic* is not parallel in structure to the noun *confidence*.

Are all three compound elements parallel in the sentence below?

The construction worker **looked** at the plans, **thought** about his options, and **he called** the supervisor.

The sentence above is not parallel in structure. How can you tell? Look at the three elements in boldface—*looked, thought, he called*. Can you see that the last element does not match the others? Here is the same sentence corrected:

The construction worker **looked** at the plans, **thought** about his options, and **called** the supervisor.

Is this sentence parallel in structure?

> We have developed a program that can be used by elderly people, by children, and that is good for disabled people as well.

If you are unsure, first underline the elements of the compound. You should underline *elderly people, children,* and *that is good for disabled people.*

Can you see that these three elements are not parallel in structure? Here is the same sentence corrected:

> We have developed a program that can be used **by elderly people, by children, and by disabled people** as well.

To check for parallel structure, first look for the conjunction *and, or,* or *nor.* Then decide what words the conjunction joins. After you've located the compound elements, make sure that the word forms are alike.

Remember that you are looking for the similar *form,* not similar *meaning.* Even though *reading, writing,* and *to do math* all are related in meaning, they are not alike in form.

In each of the following compounds, change one element so that all elements are parallel in structure. The first one is done as an example for you.

doctor, lawyer, and ~~engineering~~ **engineer**

to sing, dancing, and to play the piano

wearing a coat, a tie, and to have a hat on

typing a report and to save a file

to wash the dishes and drying them

Your lists should be similar to these: *to sing, to dance, and to play the piano; wearing a coat, tie, and hat; typing a report and saving a file;* and *to wash the dishes and to dry them.*

EXERCISE 6

<u>Part A</u> **Directions:** Underline the compound elements in each sentence below and cross out the element that is not parallel in structure to the others. Then rewrite the sentence to create parallel structure.

Example: My coworkers are <u>helpful</u>, <u>hardworking</u>, and ~~friends~~.
                                                                friendly

1. A parent needs to be patient and a firm disciplinarian.

2. Eating good food, to swim in the ocean, and sleeping are great vacation activities.

3. The featured speaker was unprepared, rude, and a disappointment during our annual conference.

4. We can solve math problems by adding, subtracting, multiplication, and dividing.

5. Why does Ms. Santorelli treat the staff like slaves but she acts as if she is the world's nicest boss?

6. The movers lifted the desks from the truck, carried them into the building, and they placed them in offices.

<u>Part B</u> **Directions:** There are errors in parallel structure in the memo below. Cross out the errors and rewrite the sentences correctly.

February 18, 2001

To all service staff:

Due to your hard work, dedication, and being diligent, this past week was one of Interior Hotel's best ever. Our rooms were fully booked, and we received no customer complaints. The entire management team thanks you for your efforts. In honor of your teamwork, we plan to give an extra paid day off next month, offering a free night's stay at any of our partner hotels, and to schedule a celebration banquet over the holiday season. Thank you again for all you do for the hotel, management, and each other.

Sincerely,

Your management team

Answers are on page 377.

Unclear Pronouns

Avoiding misplaced and dangling modifiers is one way to make your meaning clear. Another way to make your writing easy to understand is to use pronouns that can be clearly understood.

You may remember from Chapter 1 that an **antecedent** is the word that a pronoun refers to. What is the antecedent for the pronoun in the sentence below?

The waitress left her pen in the booth by the window.

The prounoun *her* is a possessive pronoun referring back to *waitress*. It is clear in the sentence to whom the pen belongs.

Now look at the sentence below. Is its meaning clear to you?

Mr. Thompson spoke to my father, and he agreed to give me more time.

To whom does the pronoun *he* refer? *Who* agreed to give more time—*Mr. Thompson or my father?*

As you can see, the pronoun *he* is unclear in this sentence. It can refer to either of the masculine nouns preceding it. On the Language Arts, Writing Test, you will be asked to identify and correct this kind of unclear pronoun.

Here are two ways to rewrite this sentence:

After he spoke to my father, Mr. Thompson agreed to give me more time.

After Mr. Thompson spoke to him, my father agreed to give me more time.

In the first sentence, the pronoun *he* refers to *Mr. Thompson*. In the second sentence, the pronoun *him* refers to *my father*.

The following sentence contains another type of unclear pronoun. To whom or what does the pronoun *they* refer?

Our system of government should be completely overhauled because they have no idea what it is like to be poor in America.

In this sentence, who are *they?* Members of Congress? State legislators? Welfare workers? To avoid this kind of unclear pronoun, replace the pronoun with a more precise noun:

Our system of government should be completely overhauled because **our elected officials** have no idea what it is like to be poor in America.

EXERCISE 7

Directions: Rewrite each incorrect sentence below, getting rid of any unclear pronouns. If the sentence is correct as written, write *correct* on the line provided.

Example: My mother never sees my sister since she lives in Alaska now.

My mother never sees my sister since my mother lives in Alaska now.

1. With the growing technology industry, they'll need more and more skilled workers in the months ahead.

   _____

2. The manager told my colleague that he would need to travel to Houston at least once a month.

   _____

3. I gave the report to the new salespeople on Friday because they needed this information.

   _____

4. Sam and Ted got into a terrible argument after he called him a liar.

   _____

5. The assembled products are sitting on their pallets ready to be shipped.

   _____

6. In the memo, they say that there is a hiring freeze in effect until the first of the year.

   _____

7. The files and the disks were late getting to the office because they had been lost in our warehouse.

   _____

8. As she approached the woman behind the desk, she said, "May I help you?"

   _____

Answers are on page 378.

Agreement in Number

A pronoun must agree with, or match, its antecedent, just as a verb must agree with its subject. Do the pronoun and antecedent agree in the sentence below?

The speeches accomplished its purpose by inspiring the crowd.

No, the pronoun *its* does not agree with its antecedent *speeches*. *Its* is a singular pronoun, while *speeches* is plural. On the Language Arts, Writing Test, you will be required to identify and correct this kind of error in pronoun agreement. Here is the corrected sentence:

The speeches accomplished their purpose by inspiring the crowd.
PLURAL NOUN   PLURAL PRONOUN

When a pronoun and an antecedent are both singular or both plural, they are said to **agree in number.**

Look at the following chart to remind yourself which pronouns are singular and which are plural.

Singular Pronouns	Plural Pronouns
I, me, my, mine	we, us, our, ours
you, your, yours	you, your, yours
he, she, it, him, her, his, hers, its	they, them, their, theirs

To check for agreement in number, follow these three steps:

1. Find the antecedent of the pronoun.
2. Decide whether the antecedent is singular or plural.
3. Make sure the pronoun agrees in number with the antecedent.

Use these steps to decide if *they* is the correct pronoun to use in the sentence below:

Management had become so huge that they didn't respond effectively to employee concerns.

What is the antecedent of *they*? The antecedent is *management*. Is *management* singular or plural? It is singular. Does the pronoun *they* match a singular noun? No, it does not. *They* is plural and does not agree with the singular noun *management*. Here is the corrected sentence:

Management had become so huge that it didn't respond effectively to employee concerns.

The antecedent of a pronoun may appear in a sentence that comes earlier in a paragraph. Watch out for agreement issues in paragraphs as well as in individual sentences. Look at the following example:

> Joe is an independent taxi driver. He owns his own cab and sets his own work hours. The city licenses them to operate within the metropolitan area.

Are all pronouns correct as written? Do they all agree in number with their antecedents?

The pronoun *them* in the third sentence is incorrect. It is a plural pronoun, and its antecedent is *taxi driver*, a singular noun. To correct this paragraph, replace *them* with *him*.

> Joe is an independent taxi driver. He owns his own cab and sets his own work hours. The city licenses **him** to operate within the metropolitan area.

Suppose you were talking about taxi drivers in general, not Joe in specific. Would it be correct to use *he* and *his?* Yes, but then the sentence would imply that all taxi drivers are men. What if you wanted to refer to both male and female taxi drivers? It would be grammatically correct to say *He or she owns his or her own cab*, but you can see how awkward and wordy that is. *He or she* works best when there's only one pronoun in the sentence. To fix a problem with agreement in gender, rewrite the sentence so the antecedents are plural. That way the pronouns can be plural and include both males and females:

> **Taxi drivers** are independent **workers. They** own **their** own cabs and set **their** own work hours.

Other pronoun agreement problems can arise with compound subjects joined with *both* or *neither*. The same rule used in Chapter 2 for subject-verb agreement applies to pronoun agreement as well.

> <u>Both the clerk and the treasurer</u> <u>attend</u> meetings regularly.
>   PLURAL SUBJECT   VERB NOT ENDING IN *S*

> <u>Both the clerk and the treasurer</u> bring <u>their</u> reports with them.
>   PLURAL ANTECEDENT   PLURAL PRONOUN

You may remember that when a compound subject is joined with *neither*, the verb agrees with the subject closer to it. The same rule applies to a pronoun and its antecedents.

> Neither Mary nor her <u>parents</u> want <u>their</u> names included on this list.
>   PLURAL   PLURAL
>   ANTECEDENT   PRONOUN

> Neither her parents nor <u>Mary</u> wants <u>her</u> name included on this list.
>   SINGULAR   SINGULAR
>   ANTECEDENT   PRONOUN

Notice how the meaning changes depending on the order of the simple subjects.

When an indefinite pronoun serves as an antecedent to another pronoun, you'll need to pay careful attention to agreement. Look at this example and decide which pronoun in parentheses is correct.

Somebody left (his, their) shoes in the front hallway.

Perhaps you remember from Chapter 2 that *somebody* is a singular pronoun. Therefore, the singular pronoun *his* is correct.

Use the chart below to review which antecedents are singular, which are plural, and which can be either.

Singular Indefinite Pronouns		
each	no one	everyone
either	nothing	everything
neither	nobody	everybody
one	anyone	
someone	anything	
something	anybody	
somebody		

Plural Indefinite Pronouns			
both	few	many	several

Singular or Plural Indefinite Pronouns				
some	most	any	none	all

Which pronoun in parentheses is correct in the sentence below?

Everyone we saw at the Women's Weekend thought (her, their) work was appreciated.

Since *everyone* is singular, the singular pronoun *her* is the correct choice.

EXERCISE 8

Part A **Directions:** For each sentence, underline the pronoun that agrees with the antecedent in number. Underline the antecedent.

Example: Each <u>woman</u> must bring (*her*, *their*) own supplies.

1. The company expects to earn several million dollars from the sale of (*its*, *their*) new product.

2. Neither woman wanted to spend (*her*, *their*) day off cooking and cleaning.

3. Both Mr. Jones and his sons plan to make (*his*, *their*) trip worthwhile.

4. Although a problem may be difficult to solve, (*it is*, *they are*) most often not impossible to surmount.

5. Runners must train to be competitive. (*He or she*, *they*) must run through any pain.

6. All of the staff members signed a petition to have (*his*, *their*) supervisor removed for incompetence.

7. Neither the workers nor their boss came with (*her*, *their*) mind made up.

8. When a man becomes a father, (*he begins*, *they begin*) to see life differently.

9. The insurance company sent (*its*, *their*) agent to investigate the accident.

10. Everyone needs to bring (*his or her*, *their*) own lunch to school.

Part B **Directions:** There are errors of pronoun agreement in number in the directions below. Underline the antecedents and cross out the errors. Then write in the correct pronouns.

The easiest way to get to the conference center is either by car or by subway. If you are driving from the south, try to hook up with someone from the office. They'll appreciate a ride. Take I–92 to Exit 14 and bear left at the end of the ramp. When you get to Linset Street on your right, take it for about 5 miles. Everyone should park their car in the back lot.

If you want to take the subway, use the Purple Line toward South Station. Most subway cars post its destination clearly on the display window. When you get to South Station, switch trains and take the Blue Line toward Englewood. The company will be sure that their shuttle bus is there to pick you up.

Answers are on page 378.

Agreement in Person

Personal pronouns can be grouped in three categories: **first person,** which refers to the speaker or writer *(I)*; **second person,** which refers to the audience or reader *(you)*; and **third person,** which refers to the person, thing, or group spoken about *(he, she, it, they)*. Look at the examples below:

- **First person:** I, me, my, mine, we, us, our, ours

  I gave my resignation today at work.

- **Second person:** you, your, yours

  You gave your resignation today at work.

- **Third person:** he, she, it, one, they, him, her, them, its, his, hers, their, theirs

  She gave her resignation today at work.

A common writing error is to switch from one personal pronoun to another unnecessarily.

Incorrect:	When we finally finished the job, you could feel a sense of relief.
Correct:	When we finally finished the job, **we** could feel a sense of relief.

Look at the sentence below. Is the correct personal pronoun used?

If a worker is injured on the job, you will receive workers' compensation.

The pronoun in the second clause should refer to the antecedent *worker*. Therefore, the second-person pronoun *you* is not correct. Use a third-person pronoun, *he or she*, instead:

If a worker is injured on the job, **he or she** will receive workers' compensation.

Circle the pronouns in the sentence below. Do they agree in person?

When we arrived at the crowded party, you could barely get into the kitchen.

The pronouns *we* and *you* do not agree, since *we* is first person and *you* is second person. Rewrite the sentence correctly in the space below.

_____

_____

You could have written either of the following two sentences:

> When **we** arrived at the crowded party, **we** could barely get into the kitchen.

> When **you** arrived at the crowded party, **you** could barely get into the kitchen.

Notice how the meaning of the sentence changes depending on which pronoun you use.

Watch out for sentences that contain the third-person pronoun *one*. Remember that when *one* is the antecedent, only a third-person pronoun can refer to it.

Incorrect	When one wants a job badly enough, you'll get it.
Correct:	When one wants a job badly enough, he'll (or she'll) get it.

Pronoun agreement within a paragraph is particularly important, and mistakes in this area are common. In the paragraph below, find where the writer slipped from one person to another incorrectly.

> We began the meeting with a short discussion of our goals for the afternoon. Next, we heard a presentation from human resources about the company's plans for expansion next year. You got the idea that anything was possible! In the afternoon, we broke up into small groups to talk about new ideas for increasing business.

Did you discover that *you* in the third sentence is incorrect? Replace it with the first-person plural pronoun used throughout the rest of the paragraph:

> **We** got the idea that anything was possible!

EXERCISE 9

Part A **Directions:** Underline the pronoun that agrees in person with its antecedent. Circle the antecedent.

Example: As (we) entered the room, *(you, we)* were amazed at its size.

1. My choice for mayor is Natalie Doyle because *(I, you)* know she'll always work hard for this city.

2. Most people agree that a factory in *(your, their)* backyard does not enhance property values.

3. If a person is not careful around this machinery, *(you, he or she)* could be badly injured.

4. Whenever George goes out, *(he sees, you see)* how enjoyable life can be.

5. Animals do not always pay attention to *(its, their)* masters' wishes.

Part B **Directions:** Read the paragraph below and cross out the pronouns that do not agree with their antecedents. Write the correct pronoun above the incorrect one.

If you want to build a bookcase, first decide what kind of lumber one wants to use. Then measure the place where you plan to put the bookcase. When you go to the lumberyard, the salesperson will help you figure out how much wood to buy. When you get it home, remeasure everything, using pencil to make marks on the wood. Then cut where you have put their pencil marks. Assemble the wood pieces with nails or glue. They may want to use both for added strength.

Answers are on page 378.

Using Correct Language: Editing Practice

Directions: The following propaganda contains errors in modification, parallel structure, and pronoun reference. Find and correct these errors using this checklist as your editing guide:

- ☐ Are modifying phrases close to the words they describe?
- ☐ Are commas used to set off renaming phrases and introductory modifying phrases?
- ☐ Do pronouns refer clearly to their antecedents?
- ☐ Are pronouns consistent with their antecedents?
- ☐ Is parallel structure used for compound elements?

Take Back the Neighborhood!

We, the citizens of this town, need to take back control of our streets. Crime has been increasing at an unprecedented rate over the past several years, and it is time for us to put a stop to them. Growing up, our doors were never locked. We worked, shopped, and played without worrying whether our homes would be vandalized or robbed. Nowadays, one cannot leave your house without locking it up tight as a drum.

What can we do? First of all, we can get to know your neighbors again. If someone comes to our front door and asks us to watch their home while he is away, we should say yes! Keep an eye out for people who act suspiciously around our neighborhoods, and report him to the police. Let's take care of each other's property as if it were our own.

Second, support our local police. A police officer in this town works hard for a living, and they deserve respect from the community. Please consider attending the annual Police Officers' Ball, usually held in November. It is a night of great entertainment, good cheer, and very friendly. Being unable to go, at least buy a ticket to support the cause.

Last, use the power of your vote to elect council members who care about controlling crime. After being in office for over 10 years, we believe it is time for Councilman McHenry to step down. He has consistently been in favor of reducing police salaries, cutting back on neighborhood youth programs, and he favors letting criminals get off with light sentences. McHenry has to go!

Answers are on page 378.

Chapter Review

Directions: Choose the <u>one best answer</u> to each question. Some of the sentences may contain language errors. A few, however, may be correct as written. Read the sentences carefully and then answer the questions based on them. For each question, choose the answer that would result in the most effective writing of the sentence or sentences.

Questions 1–7 refer to the following article.

Are Calculators Helpful?

(A)

(1) Calculators, once bulky and expensive machines have become much smaller and cheaper in the past 20 years; as a result, they are revolutionizing the way math is taught. (2) Because pocket calculators are now widely available at low prices, they say that elementary-school students should spend less time on their multiplication and division drills. (3) Instead, the children should be taught to analyze a word problem, they should select the information needed to solve the problem, and decide what operation to use to solve the problem. (4) The calculators will perform the mechanical operations. (5) By using them, the children will be able to concentrate on the real thinking skills one will need later.

(B)

(6) The danger in this shift, some math teachers say, is that students will lose their ability to compute on their own. (7) Would we want a society full of people who need to have a calculator on hand for even the most basic of calculations? (8) Furthermore, there is danger for the average person that you may not recognize a simple error caused by hitting the wrong key on the calculator. (9) Arguments on both sides of the calculator issue cannot dispute one obvious fact. (10) The best math students will continue to be the children who have good problem-solving skills as well as having a strong command of math facts.

1. **Sentence 1: Calculators, once bulky and expensive machines have become much smaller and cheaper in the past 20 years; as a result, they are revolutionizing the way math is taught.**

   What correction should be made to sentence 1?

   (1) remove the comma after *Calculators*
   (2) insert a comma after *machines*
   (3) change *have* to *has*
   (4) replace *they are* with *it is*
   (5) no correction is necessary

2. **Sentence 2: Because pocket calculators are now widely available at low prices, they say that elementary-school students should spend less time on their multiplication and division drills.**

   What correction should be made to sentence 2?

   (1) remove *Because pocket calculators are*
   (2) replace *they* with *some educators*
   (3) replace *elementary-school students* with *they*
   (4) change *drills* to *drilling*
   (5) no correction is necessary

3. **Sentence 3: Instead, the children should be taught to analyze a word problem, they should select the information needed to solve the problem, and decide what operation to use to solve the problem.**

   Which is the best way to write the underlined portion of the text? If the original is the best way, choose option (1).

   (1) they should select
   (2) selecting
   (3) to select
   (4) select
   (5) that they select

4. **Sentence 5: By using them, the children will be able to concentrate on the real thinking skills one will need later.**

   The most effective revision of sentence 5 would include which group of words?

   (1) thinking skills they will need later
   (2) thinking skills you will need later
   (3) thinking skills he or she will need later
   (4) thinking and skills one will need later
   (5) thinking skills that will be needed later by one

5. **Sentence 6: The danger in this shift, some math teachers say, is that students will lose their ability to compute on their own.**

   What correction should be made to sentence 6?

   (1) change *is* to *are*
   (2) change *their ability* to *his ability*
   (3) change *to compute* to *computing*
   (4) change *their own* to *his own*
   (5) no correction is necessary

6. **Sentence 8: Furthermore, there is danger for the average person that you may not recognize a simple error caused by hitting the wrong key on the calculator.**

   Which is the best way to write the underlined portion of the text? If the original is the best way, choose option (1).

   (1) that you may not recognize
   (2) that they may not recognize
   (3) that it may not recognize
   (4) that he or she may not recognize
   (5) that you, may not, recognize

7. **Sentence 10: The best math students will continue to be the children who have good problem-solving skills as well as having a strong command of math facts.**

   Which is the best way to write the underlined portion of the text? If the original is the best way, choose option (1).

   (1) as well as having
   (2) as, well as having
   (3) as well as had
   (4) as well, as having
   (5) as well as

Questions 8–15 refer to the following passage.

What Kind of Loan Is Best for You?

(A)

(1) Many people, at one time or another, want to borrow money. (2) Whether to buy a house, remodel a bathroom, sending a child to college, or take a dream vacation, a loan can help a person achieve a goal. (3) Often, getting a loan is not nearly as difficult as deciding what kind of loan is right for you. (4) Here is some information you may want to keep in the back of his mind as you familiarize yourself with the world of bank loans.

(B)

(5) If you own your own house, you may qualify for a **home equity loan**. (6) With this loan, you borrow on the equity you have in the house, which means the market value minus the amount still owed on the home. (7) The rate you pay is based on the prime interest rate, and most banks charge one or two points above the prime rate. (8) Therefore, if the prime interest rate is 8.25 percent, you might pay 9.25 or 10.25 percent, sometimes even higher. (9) Shopping for this type of loan, it is important to know what the "cap" is—the figure above which the rate cannot rise.

(C)

(10) Another type of loan you may want to consider is a **home improvement loan.** (11) These loans are usually given for five to seven years, and interest rates can range from 9 to 15 percent. (12) The disadvantage of these loans is that we are given such a short time to pay back the money, resulting in high monthly payments. (13) The advantages of this type of loan are that it is tax deductible, low cost, and an easy loan to apply for.

(D)

(14) If one does not have a lot of equity, you should consider a **HUD Home Improvement Loan**. (15) The HUD loan, a government-secured loan is available through a variety of banks. (16) The Federal Housing Authority, under their Title I program, insures loans of up to $25,000 on single-family dwellings. (17) Unlike a regular home improvement loan, this loan can be paid back in up to 15 years. (18) This type of loan is also available for multiple-family units for up to $12,000 per unit, with a $60,000 maximum.

8. **Sentence 2: Whether to buy a house, remodel a bathroom, sending a child to college, or take a dream vacation, a loan can help a person achieve a goal.**

   What correction should be made to sentence 2?

   (1) remove the comma after *house*
   (2) change *sending* to *to send*
   (3) change *sending* to *send*
   (4) remove the comma after *vacation*
   (5) add a comma after *help*

9. **Sentence 4: Here is some information you may want to keep in the back of <u>his mind as you familiarize</u> yourself with the world of bank loans.**

   Which is the best way to write the underlined portion of the text? If the original is the best way, choose option (1).

   (1) his mind as you familiarize
   (2) your mind as you familiarize
   (3) his mind as he familiarizes
   (4) their mind as they familiarize
   (5) their mind as you familiarize

10. **Sentence 9: <u>Shopping for this type of loan, it is</u> important to know what the "cap" is—the figure above which the rate cannot rise.**

    Which is the best way to write the underlined portion of the text? If the original is the best way, choose option (1).

    (1) Shopping for this type of loan, it is
    (2) Shopping for this type of loan, they are
    (3) When he shops for this type of loan, it is
    (4) When they shop for this type of loan, they are
    (5) When you shop for this type of loan, it is

11. **Sentence 12: The disadvantage of these loans is that we are given such a short time to pay back the money, resulting in high monthly payments.**

    What correction should be made to sentence 12?

    (1) change *is* to *are*
    (2) change *we* to *you*
    (3) change *we* to *they*
    (4) remove the comma after *money*
    (5) no correction is necessary

12. **Sentence 13: The advantages of this type of loan are that it is tax deductible, low cost, and an easy loan to apply for.**

    What correction should be made to sentence 13?

    (1) change *are* to *is*
    (2) replace *it is* with *they are*
    (3) remove the comma after *deductible*
    (4) replace *an easy loan* with *easy*
    (5) change to *apply* to *applying*

13. **Sentence 14: <u>If one does not have a lot of equity,</u> you should consider a HUD Home Improvement Loan.**

    Which is the best way to write the underlined portion of the text? If the original is the best way, choose option (1).

    (1) If one does not have a lot of equity,
    (2) If one does not have a lot of equity
    (3) If you do not have a lot of equity,
    (4) Although one does not have a lot of equity,
    (5) So that one does not have a lot of equity,

14. Sentence 15: **The HUD loan, a government-secured loan is available through a variety of banks.**

What correction should be made to sentence 15?

(1) remove the comma after *HUD loan*
(2) add a comma after *government-secured loan*
(3) change *is* to *are*
(4) change *is* to *was*
(5) no correction is necessary

15. Sentence 16: **The Federal Housing Authority, under their Title I program, insures loans of up to $25,000 on single-family dwellings.**

What correction should be made to sentence 16?

(1) change *their* to *its*
(2) remove the comma after *program*
(3) change *insures* to *insure*
(4) insert a comma after *single-family*
(5) no correction is necessary

Answers are on page 379.

Cumulative Review

Directions: Choose the <u>one best answer</u> to each question. Some of the sentences may contain errors. A few sentences, however, may be correct as written. Read the sentences carefully and then answer the questions based on them. For each question, choose the answer that would result in the most effective writing of the sentence or sentences.

Questions 1–8 refer to the following letter.

March 2, 2001

Mr. Ronald Carleton
Customer Service Manager
Twinways Bus Co.
10 Soldiers Field Rd.
Scarsdale, NY 10583

Dear Mr. Carleton:

(A)

(1) I am writing to let you know of problems my family encountered on two different travel occasions with your bus line. (2) I hope that you will be able to help me, and perhaps some other family might avoid similar mishaps. (3) It's a shame that a bus service as well known as yours provide such poor service to good customers.

(B)

(4) The first event occurred last October. (5) In October, my family and I took a trip to New Orleans. (6) We boarded a Twinways bus in New York, prepared for the 17-hour trip. (7) As instructed by the porter, we stored our luggage in the compartment below. (8) Upon our arrival in New Orleans, however, two out of the four suitcases were missing. (9) After waiting what seemed like hours, our suitcases were found at the bus depot in Washington, D.C. (10) As if this delay were not bad enough, the people in the Twinways office were rude and unhelpful. (11) The second upsetting event took place on a Twinways trip just last week.

(C)

(12) I planned to take a bus trip from New York to Boston on February 26 to visit a relative. (13) I called the Twinways station and the schedule manager told me that there was a 10:24 bus leaving that morning for Boston. (14) I arrived a half-hour early, only to find out that the morning bus had left at 9:00! (15) The next bus would have gotten me to Boston much too late, yet I canceled my trip. (16) The people who answer the telephone are expected to know your bus schedule and should not make this kind of mistake. (17) If people do not take they're jobs seriously, customers pay the price. (18) My family and I deserve an explanation, apologizing, and some monetary recompense.

Sincerely,
Arlene Davenport

1. **Sentence 3: It's a shame that a bus service <u>as well known as yours provide</u> such poor service to good customers.**

   Which is the best way to write the underlined portion of the text? If the original is the best way, choose option (1).

   (1) as well known as yours provide
   (2) as well known as your's provide
   (3) as well known as yours provides
   (4) as well knew as yours provide
   (5) as well known as your provides

2. **Sentences 4 and 5: The first event occurred last October. In October, my family and I took a trip to New Orleans.**

   The most effective combination of sentences 4 and 5 would include which group of words?

   (1) last October, and my family
   (2) last October when my family
   (3) last October, but my family
   (4) last October having taken a trip
   (5) last October, in October my family

3. **Sentence 9: <u>After waiting what seemed like hours, our</u> suitcases were found at the bus depot in Washington, D.C.**

   Which is the best way to write the underlined portion of the text? If the original is the best way, choose option (1).

   (1) After waiting what seemed like hours, our
   (2) After waiting what seemed like hours our
   (3) After having waited what seemed like hours, our
   (4) After waiting what seemed like hours, their
   (5) After we waited what seemed like hours, our

4. **Sentence 11: The second upsetting event took place on a Twinways trip just last week.**

   Which revision should be made to sentence 11?

   (1) move sentence 11 to the end of paragraph C
   (2) move sentence 11 to the end of paragraph A
   (3) move sentence 11 to the beginning of paragraph C
   (4) move sentence 11 to follow sentence 12
   (5) remove sentence 11

5. **Sentence 13: I called the Twinways station and the schedule manager told me that there was a 10:24 bus leaving that morning for Boston.**

   What correction should be made to sentence 13?

   (1) add a comma after *station*
   (2) replace *and* with *but*
   (3) change *manager* to *Manager*
   (4) replace *told* with *will tell*
   (5) change *was* to *were*

6. **Sentence 15: The next bus would have gotten me to Boston much too late, yet I canceled my trip.**

   What correction should be made to sentence 15?

   (1) change *Boston* to *boston*
   (2) remove the comma after *late*
   (3) replace *yet* with *so*
   (4) replace *yet* with *although*
   (5) change *canceled* to *was canceling*

7. **Sentence 17: If people do not take they're jobs seriously, customers pay the price.**

   What correction should be made to sentence 17?

   (1) replace *If* with *So that*
   (2) change *do* to *did*
   (3) replace *they're* with *their*
   (4) remove the comma after *seriously*
   (5) no correction is necessary

8. **Sentence 18: My family and I deserve an explanation, apologizing, and some monetary recompense.**

   What correction should be made to sentence 18?

   (1) change *My* to *Mine*
   (2) change *me* to *I*
   (3) change *deserve* to *deserves*
   (4) remove the comma after *explanation*
   (5) replace *apologizing* with *an apology*

Questions 9–15 refer to the following directions.

How to Light a Charcoal Grill

(A)

(1) Charcoal grilling is still one of the tastiest and easiest ways to cook food outdoors. (2) There are as many different grilling techniques as there are cooks, so experiment and see what method works best for you. (3) Both these basic instructions and our handy guide is intended to help you get started.

(B)

(4) Choose a spot for your grill that is well-ventilated and it is far away from anything flammable. (5) Keep all your tools nearby, such as spatulas, a fire extinguisher, tongs, and a spray bottle. (6) Spread a single layer of charcoal across the bottom of the grill, adding a few extra coals if the weather is humid or windy. (7) Humidity is a plague of the South and East that does not seem to affect the North and West regions as much.

(C)

(8) Your next step is to choose a lighting method. (9) One way is to use a charcoal chimney, which can be purchased at a hardware store or easily made from an old coffee can. (10) Another lighting method is filling a half-gallon paper milk carton with charcoal and lighting the bottom of the carton. (11) Another method is to use lighter fluid, a method that many cooks do not like because the fluid can diminish the flavor of the food. (12) One last method, or way, that is the final method we present and offer for you here at this time is the use of self-igniting briquettes. (13) Simply stack these briquettes in a pyramid and light at the base.

(D)

(14) Once you have lit the charcoal, it is time to wait, it will take somewhere between 15 and 45 minutes for the charcoal to burn evenly. (15) Avoid the temptation to pour on more lighter fluid or strike another match. (16) Once you see a light coating of gray ash across the coals, it's time to rearrange the coals into a single layer at the bottom of the grill. (17) Coat your cooking rack with a little cooking oil, and You're ready to grill!

9. **Sentence 3: Both these basic instructions and our handy guide is intended to help you get started.**

   What correction should be made to sentence 3?

   (1) replace *our* with *their*
   (2) change *is* to *are*
   (3) change *is* to *was*
   (4) change *you* to *us*
   (5) no correction is necessary

10. **Sentence 4: Choose a spot for your grill that <u>is well-ventilated and it is far</u> away from anything flammable.**

    Which is the best way to write the underlined portion of the text? If the original is the best way, choose option (1).

    (1) is well-ventilated and it is far
    (2) are well-ventilated and it is far
    (3) is well-ventilated, but it is far
    (4) is well-ventilated, so it is far
    (5) is well-ventilated and far

11. **Sentence 7: Humidity is a plague of the South and East that does not seem to affect the North and West regions as much.**

    Which revision should be made to sentence 7 to improve paragraph B?

    (1) move sentence 7 to the beginning of paragraph B
    (2) remove sentence 7
    (3) move sentence 7 to follow sentence 4
    (4) move sentence 7 to follow sentence 5
    (5) move sentence 7 to follow sentence 8

12. **Sentence 9: One way is to use a charcoal chimney, which can be purchased at a hardware store or easily made from an old coffee can.**

    What correction should be made to sentence 9?

    (1) change *is* to *was*
    (2) replace *can be* with *was*
    (3) change *made* to *make*
    (4) change *coffee* to *Coffee*
    (5) no correction is necessary

13. **Sentence 12: One last method, or way, that is the final method we present and offer for you here at this time is the use of self-igniting briquettes.**

    If you rewrote sentence 12 beginning with

    The final method we present

    The next words should be

    (1) and offer at this time
    (2) and the last method
    (3) as the last way
    (4) is the use of
    (5) is at this time the way to use

14. **Sentence 14: Once you have lit the charcoal, it is time to wait, it will take somewhere between 15 and 45 minutes for the charcoal to burn evenly.**

    What correction should be made to sentence 14?

    (1) remove the comma after *charcoal*
    (2) replace *it is* with *they are*
    (3) insert *because* after *wait*
    (4) replace *will take* with *took*
    (5) no correction is necessary

15. **Sentence 17: Coat your cooking rack with a little cooking <u>oil, and You're</u> ready to grill!**

    Which is the best way to write the underlined portion of the text? If the original is the best way, choose option (1).

    (1) oil, and You're
    (2) oil and You're
    (3) oil, and your
    (4) oil, and you're
    (5) oil, and Your

Answers are on page 379.

CHAPTER 6

Mechanics

Capitalization Review

In Chapter 1, you learned the two basic rules of capitalization that you need to know for success on the GED Language Arts, Writing Test as well as in your own writing. Here are those rules for review:

1. **Capitalize the first letter of the first word of every sentence.**

   You have been chosen as the best leader for this team.

2. **Capitalize proper nouns.** A proper noun is a noun that names a specific person, place, or thing.

   The bus takes a left on **Hillside Avenue.**

In this sentence, *Hillside Avenue* names a specific street.

Some words are always capitalized because they always name something or someone specific. The following chart shows some examples.

Category	Example
Days and months	Monday, Tuesday, March, July, November
Cities, states, countries	Boston, San Diego, Maine, North Dakota, Guatemala, China, South Korea
People's names	Naomi, Jorge, Harry, Shanelle, Paul, Patrice
Words derived from specific places	English, Vietnamese, American, Mexican

Other words are capitalized sometimes, depending on how they are used in a sentence. Notice the noun *aunt* in the two sentences below.

The children were discussing their favorite **aunt.**

The winner of the popularity contest was **Aunt Meg.**

Why is *aunt* not capitalized in the first sentence but capitalized in the second? In the second sentence, the word *Aunt* is used as a title to name a *specific* person, but in the first sentence, *aunt* is used as a general reference.

Here's another example. In which sentence should *doctor* be capitalized?

The best person to call is (*doctor, Doctor*) Leichtman.

The patient tried to reach her (*doctor, Doctor*) on his beeper.

You are correct if you capitalized *Doctor* in the first sentence because it is part of a specific title. The word *doctor* in the second sentence should not be capitalized.

EXERCISE 1

Part A   **Directions:**   Correct the capitalization errors in the sentences below. Some words are capitalized when they should not be. Other words should be capitalized and are not. Some words are correct as written. Cross out any errors and write the correct word above.

Example: Last ~~Year,~~ *year* our clients moved their offices to Main ~~street.~~ *Street*

1. The Mississippi is the longest River in the united states but not the longest in the world.

2. The mayors from both Cities will attend the funeral service.

3. Please send me copies of the report before next thursday.

4. The best part about Winter is the annual company holiday bash.

5. You should head north when you reach the Town Hall.

Part B   **Directions:**   Correct the errors in capitalization in the memo below.

june 5, 2002

To: Ms. Sanders

From: Renée Armstrong

I would like to request the following days off: Monday, july 6; thursday, august 10; and two Days in September that I have not yet chosen. My Mother has been sick, and I need the time off to help care for her. Since I will have to travel to south Carolina on these dates, simply an afternoon off is not sufficient.

Please let me know, ms. Sanders, if these dates are okay with you.

Renée

Answers are on page 380.

Spelling Homonyms

As you know, accurate spelling is an important skill in effective writing. You'll also need to use correct spelling in order to ensure success on the Language Arts, Writing Test.

Part I will test your knowledge of spelling homonyms. A **homonym** is a word that sounds the same as another word but is spelled differently. You saw some examples of homonyms in Chapter 1 when you studied pronouns, possessives, and contractions. Here are some more examples:

Members of the committee should bring **their** surveys to tonight's meeting.

There are several ideas for new products that we need to talk about.

I know **they're** going to be late again.

The words *their, they're,* and *there* are homonyms. They all sound the same, but they are spelled differently and have different meanings. A common writing error is to use the wrong homonym in a sentence. What is the spelling mistake in the sentence below?

There should be an announcement telling the employees to bring they're handbooks.

The spelling error in this sentence is *they're*. This homonym is the contraction meaning *they are*, which makes no sense in this sentence. The correct word is *their*, a possessive pronoun that shows the ownership of *handbooks*.

There should be an announcement telling the employees to bring **their** handbooks.

Here is a review of some confusing homonyms—contractions and possessive pronouns. Notice how they follow this simple rule: contractions need apostrophes; possessive pronouns <u>do not</u> use apostrophes.

Possessive Pronouns	**Contractions**
its (the dog's)	it's (it is, it has)
theirs (the Joneses')	there's (there is)
your (Joe's)	you're (you are)
whose (Mr. Smith's)	who's (who is)

Another common homonym error is using an apostrophe to form a plural noun. This error is often made because a plural noun sounds just like a possessive noun.

Incorrect: The book's are being held at the front desk.

Correct: The books are being held at the front desk.

Correct: The books' covers have all been torn.

The first sentence is incorrect because it uses an apostrophe in a plural noun that does not show possession. The next two sentences are correct. One shows a simple plural; the other shows a plural possessive with an apostrophe.

In the English language, there are many homonyms that are not contractions, possessives, or plurals. Some of these homonyms may appear on the Language Arts, Writing Test as spelling errors. The following list provides you with *some* examples of homonyms but not all of them. Use this list as a guide as you prepare for the test.

Homonym	Meaning	Example Sentence
affect	act upon	The new plan will **affect** everyone.
effect	result	The **effect** of the plan was disaster.
all ready	completely ready	I'm **all ready** for vacation.
already	previously	He's **already** gone to work.
brake	stopping device	The driver stepped on the **brake**.
break	fall to pieces; take a rest	Let's take a coffee **break**.
hear	listen; use one's ears	Did you **hear** what he said?
here	in this place	The mail is finally **here**.
knew	was aware of	He **knew** how to drive a car.
new	not old	She asked for a **new** car.
know	be aware of	I **know** what you're thinking.
no	opposite of yes	**No** food is allowed in the gym.
passed	went by; succeeded	Andrew **passed** me in the hall.
past	before the present; gone by	That happened in the **past**.

Homonym	Meaning	Example Sentence
principal	main; most important	The **principal** goal is higher sales.
principle	theory; belief	This is a **principle** I believe in.
right	opposite of left; correct	This is the **right** way to go.
write	put words on paper or screen	Please **write** your name clearly.
through	finished; into and out of	I took him **through** the plan.
threw	did throw	She **threw** the files away.
to	word before a verb; in a direction	They went **to** work.
two	number after one	There will be **two** speakers.
too	also; more than enough	I'd like her to come **too.**
weather	atmospheric conditions	We had great **weather.**
whether	if	Tell me **whether** you can go there.
week	seven days	My boss took a **week** off.
weak	not strong	Your performance is **weak.**
whole	entire	The **whole** pie was eaten!
hole	empty place	There is a **hole** in this paper.
wood	product of trees	This chair is made of **wood.**
would	helping verb	The judge **would** like to see you.

EXERCISE 2

<u>Part A</u> **Directions:** Underline the word in parentheses that will correctly complete each sentence.

Example: The conference date is *(to, two, <u>too</u>)* far ahead to think about now.

1. Using your own ideas is the *(right, write)* thing to do on this test.

2. Your actions today will *(effect, affect)* your future.

3. The lawyer *(past, passed)* around the documents to be signed.

4. The children will be *(all ready, already)* to go when you arrive.

5. Be sure to let us know *(weather, whether)* the slides are readable.

6. Let's go *(through, threw)* this procedure one more time.

7. The workers should always take a *(brake, break)* when they are tired.

8. The *(principal, principle)* causes of obesity are overeating and lack of exercise.

9. We will move into a *(new, knew)* building.

10. The plan you propose is *(to, too, two)* ambitious for us to consider right now.

<u>Part B</u> **Directions:** Find and correct the spelling errors in the report below.

This report summarizes the sales events we have planned for the month of January. It was decided that all holiday merchandise all ready marked down will be sold for an additional 25 percent off. Our hole inventory of men's and women's clothing will be 30 percent off, now threw February 1. Its important for all employees to be present to help with labeling. Customers should be informed that there discounts will be taken at the register. This coming weak will be an important one for the sales department.

Answers are on page 380.

Comma Review

In earlier chapters of this book, you learned many ways to use a comma correctly. In general, commas are used to make writing easier to read and understand. The next few pages will give you a quick review of how commas are used correctly in writing. All of these rules are important for success on the Language Arts, Writing Test.

1. **Use commas to separate items in a series.**

   When more than two nouns, verbs, adjectives, adverbs, or phrases are joined by a conjunction, a comma should separate them.

   > The waiter put salt, pepper, bread, and butter on the table.

   > This document was written by workers, for workers, and about workers.

   > Angela washed, waxed, and vacuumed the car.

   Do not use a comma with only two items joined by *and*.

Incorrect:	Your supervisor called, and asked for your personnel folder.
Correct:	Your supervisor called, asked for your folder, and hung up.
Correct:	Your supervisor called and asked for your personnel folder.

2. **Use a comma after an introductory element.**

   An introductory element can be a prepositional phrase that begins a sentence.

   > In the annual report, the board of trustees reported several changes.

   > For several of our clients, these changes represent good news.

   Another introductory element you have learned about is a modifier.

   > Skillfully, the machinist slipped the device into gear.

   > Annoyed by all the complaints, the nurse quit her job on Friday.

3. **Use commas to separate an appositive from the rest of a sentence.**

   An **appositive**, or renaming phrase, is another type of modifier, as you learned in Chapter 5.

   > The cabinet was assembled by Mr. Torrence, the late-shift supervisor.

   > This file, a report about fire hazards, should be printed on card stock.

4. **Use a comma between independent clauses joined by a conjunction.**

   Remember that an independent clause is a subject-verb pair. See page 87 for more of a review.

   > The children did not want to stay, nor did they ask to be there.

   > We knew the consequences, but we decided to speak up anyway.

   > Jane met the new teacher, and she liked him immediately.

   Be careful not to use a comma with compound predicates.

Incorrect:	The desserts were prepared at home, and were delicious.
Correct:	The desserts were prepared at home and were delicious.
Correct:	The desserts were prepared at home, and they were delicious.

5. **Use a comma in a complex sentence when the dependent clause precedes the independent clause.**

   A complex sentence is one in which a subordinating conjunction is used to join two clauses. See page 93 for more of a review.

   > When my son gets home, I need to talk to him right away.

   > If you are going to be late, please call your supervisor.

   When a dependent clause follows the independent clause, do not use a comma.

   > I need to talk to my son when he gets home.

   > Please call your supervisor if you are going to be late.

6. **Unless you can state the reason for using a comma, don't put one in.**

   Using a comma when it is not necessary is as common an error as omitting a necessary comma.

EXERCISE 3

Directions: Insert commas where they are needed in the sentences below. Some sentences are correct as written. On the space beside each sentence, write the number of the rule on pages 183–184 that you used to make your decision.

Example: We are out of time, but let's finish what we have started. Rule # _4_

1. The change order requested that the part be measured polished and shipped.
   Rule # _____

2. The train will depart as soon as all passengers are aboard.
   Rule # _____

3. Martha's manager a great guy is planning to retire next year.
   Rule # _____

4. The kitchen was out of potatoes so the assistant chef went to the market.
   Rule # _____

5. Although the meeting is in Philadelphia a teleconference is planned as well.
   Rule # _____

6. Please set up all the folding chairs so that there is room for everyone.
   Rule # _____

7. Immediately the fire department was called to the scene.
   Rule # _____

8. My uncle my brother and my stepfather all work for United Companies.
   Rule # _____

9. Sandra wants to see the new movie but we would like to go out to eat.
   Rule # _____

10. Ms. Ortega an immigrant from Chile came to our class yesterday.
    Rule # _____

Answers are on page 380.

Mechanics: Editing Practice

Directions: Find and correct the errors in capitalization, spelling homonyms, and punctuation in the memo below. Use this checklist as your editing guide:

☐ Are specific names of people and places capitalized?

☐ Are general names not capitalized?

☐ Are all homonyms spelled correctly?

☐ Are commas used properly with items in a series, introductory elements, appositives, and dependent and independent clauses?

☐ Are there any unnecessary commas?

To: Support Group Attendees

From: Jane Eaton

Here is the information about the support group meeting that will take place on saturday, June 2, this year. Please try to be there, for we will be discussing some very important issues all day. They're will be lots of opportunities to visit with old friends and meet new ones. We will talk laugh and work together in support of each other's growth and development.

First of all, the meeting will be held at the Western Conference Center on Foley Avenue from 8:00 A.M. until 4:00 P.M. If you have not registered please send your $25 registration fee to Mrs. Eileen Smith. Paying at the door is also an option, although the fee will then be $30. You should park in the lot to the right of the Building.

To get to the conference center, travel north on Route 60 until you see signs for Millwood. Take Exit 12, and bear right at the blinking yellow light. Go approximately 4 miles turn left onto Brook Street and take your first right onto Main Street. The conference center is on you're left.

It is a good idea to bring your own beverages for the day, and cash for lunch. We plan to get threw our morning agenda by noon to enjoy a group-sponsored buffet lunch. Several brakes are also scheduled throughout the day.

Answers are on page 381.

Chapter Review

Directions: Choose the <u>one best answer</u> to each question. Some of the sentences may contain errors in mechanics. A few, however, may be correct as written. Read the sentences carefully and then answer the questions based on them. For each question, choose the answer that would result in the most effective writing of the sentence or sentences.

Questions 1–7 refer to the following instructions.

Cooking a Turkey

(A)

(1) Its holiday time, and the experts at Turkey Talk are here to offer you some hints on cooking that delicious meal you have been dreaming about. (2) With a little bit of advance planning and some extra time in the Kitchen, you can impress your family and guests and treat them to the meal of a lifetime. (3) Just follow the steps outlined below and call 1-800-TURKEYS for additional information.

(B)

(4) Before you begin, preheat your oven to 325 degrees take the turkey from the refrigerator, and remove the plastic wrappings. (5) While the oven heats up, the turkey can come a bit closer to room temperature. (6) Next, remove the giblets and neck from the turkey's main cavity. (7) If the turkey is very juicy pat it dry with paper towels.

(C)

(8) Your next step is to stuff the turkey. (9) Stuff the main cavity first but do not pack it too tightly. (10) Overstuffing a turkey can result in soggy pasty, and undercooked stuffing. (11) If you are not using stuffing, you can add some herbs or vegetables to the cavity to improve the flavor of the meet. (12) Next, use metal or wooden skewers to fasten the flap of skin over the cavity. (13) Tie the legs together with cotton string. (14) As a final step rub the turkey all over with vegetable oil or butter to create a crispy, brown skin while roasting.

1. **Sentence 1: <u>Its holiday time, and</u> the experts at Turkey Talk are here to offer you some hints on cooking that delicious meal you have been dreaming about.**

   Which is the best way to write the underlined portion of the text? If the original is the best way, choose option (1).

   (1) Its holiday time, and
   (2) It's holiday time, and
   (3) Its holiday time and
   (4) Its holiday time, but
   (5) Its Holiday time, and

2. **Sentence 2: With a little bit of advance planning and some extra time in the Kitchen, you can impress your family and guests and treat them to the meal of a lifetime.**

   What correction should be made to sentence 2?

   (1) insert a comma after *planning*
   (2) insert a comma after *time*
   (3) change *Kitchen* to *kitchen*
   (4) remove the comma after *Kitchen*
   (5) change *your* to *you're*

3. **Sentence 4: Before you begin, preheat your oven to 325 degrees take the turkey from the refrigerator, and remove the plastic wrappings.**

    What correction should be made to sentence 4?

    (1) insert a comma after *325 degrees*
    (2) remove the comma after *begin*
    (3) change *turkey* to *Turkey*
    (4) remove the comma after *refrigerator*
    (5) no correction is necessary

4. **Sentence 7: If the turkey is very juicy pat it dry with paper towels.**

    What correction should be made to sentence 7?

    (1) replace *If* with *Although*
    (2) insert a comma after *very*
    (3) insert a comma after *juicy*
    (4) replace *it* with *them*
    (5) insert a comma after *dry*

5. **Sentence 10: Overstuffing a turkey <u>can result in soggy pasty, and</u> undercooked stuffing.**

    Which is the best way to write the underlined portion of the text? If the original is the best way, choose option (1).

    (1) can result in soggy pasty, and
    (2) did result in soggy pasty, and
    (3) has resulted in soggy pasty, and
    (4) can result in soggy, pasty, and
    (5) can result in, soggy, pasty, and

6. **Sentence 11: If you are not using stuffing, you can add some herbs or vegetables to the cavity to improve the flavor of the meet.**

    What correction should be made to sentence 11?

    (1) remove the comma after *stuffing*
    (2) replace *some* with *sum*
    (3) insert a comma after *herbs*
    (4) replace the first *to* with *too*
    (5) replace *meet* with *meat*

7. **Sentence 14: As a final step rub the turkey all over with vegetable oil or butter to create a crispy, brown skin while roasting.**

    What correction should be made to sentence 14?

    (1) insert a comma after *step*
    (2) insert a comma after *oil*
    (3) insert a comma after *butter*
    (4) remove the comma after *crispy*
    (5) insert a comma after *skin*

Items 8–15 refer to the following letter.

Dear Mrs. Jansen:

(A)

(1) On behalf of all the relatives involved in Englewood Nursing Facility, the residence of my grandmother I would like to thank you for the care you have given to the residents over the past 15 years. (2) Your hard work, and dedication have been an inspiration to us all. (3) Each and every one of us owes you a debt of gratitude that is difficult to put into words.

(B)

(4) Before you came to Englewood, staff morale was very low. (5) The facilities themselves were run down and dirty. (6) Residents were not being cared for appropriately, and we new we needed help. (7) Although we complained often to the department of human Services, we never saw any significant results.

(C)

(8) Since 1986, we have seen you make steady improvements at Englewood. (9) The renovation of the dining room the installation of a new fitness center, and the establishment of a residents' rights program are all examples of your excellent work. (10) We can happily say that our mothers, fathers, grandparents, uncles, and aunts are all well cared for hear at Englewood. (11) This was not the case before you came to work at this facility.

(D)

(12) As you enter you're retirement years, we hope that you will carry with you the satisfaction of a job well done. (13) The love and caring you have shown us cannot be beat. (14) Thank you for all you have done for this Community.

Sincerely,

Deborah Johnson

8. Sentence 1: **On behalf of all the relatives involved in Englewood Nursing Facility, the residence of my grandmother I would like to thank you for the care you have given to the residents over the past 15 years.**

   What correction should be made to sentence 1?

   (1) change *Englewood Nursing Facility* to *englewood nursing facility*
   (2) remove the comma after *Facility*
   (3) replace *past* with *passed*
   (4) insert a comma after *grandmother*
   (5) no correction is necessary

9. Sentence 2: **Your hard work, and dedication have been an inspiration to us all.**

   What correction should be made to sentence 2?

   (1) change *your* to *you're*
   (2) remove the comma after *work*
   (3) change *have* to *has*
   (4) replace *been* with *bin*
   (5) insert a comma after *inspiration*

10. Sentence 6: **Residents were not being cared for <u>appropriately, and we new we</u> needed help.**

Which is the best way to write the underlined portion of the text? If the original is the best way, choose option (1).

(1) appropriately, and we new we
(2) appropriately and we new we
(3) appropriately, and we knew we
(4) appropriately, and we new, we
(5) appropriately, and we new us

11. Sentence 7: **Although we complained often to the <u>department of human Services, we</u> never saw any significant results.**

Which is the best way to write the underlined portion of the text? If the original is the best way, choose option (1).

(1) department of human Services, we
(2) department of human services, we
(3) department of human Services we
(4) Department of Human Services, we
(5) department of human Services, but we

12. Sentence 9: **The renovation of the dining room the installation of a new fitness center, and the establishment of a residents' rights program are all examples of your excellent work.**

What correction should be made to sentence 9?

(1) insert a comma after *room*
(2) replace *new* with *knew*
(3) insert a comma after *program*
(4) change *are* to *is*
(5) change *your* to *you're*

13. Sentence 10: **We can happily say that our mothers, fathers, grandparents, uncles, and aunts are all well cared for hear at Englewood.**

What correction should be made to sentence 10?

(1) remove the comma after *mothers*
(2) remove the comma after *fathers*
(3) remove the comma after *uncles*
(4) insert a comma after *aunts*
(5) replace *hear* with *here*

14. Sentence 12: **As you enter <u>you're retirement years, we hope</u> that you will carry with you the satisfaction of a job well done.**

Which is the best way to write the underlined portion of the text? If the original is the best way, choose option (1).

(1) you're retirement years, we hope
(2) your retirement years, we hope
(3) you're retirement years, then we hope
(4) you're retirement years we hope
(5) you're retirement years, we hoped

15. Sentence 14: **Thank you for all you have done for this Community.**

What correction should be made to sentence 14?

(1) insert a comma after *you*
(2) replace *for* with *four*
(3) replace *have done* with *will do*
(4) insert a comma after *done*
(5) change *Community* to *community*

Answers are on page 381.

Cumulative Review

Directions: Choose the <u>one best answer</u> to each question. Some of the sentences may contain errors in organization, sentence structure, usage, and mechanics. A few sentences, however, may be correct as written. Read the sentences carefully and then answer the questions based on them. For each question, choose the answer that would result in the most effective writing of the sentence or sentences.

Questions 1–8 refer to the following document.

Grievance Policy and Procedures

(A)

(1) This document provides all employees with the proper steps to follow to lodge a complaint about a fellow employee, a supervisor, or a company policy. (2) These steps are in place to protect all members of this workplace and they should be followed with careful thought and attention. (3) A worker should have the confidence to express their viewpoint in this manner without fear of disciplinary action or retribution. (4) Please read the following information, sign both copies, and to return one copy to the Office for Human Resources.

(B)

(5) The remaining copy should be kept in a safe place for your own referral. (6) If you have a concern with the actions of either a coworker or a supervisor, your first step should be to speak directly with the person involved; if you have a concern regarding company policy, speak to your supervisor. (7) Present your point of view in a courteous manner. (8) And respectfully and honestly. (9) Try to remember that it is as important to listen as it is to speak. (10) In many cases, if this step is handled well, there was no need to take further action. (11) If, however, you feel that the person you have addressed is unwilling or unable to respond effectively to your concern, the next step is to put your complaint in writing.

(C)

(12) Your formal letter of complaint should be as specific as possible. (13) Provide specific names, dates, and locations for all situations you are addressing. (14) For example, you might be concerned that a safety code has been violated. (15) Give the violator's name, date of violation, and where the violation allegedly took place. (16) Also include the names of any witnesses you believe might have information. (17) One copy of your letter should be sent to your supervisor and another copy should be sent to the person involved in the complaint. (18) Someone from Human Resources will respond after they have reviewed the case.

1. **Sentence 2: These steps are in place to protect all members of this <u>workplace and they should be followed</u> with careful thought and attention.**

    Which is the best way to write the underlined portion of the text? If the original is the best way, choose option (1).

    (1) workplace and they should be followed
    (2) workplace, and they should be followed
    (3) Workplace and they should be followed
    (4) workplace and it should be followed
    (5) workplace and it should have been followed

2. **Sentence 3: A worker should have the confidence to express their viewpoint in this manner without fear of disciplinary action or retribution.**

    What correction should be made to sentence 3?

    (1) change *fear* to *Fear*
    (2) insert a comma after *confidence*
    (3) change *their* to *they're*
    (4) change *a worker* to *Workers*
    (5) insert a comma after *action*

3. **Sentence 4: Please read the following information, sign both copies, and to return one copy to the Office for Human Resources.**

    What correction should be made to sentence 4?

    (1) remove the comma after *information*
    (2) change *sign* to *signed*
    (3) change *to return* to *return*
    (4) replace *one* with *won*
    (5) change *Resources* to *resources*

4. **Sentence 5: The remaining copy should be kept in a safe place for your own referral.**

    Which revision should be made to sentence 5?

    (1) move sentence 5 to follow sentence 3
    (2) move sentence 5 to follow sentence 6
    (3) remove sentence 5
    (4) move sentence 5 to the end of paragraph A
    (5) move sentence 5 to the beginning of paragraph C

5. **Sentences 7 and 8: Present your point of view <u>in a courteous manner. And respectfully and honestly</u>.**

    Which is the best way to write the underlined portion of the text? If the original is the best way, choose option (1).

    (1) in a courteous manner. And respectfully and honestly.
    (2) in a courteous manner, and respectfully and honestly.
    (3) in a courteous manner but respectfully and honestly.
    (4) in a courteous manner. But respectfully and honestly.
    (5) courteously, respectfully, and honestly.

6. **Sentence 10: In many cases, if this step is handled well, there was no need to take further action.**

    What correction should be made to sentence 10?

    (1) replace *is* with *will be*
    (2) remove the comma after *well*
    (3) replace *there* with *their*
    (4) replace *there* with *they're*
    (5) replace *was* with *will be*

7. Sentences 14 and 15: **For example, you might be concerned that a safety code has been violated. Give the violator's name, date of violation, and where the violation allegedly took place.**

    The most effective combination of sentences 14 and 15 would include which group of words?

    (1) For example, if you are concerned that
    (2) For example, even though you are concerned that
    (3) The fact that you are concerned that
    (4) So that you will be concerned that
    (5) Despite the fact that you are concerned that

8. Sentence 18: **Someone from Human Resources will respond after they have reviewed the case.**

    What correction should be made to sentence 18?

    (1) replace *will respond* with *respond*
    (2) replace *will respond* with *responded*
    (3) replace *after* with *although*
    (4) replace *they have* with *he or she has*
    (5) no correction is necessary

Questions 9–15 refer to the following passage.

Hear Ye, Hear Ye!

(A)

(1) There is several important reasons to attend next week's town meeting. (2) You have a voice in this town, being a member of the community. (3) Your presence at the meeting sends a clear signal, wherever you stand on the important issues to be addressed, that you care about this town and the people who live here. (4) Furthermore, we need a quorum of voting-age citizens to attend the meeting in order to pass important legislation. (5) Your fellow citizens are counting on you to make sure their efforts are not fruitless. (6) Lastly, your vote at this meeting is an important one for our future. (7) Because one of the most pressing issues we will debate is the need for improved schools in Rockland, you will be making a decision that will effect generations to come. (8) In short, we must take responsibility for the people in our community who cannot cast a vote—our children and grandchildren.

(B)

(9) Basically, the choice is either renovate Lincoln Junior High to make it a sufficient place of learning or build a new school on land currently owned by the town. (10) Our junior high enrollment have increased 75 percent since 1998, and Lincoln is simply not adequate to serve our needs any longer. (11) The question is whether we spend roughly $2 million to create a moderately useful facility or spend $4 million to build a spectacular school that will serve us well into the new millennium. (12) The choice is your's.

9. **Sentence 1: There is several important reasons to attend next week's town meeting.**

   What correction should be made to sentence 1?

   (1) change *There* to *They're*
   (2) change *is* to *are*
   (3) replace *to* with *two*
   (4) replace *week's* with *weaks*
   (5) no correction is necessary

10. **Sentence 2: <u>You have a voice in this town, being a member of the community.</u>**

    Which is the best way to write the underlined portion of the text? If the original is the best way, choose option (1).

    (1) You have a voice in this town, being a member of the community.
    (2) Being a member of the community, you have a voice in this town.
    (3) You had a voice, being a member of the community, in this town.
    (4) Being a member of the community, your voice is in this town.
    (5) Your voice is being a member of the community in this town.

11. Sentence 3: **Your presence at the meeting sends a clear signal, wherever you stand on the important issues to be addressed, that you care about this town and the people who live here.**

The most effective revision of sentence 3 would begin with which group of words?

(1) This town and the people who live here
(2) If you care about this town and important people,
(3) Wherever you stand on the important issues,
(4) Coming sends a clear signal about the town and the people
(5) Important issues to be addressed

12. Sentence 7: **Because one of the most pressing issues we will debate is the need for improved schools in Rockland, you will be making a decision that will effect generations to come.**

What correction should be made to sentence 7?

(1) change *is* to *are*
(2) change *Rockland* to *rockland*
(3) remove the comma after *Rockland*
(4) replace *will be* with *were*
(5) replace *effect* with *affect*

13. **Which sentence below would be most effective if inserted at the beginning of paragraph B?**

(1) This town of Rockland is in bad shape.
(2) The schools in Rockland are decrepit, inadequate in terms of educating children, and unsafe.
(3) The facts about the schools in Rockland are complex, but this is an attempt to simplify them for you.
(4) Let's think about taxes, municipal government, and schools.
(5) Junior high schools should have a student-teacher ratio of 15:1.

14. Sentence 10: **Our junior high enrollment <u>have increased 75 percent since 1998, and Lincoln</u> is simply not adequate to serve our needs any longer.**

Which is the best way to write the underlined portion of the text? If the original is the best way, choose option (1).

(1) have increased 75 percent since 1998, and Lincoln
(2) have increased 75 percent, since 1998, and Lincoln
(3) has increased 75 percent since 1998, and Lincoln
(4) have increased 75 percent since 1998 and Lincoln
(5) have increased 75 percent since 1998, and Lincoln

15. Sentence 12: **The choice is your's.**

What correction should be made to sentence 12?

(1) change *is* to *was*
(2) change *choice* to *Choice*
(3) change *is* to *are*
(4) change *your's* to *yours*
(5) no correction is necessary

Answers are on page 381.

Evaluate Your Progress

On the following chart, circle the number of any item you answered incorrectly in the Cumulative Reviews for Chapters 5 and 6. Next to each group of item numbers, you will see the pages you can review to learn how to answer the items correctly. Pay particular attention to reviewing skill areas in which you missed half or more of the questions.

Skill Area	Chapter 5 Item Number (pages 172–176)	Chapter 6 Item Number (pages 191–195)	Review Pages
ORGANIZATION			
Text divisions	4	4	120–126
Topic sentences		13	115–119
Unity/coherence	11		127–133
SENTENCE STRUCTURE			
Complete sentences, fragments and sentence combining		5	19–24, 83–104
Run-on sentences/ comma splices	14		86–88, 96
Wordiness/repetition	2, 13		97–98, 103–104
Coordination/subordination	6	7, 11	83–84, 89–98
Modification	3	10	145–153
Parallelism	8, 10	3	154–156
USAGE			
Subject-verb agreement	1, 9	9, 14	51–59, 62–73
Verb tense/form	12	6	51–61, 101–102
Pronoun reference/ antecedent agreement		2, 8	38–42, 157–165
MECHANICS			
Capitalization	15		29, 34–35, 177–178
Punctuation (commas)	5	1	31, 87, 93, 96, 183–185
Spelling (possessives, contractions, and homonyms)	7	12, 15	43, 179–182

CHAPTER 7

Test-Taking Strategies

What Will the Test Be Like?

You already have a good sense of what Part I of the GED Language Arts, Writing Test looks like because you have worked through this book. The passages and questions on this portion of the GED Test will look very similar to the passages and questions you have worked on in the Cumulative Review at the end of each chapter of this book.

In Part I of the Language Arts, Writing Test, you will be given **75 minutes to answer 50 questions.** The questions will all be multiple choice with five answer choices. The questions will be based on short passages, each approximately 200–300 words in length. The passages will be business documents, instructional documents, and informational documents. The questions will check your knowledge of organization, sentence structure, standard usage, and mechanics (punctuation, capitalization, and spelling of homonyms).

Your score on Part I will be based on the number of correct answers you record over the 75-minute test period. This means that **there is no penalty for guessing.** The number of items you answered correctly will be converted into a standard score. This standard score will be combined with your score on Part II of the test (the Essay). This combined score will apply to the overall points you will need to pass the entire battery of GED tests.

If you understand the material covered in this book and you have done well in the Cumulative Review tests, you should do well on Part I of the Language Arts, Writing Test. However, there are some additional strategies that you might be able to use to boost your score. These strategies are included in this chapter. Keep in mind, however, that no amount of "test-wiseness" can substitute for a real understanding of the material in this book. Be sure you work carefully through all chapters before you attempt the practice test or the actual GED Test!

Know the Common Errors

Before you begin to answer the questions, first read the passage that the questions are based on. It helps to get an idea of what the passage is about, what verb tense it is written in, and what the basic style of the writing is. As you read through the passage, see if you can spot sentences in which there might be an error. You may not be able to tell exactly what the error is, but you may have an idea that something just doesn't sound right.

It may seem that there are millions of different errors that can appear in the passages on the Language Arts, Writing Test. In fact, this is not so. The chart below reviews the main skill areas tested. Read them and decide which areas you are most confident in.

Type of Error	Example
SENTENCE STRUCTURE	
Sentence fragment	Because it was a holiday.
Run-on sentence or comma splice	He left early, we met him at the train.
Wordy or repetitive sentence	I went to the grocery store to buy some milk, and I went to the grocery store to buy some eggs.
Incorrect coordination or subordination	Computers are easy to use, so people are afraid of them.
Misplaced or dangling modifier	Sitting in front of the television, her eyes became glassy.
Lack of parallel structure	The report is intended to inform, amuse, and being instructional.
USAGE	
Subject-verb disagreement	Jim and Raoul was at the meeting today.
Incorrect verb tense	Tomorrow, the fun was just beginning.
Pronoun-antecedent disagreement	Everyone should bring their driver's license.
MECHANICS	
Incorrect capitalization	The country of south africa is South of the equator.
Missing comma	Whenever we see each other we are surprised.
Unnecessary comma	Yesterday we walked, and biked.
Misspelled homonym, possessive, or contraction	They took they're film to the convenience store.

Of course, this list does not include every single skill and rule you need to know to succeed on Part I of the test, but these are the important categories.

Organization Errors

Some sentences on the Language Arts, Writing Test will not contain grammatical errors. But some of these grammatically correct sentences will need to be moved or deleted in order to create an effective piece of writing. In addition, some paragraphs will need to be divided or combined to make an effective piece of writing.

These organization errors fall into the following categories:

1. Divide a Paragraph

Sometimes a paragraph as written will be too long. It will contain more than one main idea. If this is the case, there will be a question that asks *What revision would make this paragraph more effective?* Five options for dividing the paragraph will follow.

2. Combine Two Paragraphs

At other times, two paragraphs actually relate to the same main idea. The writing would be more effective if the two paragraphs were combined. In this case, a question will ask *Which revision should be made to sentence x to improve the paragraph?* The correct response is one in which two paragraphs are combined.

3. Add a Topic Sentence

Sometimes a paragraph will be missing a topic sentence—a sentence that unifies all of the other sentences. In this case, the question *Which sentence would be most effective at the beginning of the paragraph?* will be asked. Following this question, there will be five possible topic sentences, one of which will be the correct response.

4. Move a Sentence

If a sentence is out of place in a paragraph, you will be asked *Which revision would make the paragraph more effective?* Your options will be places to move the sentence within the piece of writing.

5. Remove a Sentence

Occasionally, a sentence simply does not belong anywhere in a piece of writing. It does not support any of the main ideas. In this case, one of the answer choices will be to *remove sentence x.*

Understanding these five types of organization questions will help you focus on some of the errors you will find in the documents in the Language Arts, Writing Test.

Understand the Question Types

There are three different types of questions on Part I of the Language Arts, Writing Test. Recognizing and understanding these item types will help you prepare.

Sentence Correction

Of the 50 questions on the test, fewer than half (45 percent) will be the sentence correction type. In this type of question, you'll see a sentence from the passage followed by the question *What correction should be made to sentence x?* The five possible answers will focus on different parts of the sentence. One choice might deal with a homonym error, another with punctuation, a third with usage, and a fourth with sentence structure. Sometimes the fifth choice will be *no correction is necessary*. This fifth choice is sometimes correct, meaning that the sentence was correct as written in the passage. Look at the example below:

Sentence 1: Mr. Anderson, why does all the files need to be printed now?

What correction should be made to sentence 1?

(1) remove the comma after *Anderson*
(2) change *does* to *do*
(3) insert a comma after *files*
(4) change *need* to *needed*
(5) no correction is necessary

If you recognize the error in the sentence right away, just look for the answer that corrects that error. Otherwise, the key to answering this type of question is flexibility. Look carefully at the suggested change in each choice and see how it would fit into the sentence. Sometimes you will have to check the paragraph as a whole for verb tense or pronoun choice. Take some time to try out each possibility to see if it makes sense.

Let's evaluate each of the choices above. Answer choice (1) is not correct because a comma is needed after the direct address introduction. Answer (3) is not correct because a comma is not needed between a subject and a predicate. Answer (4) is incorrect because the past tense *needed* is not necessary. Since there is an error in the sentence, answer (5) is not correct. Answer (2) is correct. The correct verb to agree with the plural subject *files* is *do*.

Sentence Revision

Out of 50 writing skills questions, about one-third (35 percent) will be of the sentence revision variety. In this type of question, text from the passage will be presented with one section of it underlined. You'll be asked to choose the best way to rewrite the underlined portion. The first answer choice will always be the original wording; the other four choices give you alternative versions. You choose option (1) if the original sentence is correct as written.

> **Sentence 2: Several improvements have been made to <u>our office, it's a</u> more pleasant place to work.**
>
> Which is the best way to write the underlined portion of the text? If the original is the best way, choose option (1).
>
> (1) our office, it's a
> (2) our office it's a
> (3) our office, but it's a
> (4) our office, in fact it's a
> (5) our office, so it's a

Since only one part of the sentence contains an error, this kind of question will probably focus on one or two rules rather than several. In the above example, you can see that the question deals with the correct way to join two clauses together. Is the original sentence correct, or is it a comma splice? Which of the alternatives is correct? See if you can eliminate the wrong answer choices.

Answer choice (5) is correct. Adding a conjunction that shows a cause-effect relationship between the two clauses corrects the comma splice. The other choices create either a run-on sentence, a comma splice, or a sentence with an inaccurate conjunction.

Construction Shift

The last type of question on the Language Arts, Writing Test is called a construction shift. There will be about 10 of these items on the test (20 percent). This type of question will ask you to choose the best way to rewrite a sentence or to combine two sentences. A construction shift question is different from the other two types in that it asks you to improve a sentence by choosing an alternative structure. The correct answer should be an obvious improvement over the original, while retaining the same meaning. Look at the examples on the next page.

Sentences 3 and 4: The meeting should be attended by all salespeople. Managers and support staff should also attend the meeting.

The most effective combination of sentences 3 and 4 would include which group of words?

(1) The meeting should be attended by all salespeople, and managers
(2) Salespeople, managers, and support staff should attend
(3) To attend the meeting is required by salespeople, managers, and
(4) Salespeople should attend the meeting, and managers and support staff
(5) Attending the meeting should be all salespeople, and managers

As you can see, there are no errors in sentences 3 and 4. However, together they are a bit awkward and repetitive. Which revised sentence is the most effective combination? Answers (1), (3), (4), and (5) would combine the sentences, but the resulting sentences would be long and still repetitive. Answer (2) effectively joins the common elements of the two sentences to make one simple sentence with no repetition.

Another type of construction shift item asks you to think about rewriting a sentence starting with a different group of words. Again, there is no error in the original sentence, but the revised sentence should result in an improvement over the original.

Sentence 5: We left the house so that we would be on time for the conference, but we arrived late for the conference.

If you rewrote sentence 5 beginning with

Although we left the house,

The next words should be

(1) on time for the conference, but we
(2) we arrived late for the conference
(3) so that we would be on time, but we arrived
(4) on time, we arrived late for
(5) on time for the conference, we arrived late for the conference

Read each answer carefully. Some of them leave out important parts of the original sentence. Others are still repetitive. Only answer (4) includes all the meaning of the original sentence without unnecessary repetition.

Look at the Whole Passage

Consider the context of the entire passage before choosing the correct answer. Questions that deal with consistent verb tense and pronoun reference often require you to see the sentence as part of a whole.

The question below is based on the following short passage.

(1) The senior managers at Century Fund would like to donate the enclosed check to your organization. (2) As you may know, several of our employees volunteer their time at Hannah's House, participating in repair work, maintenance, and cooking for the residents. (3) We would like to pay tribute to them, and to you, for the fine work this worthwhile organization does on behalf of the homeless. (4) We are pleased to say that our collection among managerial staff was more successful than ever before, netting a total of $4,800. (5) We are sure that you were able to put this money to excellent use at Hannah's House.

Sentence 5: <u>We are sure that you were</u> able to put this money to excellent use at Hannah's House.

Which is the best way to write the underlined portion of the text? If the original is the best way, choose option (1).

(1) We are sure that you were
(2) We were sure that you were
(3) We are sure that you had been
(4) We will be sure that you were
(5) We are sure that you will be

All of the choices would make grammatically correct sentences. However, only one choice makes sense with the rest of the paragraph. The paragraph as a whole is written in the present tense, so *are* is the correct verb to follow *we*. Since the money will be used in the future, *will be* is the correct verb form to use with the subject *you*. Choice (5) is correct.

Answer All Fifty Questions

Be sure to answer all the questions on the Language Arts, Writing Test. There is no penalty for guessing, so a wrong answer won't count against your score any more than a blank answer. If you are unsure of an answer, try to eliminate some of the answer choices that you know are incorrect. Then guess among the remaining choices.

Now that you have completed a review of Part I of the Language Arts, Writing Test, go on to the next chapter to begin a review of Part II (the Essay).

PART II

The Essay

CHAPTER 8

Preparing for the GED Essay

> This section of the book presents a simple strategy for writing a passing GED essay.
>
> ☐ Gathering Ideas
>
> ☐ Organizing
>
> ☐ Writing
>
> ☐ Revising

The GED Language Arts, Writing Test has two parts. Part I, Editing, is a multiple-choice section covering organization, sentence structure, usage, and mechanics. The first part of this book will help you pass Part I of the test. Part II, the Essay, is a writing section in which you will be asked to write a well-developed essay on a specified topic. This section of the book will help you develop the skills you need to score well on Part II.

To write a good GED essay, you need several skills. You need to know how to express yourself clearly on paper—how to make a point, support it with specific examples, organize your ideas logically, and link them smoothly. You also need a good command of standard written English—knowledge of the rules that good writers use to decide what makes a complete sentence, where commas belong, which words to capitalize, and when to use a particular word form.

By sharpening these skills, you will be much closer to your goal of passing the GED. In addition, you will give yourself a gift that you can use for the rest of your life—the ability to write clearly and effectively. For example, when you apply for a job, you need to write about your previous experience. Put yourself in the place of an employer looking for a new worker. Which of the following statements would impress you more?

I done alots of Restrant work, so I wants to be a Manger.

After ten years as a hostess, waitress, cook, and assistant manager in two different restaurants, I feel qualified to become a manager.

There are many times when you need to write, both on the job and at home. No matter what you write, you want your writing to reflect well on you. Improving your writing will not only help you pass the GED but also help you communicate clearly and present yourself as a careful, well-educated person.

What the GED Essay Is Like

In Part II of the Language Arts, Writing Test, you will have 45 minutes to write a well-developed essay on an assigned topic. An **essay** is a group of related paragraphs about one topic. The assigned topic will draw on your personal observations, knowledge, and experiences. The question will require you to explain something, such as your opinion about a common issue or the causes and effects of an everyday problem. Here is a sample topic:

TOPIC

What is the perfect way for you to spend a day off?

In your essay, describe a perfect day off. Explain the reason for your choice.

As you can see, this essay topic draws on your general knowledge. You do not have to know any special information in order to write your essay. In fact, just being an adult should give you enough knowledge to handle it.

Your score on the essay portion represents 35 percent of your total score on the Language Arts, Writing Test. The remaining 65 percent is from the multiple-choice portion of the test.

Two readers trained to use holistic scoring will evaluate your completed essay. With holistic scoring, readers do not read your paper and mark each misspelled word or missing comma, nor do they write comments about the content and structure of your writing. Rather, they read your paper and rate its overall effectiveness. The readers will consider features such as these as they read each essay:

- Does the essay have well-focused main points?

- Does the essay have clear organization?

- Does the essay develop its main ideas with specific details?

- Does the essay have correct sentence structure, punctuation, grammar, word choice, and spelling?

The two readers will read your paper and each will rate it on a four-point scale. A copy of this scale appears on the following page. A rating of 1, the lowest score, indicates inadequate writing; a rating of 4, the highest score, indicates effective writing. The two readers' scores are averaged to produce a final score for Part II.

Your final score from Part II is combined with the score from Part I to produce a single total score on the test. Though the essay portion is only 35 percent of the total score, you must achieve a score greater than 1.5 in order to obtain a passing score on the Language Arts, Writing Test. Otherwise, you will have to take both parts of the test again.

LANGUAGE ARTS, WRITING, PART II

Essay Scoring Guide

	1 Inadequate	2 Marginal	3 Adequate	4 Effective
Response to the Prompt	Reader has difficulty identifying or following the writer's ideas.	Reader occasionally has difficulty understanding or following the writer's ideas.	Reader understands the writer's ideas.	Reader understands and easily follows the writer's expression of ideas.
	Attempts to address prompt but with little or no success in establishing a focus.	Addresses the prompt, though the focus may shift.	Uses the writing prompt to establish a main idea.	Presents a clearly focused main idea that addresses the prompt.
Organization	Fails to organize ideas.	Shows some evidence of an organizational plan.	Uses an identifiable organizational plan.	Establishes a clear and logical organization.
Development and Details	Demonstrates little or no development; usually lacks details or examples or presents irrelevant information.	Has some development but lacks specific details; may be limited to a listing, repetitions, or generalizations.	Has focused but occasionally uneven development; incorporates some specific detail.	Achieves coherent development with specific and relevant details and examples.
Conventions of EAE	Exhibits minimal or no control of sentence structure and the conventions of Edited American English (EAE).	Demonstrates inconsistent control of sentence structure and the conventions of EAE.	Generally controls sentence structure and the conventions of EAE.	Consistently controls sentence structure and the conventions of EAE.
Word Choice	Exhibits weak and/or inappropriate words.	Exhibits a narrow range of word choice, often including inappropriate selections.	Exhibits appropriate word choice.	Exhibits varied and precise word choice.

How This Section Will Help You

This section of the book will give you three specific strategies for writing a strong essay.

1. **You will learn a simple four-step writing process you can use to write a good essay in 45 minutes.**

   Forty-five minutes does not allow time to write a first draft and then write a final draft. Instead, you need to plan your work so that you can write a good final draft. In this book, you will learn to follow these four simple steps in order to plan, write, and check your essay:

   - **Gathering ideas** (figuring out the main idea of your essay and making a list of supporting details from your personal experiences)

   - **Organizing** (putting your ideas in an order that makes sense; making sure that you have enough supporting details, and ensuring that your details are all about your main idea)

   - **Writing** (using your organized list to write your essay)

   - **Revising** (reviewing and correcting your essay)

2. **You will learn a standard, five-paragraph pattern you can use to organize an essay on any topic.**

   One of the rating criteria on the scoring guide is organization. The five-paragraph essay is a pattern many writers use to organize their writing. It consists of an introductory paragraph, three body paragraphs, and a concluding paragraph.

3. **You will learn to check your essay to see how well it matches the requirements of the GED scoring guide.**

   By comparing your work to the GED scoring guide, you will learn specific ways you can raise your score to ensure that you will score well on Part II of the Language Arts, Writing Test.

The Writing Process

Most good writers follow the steps of gathering ideas, organizing, writing, and revising when they write. Following these steps will ensure that you write a good essay in 45 minutes.

Gathering Ideas

When a writer gathers ideas, he or she thinks of specific things to write about the assigned topic. Although this is a thinking stage, it helps to write your ideas on paper. First, examine the writing assignment and decide what you want to say about it. Then, begin to jot down notes on the topic. Write words and phrases. Use your experiences to help you think of ideas. Do not worry about organizing your list, spelling words correctly, or writing complete sentences. You will take care of these details in later steps.

Using the question on page 208, here is a sample idea list for a paragraph about the morning of a perfect day off:

> take a long shower and read the newspaper and drink a cup of coffee
>
> take my time getting ready
>
> sleep late
>
> not have to get up at 4:30 as on a workday
>
> cook dinner
>
> get up at 10:00
>
> _____
>
> _____

Notice that the writer simply jotted down a few specific ideas to use in the paragraph. What else might the writer add to the list? Write one or two ideas on the lines above.

Organizing

In the organizing stage, the writer checks the ideas and puts them in a logical order. In this stage, the writer makes sure that there are plenty of good ideas on the list, crosses off ideas that are not about the topic, and then puts the items on the list in the order in which he or she will use them. Look again at the list about the morning of a perfect day off. Cross off any ideas that are not about the topic.

If you crossed off *cook dinner*, your answer is correct. *Cook dinner* does not fit the topic of the morning of a perfect day off.

Now look at how the writer organized the list.

> 5. take a long shower and read the newspaper and drink a cup of coffee
>
> 4. take my time getting ready
>
> 1. sleep late
>
> 2. not have to get up at 4:30 as on a workday
>
> ~~cook dinner~~
>
> 3. get up at 10:00

Now the writer is ready to start writing.

Writing

In the writing stage, the writer puts the ideas he or she gathered or organized into sentence and paragraph form. For instance, the paragraph about the morning of a perfect day off might look like this:

> In the morning of a perfec day off I will sleep late. On most days I have to get up at 4:30. Then I have to rush to get to work by 5:30. When I have a day off I really like to sleep until 10:00 and then take my time getting up and geting reddy. So on my perfect day off after I get up, I will take a long shower. Then have a cup of coffee while I read the newspaper.

Notice that the writer made a few mistakes. Good writers don't worry if they make a few mistakes while they write. They just focus on getting their ideas down on paper. Then they go back and check their work in the final step of the writing process.

Revising

In this stage, good writers check their work. They make sure that the sentences are complete, the words are spelled correctly, and there are no other mistakes. Look back at the paragraph on a perfect morning off. Circle any errors you find.

Now look at the writer's revised paragraph. Notice how the writer improved the final product.

> *In the morning of a ~~perfet~~ perfect day off I will sleep late. On most days I have to get up at 4:30. Then I have to rush to get to work by 5:30. When I have a day off I really like to sleep until 10:00 and then take my time getting up and ~~geting reddy~~ getting ready. So on my perfect day off after I get up, I will take a long shower. Then I'll have a cup of coffee while I read the newspaper.*

Chapters 9–12 will each focus in detail on one of the steps of the writing process. If you use this simple four-step strategy, 45 minutes will be enough time to create a good GED essay.

EXERCISE 1

Part A **Directions:** Match the step of the writing process with what a writer does in that step. Write the letter on the appropriate line.

_____ 1. Write

_____ 2. Gather ideas

_____ 3. Revise

_____ 4. Organize

    a. check the essay to make sure it is well-written

    b. put the list of ideas in an order that makes sense

    c. create a list of ideas

    d. create a draft of the essay

Part B **Directions:** Put the steps of the writing process in order. Write numbers from 1 (first) to 4 (last) on the line.

_____ Write

_____ Gather ideas

_____ Revise

_____ Organize

The Five-Paragraph Essay

In order to score a 4, your essay needs to have a clear and logical organizational plan. Good writers can use the five-paragraph format to structure an essay on any topic. The five-paragraph essay is made up of the following components:

- **An introductory paragraph.** This paragraph indicates the issue your essay is going to address and states what your main idea is going to be. For example, the introductory paragraph of an essay on the topic of a perfect day off might say that the best way to spend a day off is relaxing and spending time with your family.

- **Three body paragraphs.** Each of these paragraphs expresses an idea that supports the main idea of your essay. For example, your body paragraphs might develop ideas on what you would do in the morning (sleep late), afternoon (go to the park with your family), and evening (watch a video).

- **A concluding paragraph.** Your concluding paragraph should summarize your essay and give a final idea about the topic. For example, a good concluding paragraph could restate the three activities you would do on your day off and conclude by saying that after such a relaxing day you would be ready for the rest of the week.

Here is an example of a good five-paragraph essay with the introduction, body paragraphs, and conclusion marked:

A Perfect Day Off

Introduction

There are many good ways to spend a day off. People like to do many different things. They like to watch TV, go shopping, or visit relatives. People also like to work in their yards or wash their pets. I love to relax and spend time with my family. So for me, a perfect day off consists of sleeping late, going to the park with my children, and staying up late to watch a good video.

Body Paragraph 1

On a perfect day off I will sleep late. On most days I have to get up at 4:30. Then I have to rush to get to work by 5:30. When I have a day off I really like to sleep until 10:00 and then take my time getting up and getting ready. So on my perfect day off after I get up, I will take a long shower and then have a cup of coffee while I read the newspaper.

Body Paragraph 2

My children and I really love going to the park. In the afternoon of my perfect day off, I will take my children to Lakeview Park. My kids love to play on the swings there. We also like to walk along the beach and watch the swimmers and boaters. If the weather is warm, we like to go swimming too. After a few hours we usually get some ice cream or drinks from the refreshment stand.

Body Paragraph 3

In the evening I will rent a nice video to watch after the kids go to bed. I love old comedies, so maybe I will rent a Charlie Chaplin video. Of course, I will make some popcorn to enjoy during the movie.

Conclusion

On my perfect day off I will rest and relax by sleeping late, spending time with my kids, and watching a good video. I am sure that after spending a day off in this way, I will be rested and ready for the rest of the week.

Chapter 11 will give more detail on writing a five-paragraph essay.

EXERCISE 2

Directions: Match each part of the five-paragraph essay with its description. Write the letter on the appropriate line.

_____ 1. Body paragraph

_____ 2. Conclusion

_____ 3. Introduction

a. states the issue the essay is about and gives the main idea

b. summarizes the ideas the reader saw in the body of the essay

c. gives details that support the main idea of the essay

Answers are on page 382.

EXERCISE 3

Directions: Label the parts of the essay. Write *introduction, body paragraph,* or *conclusion* on the appropriate line. Remember, a five-paragraph essay has three body paragraphs.

A Terrible Day

1. _____ Everyone has a bad day once in a while. Last Tuesday everything went wrong. I had trouble getting to work, work was terrible, and after work I got sick.

2. _____ The trouble started in the morning. First of all I overslept because the alarm clock didn't go off. When I looked at it, I found out that it was broken and that I needed a new one. I got ready in a hurry, but then I couldn't find my keys. It took me 20 minutes to find them. When I finally left the house, I still had time to make it to work on time. But the bus was behind schedule, so I got to work late.

3. _____ When I got to work, my boss yelled at me because I was late. The store was really busy all day, and the customers were in bad moods because they had to wait in line to check out. We were so busy at lunchtime that I could not take my break until 2:30. By that time I was hungry and had a headache. After lunch a customer's child spilled a huge bottle of cooking oil, and I had to clean it up. It took more than an hour, and I got oil on my clothes.

4. _____ By the end of work I began feeling sick. I had a sore throat, and my headache was worse. When I left work it was raining, and the bus was late again. I got completely soaked. By the time I got home, I was shivering, and my headache and sore throat were worse. I checked my temperature and found that it was 101 degrees. So I took some medicine, ate some soup, drank some juice, and got in bed.

5. _____ Last Tuesday turned out to be a really terrible day. Everything went wrong—morning, noon, and night. I hope that next Tuesday turns out better.

Answers are on page 382.

Using the GED Scoring Guide to Improve Your Work

Chapters 9–12 will each examine one or more of the criteria in the GED scoring guide and help you use it to make sure that your work is the best it can be. These strategies will appear in the section called Raising Your Score toward the end of each chapter. Remember, the higher your score on the essay, the higher your overall score on the Language Arts, Writing Test.

RAISING YOUR SCORE

Read the topic and the idea list below:

--- **TOPIC** ---

What is the perfect way for you to spend a day off?

In your essay, describe a perfect day off. Explain the reason for your choice.

take a long shower and read the newspaper and drink a cup of coffee

take my time getting ready

sleep late

not have to get up at 4:30 as on a workday

get up at 10:00

Now look at the criteria on responding to the prompt from the GED Essay Scoring Guide. Circle the number of the score that best describes the idea list.

LEVEL 4 writing presents a clearly focused main idea that addresses the prompt.

LEVEL 3 writing uses the writing prompt to establish a main idea.

LEVEL 2 writing addresses the prompt, though the focus may shift.

LEVEL 1 writing attempts to address the prompt but with little or no success in establishing a focus.

What number did you circle? If you circled 4, you are correct. The writer has listed five ideas that address the topic of a perfect morning.

Chapter 8 Highlights: Preparing for the GED Essay

- Part II of the GED Language Arts, Writing Test asks candidates to write a well-developed essay on an assigned topic in 45 minutes. The topic draws on your personal observations, experiences, and knowledge. You don't need any special information.

- The essay portion is 35 percent of the total score of the GED Language Arts, Writing Test. Candidates need to score higher than 1.5 on a scale of 4 to pass the test.

- In order to write a good essay in 45 minutes, it helps to follow the four steps of the writing process—gathering ideas, organizing, writing, and revising.

- The five-paragraph essay format is a good way to organize an essay on any topic. A five-paragraph essay consists of an introductory paragraph, three body paragraphs, and a concluding paragraph.

- Understanding the scoring guide that the readers use to evaluate your essay will help you develop ways to improve your writing and raise your score.

CHAPTER 9

Gathering Your Ideas

> In this chapter you will learn ways to gather ideas for a good
> GED essay.
>
> ☑ Gathering Ideas
>
> ☐ Organizing
>
> ☐ Writing
>
> ☐ Revising

You are about to start writing your GED essay. A clean sheet of paper is lying in front of you, and you have to fill it up. Suddenly, your mind may seem as blank as the paper. You may wonder how on earth you will ever get started. What can you do to set your pen in motion?

The answer is deceptively simple—think. When you are faced with the GED essay or any writing assignment, start by thinking about the topic. Think about the kind of information that is required to answer the question. Then jot down some ideas.

Some version of this idea-gathering process forms a part of every writer's routine. The process of gathering ideas for a good GED essay includes these three steps:

• Analyzing the GED essay question

• Choosing the main idea of your essay

• Thinking of ideas that back up your main idea

You can mentally follow the steps of the idea-gathering process. However, usually it is best to write down all of your ideas on scrap paper as you think of them. That way you will not forget anything.

During the GED Test, you will be permitted to use scrap paper to plan your essay. The readers will not evaluate anything you write on the scrap paper. They will read only your corrected draft, which you will write on separate paper. So jotting notes on the scrap paper will help you make sure that you have plenty of ideas and that you include all of your best ideas in the draft of your essay.

The rest of this chapter will give you more information and strategies for each of the three steps involved in the idea-gathering process.

Analyzing the GED Essay Question

Each GED essay question indicates the topic of the essay. Look, for example, at the sample GED essay question below. What do you think should be the topic of your essay? Circle some key words in the question.

TOPIC

Nowadays many people say that they are under more and more stress. Why do you think they feel this way?

In your essay, explain why people feel their amount of stress is increasing.

If you circled *stress* or *their amount of stress is increasing*, you are correct. A good essay will focus only on this topic.

The GED essay question also gives you a suggestion of how to respond. Look for key words in the question that will help you determine the type of response you should write. The following chart shows key words in sample GED essay questions. Additional key words are in the third column of the chart.

GED Essay Question	Type of Response	Other Key Words
Do you think that people spend too much money on their pets? In your essay, tell whether you think people spend too much money on their pets. Give specific reasons to back up your opinion.	state an opinion give reasons to explain your belief	• give your views • present your opinion • say whether you believe • state whether you agree
Most doctors say that eating too many sweets is bad for our health. In your essay, tell what happens when people eat too many sweets.	state causes and effects	• state the effect of • tell the causes of • explain what happens when • tell why • explain how • explain why
Some people prefer to live in an apartment. Others like living in a house. In your essay, tell whether you think it is better to live in a house or an apartment. Give examples.	compare and contrast two items	• compare • explain the similarities and differences

Look again at the sample GED essay topic on page 220. Underline the key words that help you determine how to respond. Then answer the question below.

How should the writer respond? Check the appropriate box.

☐ state an opinion and give reasons for the opinion

☐ state causes and effects

☐ compare and contrast

Did you underline *explain why* and check the box labeled *state causes and effects?* These answers are correct. This GED essay question asks you to state causes of people's rising stress.

After you figure out the topic and the way you will respond, write them down on a piece of scrap paper. Look at the following essay question and scrap paper:

--- T O P I C ---

Is watching television good or bad for children?

In your essay, tell whether you think that watching television is good or bad for children. Give reasons for your opinion.

Topic: Is watching TV bad for children?

How to respond: State an opinion and give reasons

Now complete the scrap paper for the essay question about stress.

Topic: _____

_____

How to respond: _____

_____

EXERCISE 1

Directions: Look at the GED essay topics that follow. Write the topic of each question on the line. What kind of information will you use to answer the question? Check the appropriate box.

1.

———————————— T O P I C ————————————

Would you rather own an economy car or a sport-utility vehicle (SUV)?

In your essay, state which kind of vehicle you think is better. State the advantages and disadvantages of each kind of vehicle.

Topic: _____

How will you respond?

☐ state an opinion and give reasons for the opinion

☐ state causes and effects

☐ compare and contrast

2.

———————————— T O P I C ————————————

Many people overeat these days. Why do you think so many people overeat?

In your essay, explain some of the causes of overeating.

Topic: _____

How will you respond?

☐ state an opinion and give reasons for the opinion

☐ state causes and effects

☐ compare and contrast

Answers are on page 382.

Choosing Your Main Idea

Once you have figured out the topic of the GED essay question and how you will respond, you need to choose your **main idea.** Your main idea is the point of view that your essay will develop. For example, look again at the essay question about watching television on page 221.

We have already said that the topic of the essay will be issues raised when children watch a lot of television. You might believe that watching TV can be good for children if they watch good programs. This would be the main idea of your essay. Another person might believe that watching TV keeps children from doing other, more valuable activities. This would be the main idea of a different essay. Whatever your main idea, you should write it down.

> Topic: Is watching TV bad for children?
> How to respond: Give reasons
> Main idea: Children watch too much TV, which keeps them from doing more valuable activities.

Look again at the sample GED essay question about stress on page 220 and think about your opinions about stress. Then complete the notes. Write down a possible main idea for the essay on stress.

Topic: Stress

How to respond: State causes and effects

Main idea: _____

_____

Look at your main idea statement. Does it focus on possible causes of people's stress? If so, you're on the right track.

EXERCISE 2

Directions: Look again at the GED essay topics in Exercise 1. Write a possible main idea for each essay on the lines below.

1. Main idea: _____

   _____

2. Main idea: _____

   _____

Answers are on page 382.

Thinking of Ideas and Supporting Details

Once you have decided what you are writing about, you can start to jot down specific details to include in your writing. The following are two ways that you can gather ideas:

- Brainstorming

- Making an idea map

Though these techniques are different, they both have one trait in common—they focus on creating, not critiquing. As you scribble notes, do not worry about wording or spelling; do not bother to write complete sentences; do not stop to decide whether each idea is good. You will take care of these issues in later steps. For now just concentrate on getting some good ideas on paper. Focusing on content helps you get a number of good ideas quickly without being distracted by phrasing, punctuation, or spelling. As a result, you are less likely to forget what you wanted to write while puzzling about how to write it.

Brainstorming

When you **brainstorm,** you simply list ideas as they come to you. As you write, think about the details you have gathered already and use them to think of new ideas. For example, if you are writing about stress, you may write that many people have to drive in heavy traffic every day. This may remind you that people have to run errands and take their children to school every day. Look at the list one writer brainstormed for an essay on stress. Can you add one or two ideas? Write them on the lines below.

Topic: Stress

How to respond: State causes and effects

Main idea: People are under a lot of stress because they have too much to do.

Ideas/Supporting details:
people have to drive in heavy traffic
people have to run errands
people have to take their kids to school
people work long hours

_____

_____

EXERCISE 3

Directions: Look at the GED essay topic below. Think
you will answer the question, and the main
Exercise 2. Brainstorm a list of ideas and c
information below.

——————————— T O P I C ———————————

Would you rather own an economy car or a sport-utility vehicle
(SUV)?

In your essay, state which kind of vehicle you think is better.
State the advantages and disadvantages of each kind of vehicle.

Topic: _____

How will you respond? _____

Main idea: _____

Ideas/Supporting details:

_____

_____

_____

_____

_____

_____

_____

_____

Answers are on page 382.

Making an Idea Map

When you make an **idea map** (also called clustering), you write your ideas in a way that shows how they relate to the main idea of your essay. To make an idea map, you write the main idea inside a circle in the center of the page. Then as you think of specific supporting details, add them in adjoining circles. Look at the idea map for the essay on stress:

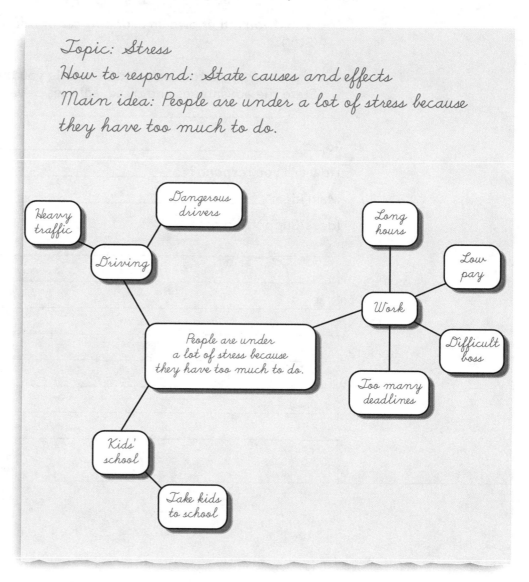

Topic: Stress

How to respond: State causes and effects

Main idea: People are under a lot of stress because they have too much to do.

[Idea map circles:]
Heavy traffic — Driving
Dangerous drivers — Driving
Driving — People are under a lot of stress because they have too much to do.
Long hours — Work
Low pay — Work
Work — People are under a lot of stress because they have too much to do.
Difficult boss — Work
Too many deadlines — Work
Kids' school — Take kids to school
Kids' school — People are under a lot of stress because they have too much to do.

Look at the ideas you added to the idea list on page 224. How would you add them to the idea map? Write them on the idea map.

No matter which method you use to gather ideas, you still need enough for a good five-paragraph essay. How many good ideas will you need? There is no exact answer. However, you need at least three general points that support the main idea (one for each of the body paragraphs) and at least two or three details to support each general point. For now, just make sure that you have thought of a number of good ideas. In the next chapter we will look at ways to develop ideas for a good five-paragraph essay.

EXERCISE 4

Directions: Look at the GED essay topic below. Think about the topic, how you will answer, and the main idea you wrote in Exercise 2. Then make an idea map and complete the information below.

—————————————— T O P I C ——————————————

Many people overeat these days. Why do you think so many people overeat?

In your essay, explain some of the causes of overeating.

——————————————————————————————————————

Topic: _____

How will you respond? _____

Main idea: _____

Idea map:

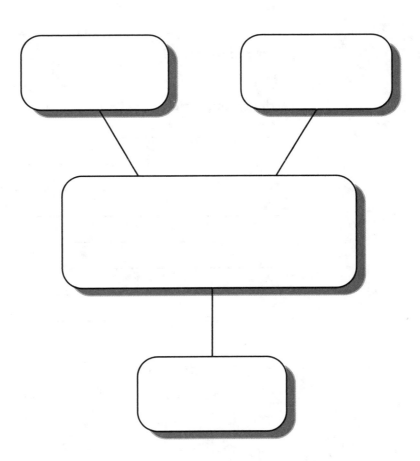

Writing a GED Essay

Directions: Look at the GED essay topic below. Analyze the question. Then decide on the topic, figure out how you will answer, and write the main idea. Complete the information below and think of supporting details. Brainstorm or make an idea map in the space provided. Save your work because you will use it again in Chapter 10.

--- T O P I C ---

Many sports stars and entertainers make millions of dollars every year. Do you believe that sports stars and entertainers make too much money?

In your essay, state whether you believe that sports stars and entertainers make too much money. Back up your opinion with specific reasons.

Topic: _____

How to respond? _____

Main idea: _____

Ideas/Supporting details:

_____

_____

_____

_____

_____

_____

_____

_____

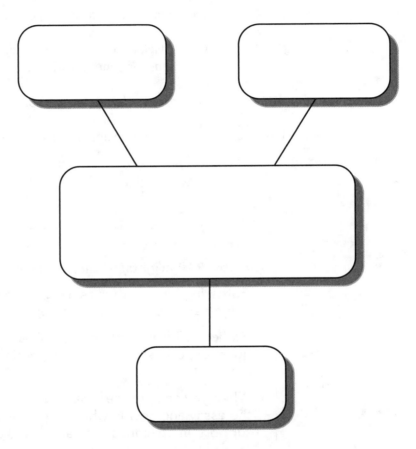

Answers are on page 382.

Look at the ideas you gathered in the GED Practice Exercise. Now look at the criteria on details from the GED Essay Scoring Guide. Circle the number of the score that best describes your list.

LEVEL **4**   writing has specific and relevant details and examples.

LEVEL **3**   writing incorporates some specific detail.

LEVEL **2**   writing lacks specific details. Details may be limited to a listing, repetitions, or generalizations.

LEVEL **1**   writing lacks details or examples or presents irrelevant information.

Now look at your list or idea map again. Add or cross off ideas to improve your score.

Chapter 9 Highlights: Gathering Your Ideas

- Gathering ideas is the first stage of the writing process. This stage helps you focus on the content of your GED essay.

- Gathering ideas has three steps—analyzing the GED essay question, choosing a main idea, and thinking of supporting details.

- When you analyze the essay question, you figure out the topic of the essay and decide whether your essay should give reasons to support an opinion, state causes and effects, or compare and contrast.

- The main idea is the point of view that you will develop in the essay. Your main idea expresses your own beliefs about the topic.

- You can brainstorm or create an idea map to think of details that support your main idea.

- As you gather ideas, jot them down so you don't forget. Don't worry about spelling, punctuation, and sentence structure. You will take care of these issues later in the writing process.

Organizing Your Ideas

In this chapter you will learn ways to organize your ideas for a good GED essay.

- ☐ Gathering Ideas
- ☑ Organizing
- ☐ Writing
- ☐ Revising

Now that your idea list is on paper, you are ready to move to the next stage of the writing process—organizing your ideas. This is important because one criterion of the GED essay scoring guide is organization. In order to score a 4 (effective), an essay must have "clear and logical organization."

Organizing your idea list consists of three steps:

- Deciding on a pattern of organization

- Arranging your ideas in three groups and naming the groups

- Making sure you have enough supporting details in each group

During the GED Test, you can organize your ideas on the same piece of scrap paper you used to gather your ideas. Remember, the readers will not evaluate anything you write on the scap paper. You should use it as much as possible to plan your essay.

The rest of this chapter will give you more information and strategies for each of the steps in the organizing process.

Deciding on a Pattern of Organization

In order to organize your ideas, you first need to decide on the pattern of organization that you will use. The best way to organize a GED essay will vary depending on the topic and main idea. In Chapter 9, you learned that in order to answer a GED essay question you must first determine the main idea. Then you must determine the pattern required to organize the supporting details. The chart below shows four main ideas:

Main Idea	Pattern of Organization
I had a terrible day yesterday.	Give reasons—time order
It's very expensive to have a pet.	Give reasons—order of importance
Eating too many sweets is bad for your health.	Cause and effect
CDs are better than cassette tapes.	Comparison and contrast

Some common terms associated with each pattern of organization are listed in the following chart:

Time Order	Order of Importance	Cause and Effect	Comparison and Contrast
how to an incident or event the process the procedure	most important least important	reasons for causes of effects of results of why	compare contrast similarities alike different favor prefer better

Each pattern of organization requires a different type of information to support the main idea.

EXERCISE 1

Directions: What pattern of organization would you use for each of the following essay questions? Write *time order, order of importance, cause and effect,* or *comparison and contrast* on the appropriate line below. Then circle the word(s) in each question that provide a clue to the pattern of organization.

_____ 1. Is baseball or football a more typically American game?

_____ 2. Is eating too many sweets bad for children?

_____ 3. Which is better, living alone or having a roommate?

_____ 4. What are the three most important tourist attractions in your state?

_____ 5. What are the causes of unemployment in your city?

Answers are on page 382.

Give Reasons

When you give reasons, you present ideas that support a particular belief. Two ways you can organize your ideas are **time order** and **order of importance.** If the reasons occurred in a certain order, such as the reasons why you had a terrible day yesterday, you can use time order. You can also use time order to list steps in a process, describe a routine, or tell about an event.

If your reasons cannot be listed in time order, you can group them in order of importance. When using order of importance, writers usually order their ideas from least important to most important.

Read the following paragraphs. Can you tell whether the writers are using time order or order of importance? Write the correct pattern of organization on the lines below.

_____

(A)

The trouble started in the morning. First of all I overslept because the alarm clock didn't go off. When I looked at it, I found out that it was broken and that I needed a new one. I got ready in a hurry, but then I couldn't find my keys. It took me 20 minutes to find them. When I finally left the house, I still had time to make it to work on time. But the bus was behind schedule, so I got to work late.

(B)

Safeguarding a dog's or cat's health is very expensive. First, dogs need vitamins, flea collars, and heartworm medicine. All of these items cost money. Second, dogs and cats need regular shots. These shots can cost $30–$40 each year. Third, if your pet gets sick or breaks a bone, vet bills can cost several hundred dollars. Even worse, if a dog or cat requires an operation, the bill may be over a thousand dollars once costs for surgery, X-rays, medicine, and animal hospital stays are added together.

If you said that paragraph A used time order and paragraph B used order of importance, you are right. Paragraph A gave reasons for the writer's bad day in the order in which the reasons happened. Paragraph B gave reasons why caring for a pet is expensive in order of importance. The writer ordered the reasons from least expensive (vitamins, flea collars, and heartworm medicine) to most expensive (an operation).

EXERCISE 2

Directions: Number each idea list in time order. The first few items in List 1 have been done for you.

1. Presidents of the United States, from <u>most</u> recent to <u>least</u> recent

   _6_ Gerald Ford

   _4_ Ronald Reagan

   _3_ George H. W. Bush

   ___ George W. Bush

   ___ Bill Clinton

   _5_ Jimmy Carter

2. Steps for starting a car at night

_____ Turn on the headlights.

_____ Open the door, get in, and close the door.

_____ Turn the key in the ignition.

_____ Put the key in the ignition.

_____ Put the car in gear and start driving.

3. How to bake a cake using a mix

_____ Pour the mixture into a greased cake pan.

_____ Bake at 350 degrees for about 30 minutes.

_____ Put the mix, two eggs, and $\frac{1}{3}$ cup of oil in a bowl.

_____ Cool completely before frosting.

_____ Mix the ingredients.

4. My trip to the airport

_____ Got up early.

_____ Walked to the gate and got on my flight.

_____ Ate breakfast and took a shower.

_____ Took a cab to the subway stop.

_____ Got off the train at the airport stop.

_____ Got on the train.

Answers are on page 382.

EXERCISE 3

Directions: A friend from another city is coming to visit you for the first time. Using a logical starting point, like the edge of town or the train station, write a paragraph describing how to reach your home from that place. Follow these steps:

1. Brainstorm a list of ideas.

2. Cross off irrelevant ideas. Number the list in time order.

3. Write a paragraph based on your list.

Answers are on page 383.

EXERCISE 4

Directions: Below is a list of ideas one writer gathered for a paragraph on reasons she likes to take public transportation to work. In your opinion, which reasons are the most important? the least important? Number the ideas from <u>least</u> important to <u>most</u> important. Add an idea of your own.

_____ Public transportation is cheaper than driving.

_____ With public transportation, I don't have to worry about parking.

_____ I can read the newspaper on the way to work.

_____ The bus stop is just a few feet from my company's front door.

_____ My idea: _____

Answers are on page 383.

EXERCISE 5

Directions: As part of a job application letter, you want to include a paragraph about your qualifications. Pick a job for which you feel qualified and write a paragraph about your qualifications. Follow these steps:

1. Think of a job you feel qualified for. Write it on the line: _____

2. Brainstorm a list of your qualifications.

3. Number your list in order from least important to most important.

4. Use your numbered list to write a paragraph.

Answers are on page 383.

Cause and Effect

There are two ways to organize information using **cause and effect.** You can tell why something happened by stating the reasons for it, or you can predict the possible results if an event or action takes place.

Suppose you have been asked to write about why teenagers smoke cigarettes regardless of the dangers of smoking. What details might you use in the article? The word *why* is the clue to the kinds of details to include. You are looking for causes of teen smoking. Look at the list of ideas below. Check the ideas that you would include in your essay.

_____ 1. Teens think smoking makes them look like adults.

_____ 2. They are rebelling against authority.

_____ 3. Smoking leads to an increased risk of lung cancer.

_____ 4. They want to do what their friends do.

_____ 5. More females smoke now than 20 years ago.

Did you check 1, 2, and 4? Good—these are reasons that teenagers might smoke. These are also three good main ideas for your essay.

Let's look at a second example of cause-and-effect thinking. Suppose that you are writing an essay on how your decision to get your GED has affected your family. What kinds of details would you include in your essay? The key word in the topic is *affected*. You want to describe the effects of your decision. Read the idea list below. Check the ideas that you would include in an essay on how your decision to get your GED has affected your family.

_____ **1.** My friends tease me, but I know they are proud of me.

_____ **2.** My kids take more responsibility for housework and cooking because they know I am busy preparing for the GED test.

_____ **3.** I need a GED in order to get a better job.

_____ **4.** My husband is a little anxious; he wonders whether I will become a different person after I get my GED.

_____ **5.** My kids are more serious about doing their homework.

You should have checked items 2, 4, and 5. These items all give effects of the decision on the family. Item 1 is an effect, but it is irrelevant because it is not about the writer's family. Item 3 is not an effect of the decision to get a GED. Rather, it is a possible cause of the writer's determination.

Later in this chapter, you will learn how to arrange your ideas for a cause-and-effect essay into three main causes or three main effects.

EXERCISE 6

Directions: Each of the topics below asks you to identify either causes or effects. For each topic, brainstorm a list of ideas you could include in a paragraph about that topic. Then read over your list and cross off any ideas that do not fit.

Example: What are some of the causes of people's overeating?

Portions are too big in restaurants.

~~Lots of people are overweight.~~

People eat too fast.

We're taught to clean our plates.

Sometimes you just feel like munching.

1. What are some of the effects of exercise?

2. What are the possible effects of getting your GED?

3. Why do some people abuse drugs and alcohol?

4. What cause some people to want to live in suburbs instead of cities?

Answers are on page 383.

Comparison and Contrast

When you want to show how things are alike and different, you use **comparison and contrast** as a pattern of organization. For example, you would use comparison and contrast to write about which is better for people's health—meat or fish.

When you compare, you talk about the similarities between the two items. For example, in an essay on whether fish is better for one's health than red meat, you might say that both meat and fish supply protein. When you contrast, you explain differences. For example, you might state that red meat is usually higher in fat than fish.

Read the list of ideas below. Write *comparison* next to the item if it states a similarity. Write *contrast* if the item states a difference.

_____ 1. CDs are more expensive than cassette tapes.

_____ 2. Chicken and beef both have protein.

_____ 3. Usually, it's more expensive to live in a house than an apartment.

_____ 4. Cats and dogs both make excellent pets.

Check your answers. Items 1 and 3 are contrasts. Items 2 and 4 are comparisons.

Later in this chapter you will learn a special technique for organizing a comparison-contrast essay.

EXERCISE 7

Part A **Directions:** People become close friends because they have something in common—background, attitudes, or interests. Yet no two people are the same. How are you and your best friend alike? different? Complete the chart below.

Items to Discuss	You	Your Best Friend
1. Background		
2. Interests		
3. Age		
4. Married or single		
5.		
6.		

Answers are on page 383.

Arranging Your Ideas

Once you know the pattern of organization you will use, you are ready to start arranging your ideas in three groups, one for each of the body paragraphs of your five-paragraph essay. Then name the groups and rank them in order of importance, from least important to most important; this is the order in which you will use them in your essay. If any of your ideas do not fit into one of your three categories or do not apply to the main topic of the essay, eliminate them. Each group represents a body paragraph. The name of the group indicates the main idea of that paragraph, which you will use to write the topic sentence. As you learned in Chapter 9, you can gather ideas by either idea mapping or brainstorming.

Idea Mapping

If you used an idea map, your ideas are already in groups. You just need to make sure that there are three groups and that the groups have names. Look again at the idea map on stress and notice that three main groups are circled. The names of these groups—work, driving, and kids' school—will be the main ideas of the body paragraphs. The list of information in each category will be used as supporting details in the paragraphs. How would you arrange the groups in the idea map below? Number the groups from 1 to 3 and compare your choices with those of another student.

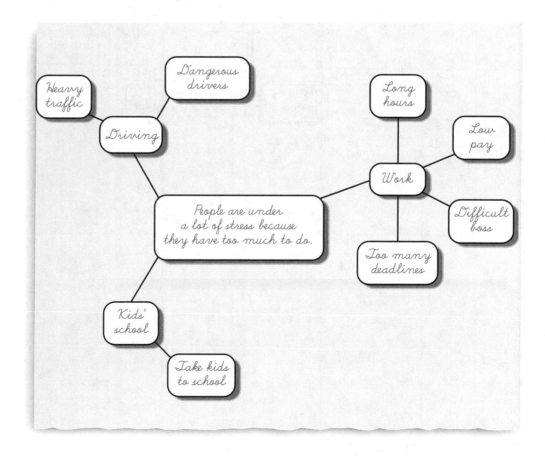

EXERCISE 8

Directions: Look at the idea map one student brainstormed for an essay on the most important tourist attractions in her state. Number the groups from 1 (least important) to 3 (most important).

Topic: Texas tourist attractions

How to respond: Give reasons

Main idea: Texas's three most important tourist attractions are historic and beautiful.

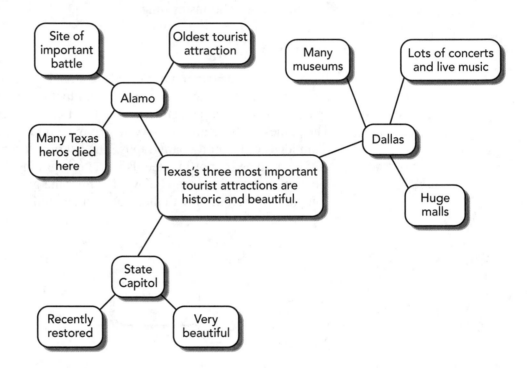

Answers are on page 383.

Circling

If you used brainstorming, one method you can use to group your ideas is **circling.** When you use circling, you draw circles to show how ideas go together into groups. You also cross off ideas that do not fit into any group. Look at the following idea list that one writer brainstormed for an essay on the benefits of watching TV. What pattern of organization would you use to organize the ideas in the list—time order, order of importance, cause and effect, or comparison and contrast?

Topic: TV

How to respond: Give examples

Main idea: TV provides many benefits.

Ideas/Supporting details:
  game shows
  movies
  comedies
  football, baseball, and basketball games
  dramas
  news shows
  biographies
  documentaries
  health programs
  GED preparation program
  Sesame Street—for kids

If you said that the writer would most likely use order of importance, you are correct. The writer would use this pattern to group reasons why watching TV is beneficial.

Now look at how the writer used circling to group the ideas, named them, and numbered them in order.

Topic: TV
How to respond: Give examples
Main idea: TV provides many benefits.
Ideas/Supporting details:

> game shows
>
> movies
>
> comedies
>
> football, baseball, and basketball games
>
> dramas

Entertainment 3

> news shows
>
> biographies
>
> documentaries
>
> health programs

Information 2

> GED preparation program
> Sesame Street—for kids

Education 1

Notice that the writer ordered the ideas in order of importance based on the number of each kind of program. There are only a few educational programs, several informational programs, and many entertainment programs.

Circling is a quick way to organize your ideas. You can use circling with any pattern of organization.

Outlining

Another way to arrange ideas you have brainstormed is to **outline** them. When you outline, you write the group names and the supporting details in the order you will deal with them. You figure out the groups, make a heading for each group, and write the details in the group that they belong to. Look at how the writer outlined his ideas about the advantages of television.

Benefits of TV

I.   A few educational programs
    A.   GED preparation program
    B.   Sesame Street—for kids

II.   Several kinds of information programs
    A.   News
    B.   Biographies
    C.   Documentaries
    D.   Health programs

III. Many entertainment programs
    A.   Game shows
    B.   Movies
    C.   Comedies
    D.   Football, baseball, and basketball games
    E.   Dramas

Outlining takes more time than idea mapping or circling, but it creates the clearest plan for writing your essay.

EXERCISE 9

Directions: Look at the ideas one writer gathered for an essay on why eating too many sweets is bad for children. Use circling or create an outline to arrange the ideas. Cross off any ideas that are not relevant.

Ideas/Supporting details:

Eating a lot of sugar causes tooth decay.

If children drink soda instead of milk, they won't get calcium for strong teeth.

Children who eat a lot of sweets may get fat.

Children who eat a lot of sweets may become hyperactive.

Usually, sweets lack vitamins.

Usually, sweets lack protein.

Ice cream, candy, cookies, and cake are delicious.

_____

_____

_____

_____

_____

_____

_____

_____

_____

_____

_____

_____

_____

_____

_____

Answers are on page 383.

Making a Chart

Writing a comparison-contrast essay takes special planning. To make sure that your ideas are clear to the reader, try arranging your ideas into a simple chart. To construct your chart, make three columns. Label the middle and right-hand columns with the subjects you are comparing. Label the left-hand column "Items to Discuss." The items to discuss are the criteria you will use to compare and contrast the two items. Your table should have three rows, one for each of three items to discuss. Each item to discuss will become a body paragraph. Look at the following example:

Items to Discuss	Subject A	Subject B
Idea 1		
Idea 2		
Idea 3		

Let's say that you are writing an essay comparing and contrasting sport-utility vehicles and cars. You brainstormed the following list:

Topic: Cars vs. SUVs
How to respond: Compare and contrast
Main idea: SUVs and cars have different
    advantages and disadvantages.
Ideas/Supporting details:
    Small cars may be less comfortable.
    The ride is bumpier in small cars.
    SUVs are more expensive.
    SUVs get poor gas mileage.
    SUVs' insurance costs more.
    In crashes, SUV passengers are safer.
    SUVs may cost $40,000 or more.
    Cars get higher gas mileage.
    Cars' insurance is cheaper.
    Cars can be cheaper.
    In crashes, SUVs sustain less damage than cars.
    In crashes, cars sustain more damage than SUVs.

To label your chart, you would fill in the "Items to Discuss" column with your three main group names—the criteria you are using to compare and contrast.

Look at the following example:

Items to Discuss	SUVs	Cars
Price	More expensive May cost $40,000 or more Insurance costs more Poor gas mileage	Less expensive Can be under $11,000 Insurance is cheaper Higher gas mileage
Comfort	Can be very comfortable Smooth ride Can seat 5-6 adults comfortably	Less comfortable Ride is bumpier A two-door car may seat only two adults comfortably
Safety		

Use the idea list on cars and SUVs to complete the section of the chart about safety.

Now compare your work to this sample. Is your organization similar?

Items to Discuss	SUVs	Cars
Safety	Passengers safer in crashes Sustain less damage in crashes	Passengers less safe in crashes Sustain more damage in crashes

EXERCISE 10

Directions: Look at the ideas one writer gathered for an essay on why it's better to have a roommate. Use the ideas to complete the chart. (The first main idea has been completed for you.) Cross off any ideas that are not relevant.

Ideas/Supporting details:

With a roommate, you can share the rent.

With a roommate, you can split the cost of utilities.

Living alone, you have to pay the rent and utilities by yourself.

You can share cleaning duties with a roommate.

When you have a roommate, you always have a friend to talk to.

It's lonely to live alone.

If you are lucky, you and your roommate will become friends.

I once had three roommates in a small apartment.

Items to Discuss	Roommate	Living Alone
Cost		

Answers are on page 384.

Making Sure All Your Ideas Are About the Main Idea

No matter how you arrange your ideas, you need to make sure that all of the ideas are about the main idea. Look at the list of reasons why John wants to go camping on his next vacation. Arrange them using either circling or outlining. Cross off any ideas that do not belong.

Topic: Camping

How to respond: Give reasons

Main idea: Camping is a good way to spend a vacation.

Ideas/Supporting details:

Camping gets you in touch with nature.

You can get fresh air and sunshine.

You can get exercise hiking.

You can swim and water ski.

You can go for walks along the beach.

Camping is inexpensive at most state parks.

Camping is usually cheaper than staying in a hotel.

Doing your laundry is a chore when you are camping.

If you crossed off *doing your laundry is a chore when you are camping*, you are correct. This is not a reason why someone would want to go camping, so it is not about the main idea of the essay. On the next page, look at how one writer organized the idea list. Are your groupings similar?

Topic: Camping

How to respond: Give reasons

Main idea: Camping is a good way to spend a vacation.

Ideas/ Supporting details:

Camping gets you in touch with nature. You can get fresh air and sunshine.

Outdoor activity

You can get exercise hiking. You can swim and water ski. You can go for walks along the beach.

Exercise

Camping is inexpensive at most state parks. Camping is usually cheaper than staying in a hotel.

Inexpensive

~~Doing your laundry is a chore when you are camping.~~

Making Sure You Have Enough Ideas

There is one final step before you begin drafting your GED essay. You need to make sure that you have enough ideas in each group in your pattern of organization so you can develop it into a strong paragraph for your essay. Each group needs two or three good supporting details. Look again at the idea map the writer gathered for an essay on stress. Circle the group that has only one supporting idea.

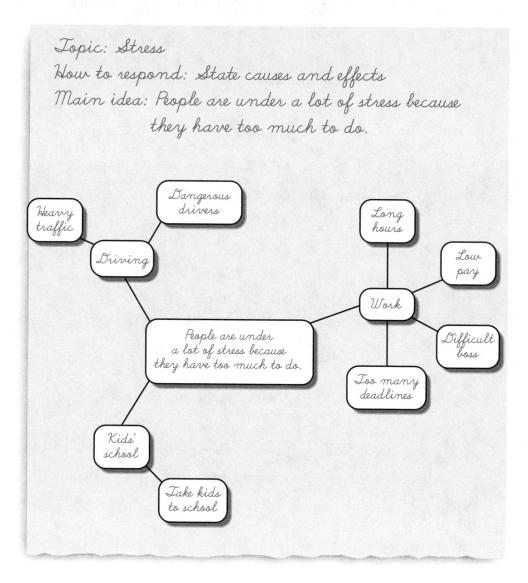

If you circled *kids' school*, you are correct. The writer needs to add at least one supporting detail to this group.

How can writers think of more ideas? Try brainstorming again. You might also use the ideas in the idea map to help you think of more ideas. For example, the idea that parents have to take their kids to school might remind you that parents have to go to meetings at school. You can also ask the *wh-* questions *(who?, what?, when?, where?, why?,* and *how?)* again. These questions might make you remember that parents need to go to parents' night once a month.

Look again at the idea map. What supporting details would you add? Use brainstorming, the ideas in the idea map, and the *wh-* questions to add at least one more idea.

EXERCISE 11

Directions: Look again at Exercise 10. Which group needs more ideas? Add at least one idea to the group.

Answers are on page 384.

GED PRACTICE
Writing a GED Essay

Directions: Look at the ideas you gathered for the GED essay at the end of Chapter 9 (page 228). Answer the following questions.

1. What pattern of organization will you use to organize your ideas? Circle your answer.

    time order

    order of importance

    cause and effect

    comparison and contrast

2. Try circling, outlining, or making a chart to arrange your ideas. Cross off any irrelevant ideas.

3. Now make sure that your essay has enough ideas. Use brainstorming, the ideas you already gathered, and the *wh-* questions to develop more ideas, if necessary.

Answers are on page 384.

Look at the ideas you organized in the GED Practice Exercise. Now look at the criteria on organization from the GED Essay Scoring Guide. Circle the number of the description that best matches your organized list.

LEVEL **4** writing establishes a clear and logical organization.

LEVEL **3** writing has an identifiable organizational plan.

LEVEL **2** writing shows some evidence of an organizational plan.

LEVEL **1** writing fails to display organized ideas.

Now look at your organized list again. What can you do to improve your score? Gather more ideas? Think of a better pattern of organization? Cross off irrelevant ideas? Use an outline?

Chapter 10 Highlights: Organizing Your Ideas

- Organizing your idea list requires three steps—figuring out your pattern of organization, arranging your ideas in three groups, and making sure you have enough ideas in each group.

- You can use time order, order of importance, cause and effect, or comparison and contrast to organize your ideas.

- If you used an idea map to gather ideas, your ideas are already in groups. You just need to arrange the groups in the order you will address them.

- When you brainstorm, you can use circling, outlining, or making a chart to organize your ideas into groups.

- As you arrange ideas, you should cross off any that are not about the main idea.

- Each group should have two or three good ideas.

- If you need to add ideas to your groups, brainstorm, review the ideas in your list, or ask yourself the *wh-* questions to think of more ideas.

CHAPTER 11

Writing Your GED Essay

In this chapter you will learn ways to use your organized list of ideas to write a good GED essay.

- ☐ Gathering Ideas
- ☐ Organizing
- ☑ Writing
- ☐ Revising

Now that you have an organized list of ideas, you are ready to begin writing your GED essay. At this point, you expand the words and phrases in your organized idea list into sentences and paragraphs.

The process of turning your organized list of ideas into a good five-paragraph essay includes these three steps:

- writing the introductory paragraph
- writing the body paragraphs
- writing the concluding paragraph

As you write your essay, be sure to use complete sentences and try your best to use good word choice, correct spelling, and proper punctuation. However, don't worry too much about these things. You will have time to correct when you revise. In this stage, you should focus on expressing your ideas in sentences and paragraphs. For more about making paragraphs effective, see Chapter 4.

Writing Paragraphs

In written English, the signal for grouped ideas is a **paragraph**. A paragraph is a set of sentences that develops a central point or main idea. When you write, you indicate the beginning of the paragraph by indenting the first line. That is, you begin the first line about half an inch to the right of the margin. This gives the reader a visual sign that a new paragraph is beginning.

Look at the examples below. Which one is a paragraph that develops a central point?

(A)

In winter, motorists in the snowbelt should always carry sand and a shovel. Driving on icy roads requires special techniques, such as pumping the brakes lightly to slow down and always steering into a spin. Wind-whipped snow can reduce visibility, and ice storms can coat trees and power lines. When the storm finally dies down, you will be in a glittering winter wonderland.

(B)

If you're planning winter travel in the snowbelt, you should always keep some winter safety supplies in the trunk of your car. Always have a warm blanket, a hooded jacket, and mittens or gloves. You should also have a snow shovel and a bag of sand or salt in case your car gets stuck in snow. If you are planning a long trip, you should take a few easily stored foods like crackers, nuts, and dried fruit. Finally, you should have a help sign or a bright orange pennant to attach to your aerial to signal for help.

Could you find any connection among the sentences in paragraph A? The sentences are all somewhat related—they are about winter in the snowbelt. But they do not develop a central point. Each sentence is about a different aspect of winter. The sentences in paragraph B, however, are related. They are all about driving in winter, and they develop the central idea that all drivers should carry certain supplies during that season.

As you know, a five-paragraph essay consists of three types of paragraphs:

- An introductory paragraph

- Three body paragraphs

- A concluding paragraph

Each type of paragraph has a different function and organization.

Writing the Introductory Paragraph

A good introductory paragraph does several things. First, it identifies the topic and main idea of the essay. Second, it captures readers' interest. Third, it indicates the organization of the essay. A good introductory paragraph is organized from general to specific. The last sentence, called the **thesis statement**, previews the content and organization by stating the topic and main idea of each of the three supporting paragraphs. Usually, the writer's notes about the topic and main idea will help him or her write the introductory paragraph.

Look at the notes the writer made about the topic and main idea of an essay on television. Compare the notes to the introductory paragraph that the writer created:

Topic: TV
How to respond:
Give examples
Main idea: TV
provides many
benefits.

Nowadays, we often hear that people spend too much time watching TV. However, people need to remember that TV can provide us with several benefits. In fact, TV has benefited my life in three main ways: it provides me with educational resources, it gives me information about the world around me, and it provides a lot of inexpensive entertainment.

Notice how the writer used the information in the notes to identify the topic *(TV)* and the main idea *(it provides several benefits)* in the introductory paragraph. Can you find the thesis statement? Underline it. What are the three main ideas of the body paragraphs that follow?

You are correct if you underlined the last sentence of the paragraph—*In fact, TV has benefited my life in three main ways: it provides me with educational resources, it gives me information about the world around me, and it provides a lot of inexpensive entertainment.* This sentence clearly indicates that the following three body paragraphs will address three different kinds of benefits that TV provides—education, information, and entertainment.

When you are writing an introduction, keep the following three points in mind:

1. **State your topic and main idea clearly.** If your readers know what point you are trying to make, they will find it easier to understand your essay. Use the topic and main idea you wrote on your scrap paper to develop the first few sentences of your introductory paragraph.

2. **Give an idea of the content and organization of your essay in the thesis statement.** Use the group names in your organized idea list to develop your thesis statement. Keep in mind that these group names not only must support the thesis but also will become the main ideas for your body paragraphs.

3. **Use the introductory paragraph to arouse the reader's interest in your essay.** An interested reader is more likely to pay attention to your essay and give it a higher score. There are many ways to grab the reader's attention. Here are two ways the writer of the essay on television could modify the introductory paragraph to make it more interesting:

(A)

What do you do when you want to see a good movie but you don't have the money for a ticket? What do you do when you wonder whether Congress has voted to raise taxes? What do you do if you want to take a GED class from home? If you are like me, you probably turn on the TV. TV is an important resource for me. In fact, TV has benefited my life in three main ways: it provides me with educational resources, it gives me information about the world around me, and it provides a lot of inexpensive entertainment.

Did paragraph A raise your interest in the topic of the essay? Why? If you said that it asked you questions about how TV relates to your life, you are right. In this example, the writer asked the reader questions to get the reader interested in the answers that will appear later in the essay. How does the paragraph on the next page raise the reader's interest?

(B)

When television was introduced in the 1940s, few people realized how quickly this invention would spread around the world. Today, nearly every American household has at least one television set, and satellites bounce programs from one continent to another. Some people may argue about whether this invention is worthwhile, but for me the answer is a definite yes. In fact, TV has benefited my life in three main ways: it provides me with educational resources, it gives me information about the world around me, and it provides a lot of inexpensive entertainment.

Paragraph B gives some background to show why the topic is important. Which introduction is better? There is no single correct answer. Your own preferences will help you decide which kind of information to write.

Problems to Avoid

Below are some standard traps to avoid when writing an introduction.

- Don't announce your plans. Your ideas and organization should speak for themselves.

Incorrect:	I am going to discuss three benefits of television in this essay.
Correct:	Television provides three benefits.

The second sentence states the main idea clearly.

- Don't apologize for your essay. You want to convince your reader that you have something to say. Never make excuses!

Incorrect:	This is a hard essay to write because I really don't watch much television, so here goes nothing.

- Don't use empty words and don't repeat yourself just to make the essay longer.

Incorrect:	Television has had several important effects on me. Its impact on my daily life has been tremendous. In fact, I have been influenced greatly by television.

• Don't assume that your reader has read the title of your essay. State or summarize the subject of your essay at the beginning.

Incorrect:	People complain a lot about it. Many people don't realize that it provides us with several benefits.
Correct:	People complain a lot about television. Many people do not realize that TV provides us with numerous benefits.

EXERCISE 1

Directions: Read the introductory paragraphs below and answer the questions that follow.

1. It is important to have pastimes. Pastimes get your mind off work and help you relax. They also help you get mental and physical exercise. There are many different kinds of pastimes. My three favorite pastimes are walking in the park, reading good books, and going to the movies.

    a. What is the topic of the essay?

    b. What is the main idea?

    c. Underline the thesis statement. Then list the main ideas of the three body paragraphs.

2. People often ask me why I made the decision to get my GED. "Why do you want to spend all of your time studying? What good will it do?" Well, in my opinion, getting a GED will help me in a variety of ways. Passing the GED test will help me get a better job, make my husband feel proud of me, and help me feel better about myself.

    a. What is the topic of the essay?

    b. What is the main idea?

    c. Underline the thesis statement. Then list the main ideas of the three body paragraphs.

3. Nowadays it seems as if more and more people are moving to the city. However, I love living in my hometown, a village of 250 people in rural New England. There are three things that make small-town life attractive: your life is simple and uncongested, you know all your neighbors, and you feel safe.

    a. What is the topic of the essay?

    b. What is the main idea?

    c. Underline the thesis statement. Then list the main ideas of the three body paragraphs.

Answers are on page 384.

Writing the Body Paragraphs

With your organized list of ideas and a clearly written introductory paragraph, you can write the body paragraphs of your essay fairly quickly. The purpose of body paragraphs is to back up the thesis statement of the introductory paragraph.

Good body paragraphs have a **topic sentence**—a sentence that clearly states the topic of the paragraph and the main idea that the author is making about the topic. The rest of the sentences are **supporting sentences**; they give details that back up the topic sentence. For more information on topic sentences, see Chapter 4, pages 115–119. Look at the paragraph about winter driving again. Underline the topic sentence.

> If you're planning winter travel in the snowbelt, you should always keep some winter safety supplies in the trunk of your car. Always have a warm blanket, a hooded jacket, and mittens or gloves. You should also have a snow shovel and a bag of sand or salt in case your car gets stuck in snow. If you are planning a long trip, you should take a few easily stored foods like crackers, nuts, and dried fruit. Finally, you should have a help sign or a bright orange pennant to attach to your aerial to signal for help.

If you underlined the first sentence, you are correct. Often the first sentence in a body paragraph is the topic sentence. Now count the number of supporting sentences. If you counted four, you are correct. Each supporting sentence gives a detail that backs up the topic sentence. In this case, the topic sentence states that in winter every driver should carry certain supplies. Each supporting sentence gives details about a kind of supply (blankets and clothing, a shovel and sand, food, and a help sign).

To be effective, the topic sentence must indicate the topic of the paragraph without being too broad or too specific. The topic sentence *If you're planning winter travel in the snow belt, you should always keep some winter safety supplies in the trunk of your car* tells the reader exactly what to expect in the rest of the paragraph. Look at the following sentence:

> You need a lot of things when you travel in winter.

This sentence is too broad to be a topic sentence of the paragraph on winter travel. This sentence could include a lot of other things besides safety supplies and could also refer to kinds of travel other than by car. Now look at this sentence:

> In winter you need to keep salt in your trunk.

This sentence is too specific to be the topic sentence of the paragraph on winter travel supplies, for the paragraph is about much more than just salt.

Good supporting sentences all back up the topic sentence. Look at the following sentences. Which one belongs in the paragraph on winter driving supplies?

When driving in a heavy snowstorm, you should slow down to a safe speed.

Every car should also have a flashlight in the glove compartment, and winter is a good time to check the batteries to make sure they are working.

If you said that the second sentence belongs in the paragraph on winter driving supplies, you are right. It names another supply that should be in every car—a flashlight. The first sentence does not belong, since it is about a related but different topic—driving in winter.

A strong body paragraph usually has at least three supporting sentences. When you write your body paragraphs, use the ideas you gathered and organized. Each group of ideas becomes a body paragraph. Use the group names to develop the topic sentence of each paragraph. Then use the details in each group to develop the supporting sentences. Each supporting idea becomes one or two sentences. Look at the organized idea list and the body paragraphs for the essay on television:

GED preparation
program
Sesame Street—
for kids

news shows
biographies
documentaries
health programs

Education

Television is a good source of education. Our public TV station has a GED preparation program every afternoon. I tape it and watch it after the kids go to bed. In addition, my kids love educational programs like Sesame Street. Both my children learned the alphabet from this show. They also love to watch The Simpsons after they do their homework.

Information

There are a lot of good news programs on TV. My husband and I always watch the news before dinner. Some channels have news 24 hours a day. There are also great health programs on TV. TV has some great

game shows
movies
comedies
Entertainment
football, baseball,
and basketball games
dramas

Entertainment

documentaries and biografies. Last night I watched a great biography of Sammy Davis, Jr.

Most importantly, TV has great entertainment. There are several exciting game shows on TV right now. You can also watch old and new movies and comedies. I Love Lucy is my husbend's favorite program, I think. I love to watch football, basketball, and baseball on TV. The World Series starting this week, and I plan to watch all the games on TV. I also saw a great program on the life of Jackie Robinson last week.

Notice that the writer used the idea list as a guide, not an absolute rule. The writer added a few ideas that were not in the idea list. For example, the writer mentioned two specific programs, *The Simpsons* and *I Love Lucy*, in the essay but not in the idea list. These ideas occurred to the writer during the actual drafting.

Also note that the writer seems to have included one or two irrelevant ideas and made a few mistakes in English. For now, do not worry about these problems. We will look at them in the last stage of the writing process, revising, in Chapter 12.

When you are writing your body paragraphs, keep these points in mind:

1. **Make sure that your topic sentence is a complete sentence.** *Television benefits* is not a good topic sentence because it is only a noun phrase. It can be the subject of a sentence but needs a predicate to be a complete sentence.

2. **Make sure that each topic sentence refers back to the thesis statement.** Notice that the topic sentence of each body paragraph refers to something that was mentioned in the thesis statement.

3. **Your body paragraphs should follow the same order that they are mentioned in the thesis statement.** In the essay on television, the body paragraphs come in the same order as in the thesis statement: education, information, and entertainment.

4. **As you write the body paragraphs, use your introductory paragraph to make sure that all of your ideas support your main idea.** If you wonder whether an idea is really relevant, reread your introductory paragraph very quickly to ensure that the idea is about the main idea. For more about deleting irrelevant sentences, see Chapter 4, pages 127–133.

EXERCISE 2

Directions: Make each group of supporting sentences into a complete paragraph by adding a topic sentence. Make sure your topic sentence states the main idea of the paragraph and is a complete sentence.

Example: *Will is slacking off on the job.* Every morning Will walks into work at least half an hour late. He uses work time to phone his girlfriends. Will's lunch hour lasts 15 minutes longer than anyone else's. He often slips away from work 10 or 15 minutes before closing time.

1. _____ Some of the money from the property tax increase could be used to give police officers and firefighters pay increases. New books could be added to the public library. We could give all of the teachers raises. The city could expand the summer employment program for teenagers.

2. _____ Sit-ups firm stomach muscles. Leg lifts tone thighs and hips. Push-ups build arm strength. Running in place strengthens legs.

3. _____ Tyrone gets up at 5:00 every morning. Then he walks the dog and takes a shower. Next he wakes up his sons and helps them get ready for school. He makes sure they eat a good breakfast. Then he walks them to school. Finally, he goes to the bus stop and takes the bus to work.

Answers are on page 384.

EXERCISE 3

Directions: Each of the following topic sentences is followed by a list of supporting sentences. Cross off the sentence that does not support the topic sentence. Then add one more sentence that does support the topic sentence. Use the idea list to write a complete paragraph.

Example: Junk foods are common in many people's diets.

a. People eat lots of sugary breakfast cereal.

b. Candy bars are a popular snack.

c. Many people have a diet rich in fruits and vegetables.

d. Lots of people order french fries at lunch.

e. *Many people like to munch on potato chips while they watch TV.*

Junk foods are common in many people's diets. In the morning, many people start their day by eating lots of sugary breakfast cereal. Candy bars are a popular snack when people get hungry between meals. Then at lunch time, lots of people order fast food, such as french fries. Even at the end of the day, many people continue to eat junk food by munching on potato chips while they're watching TV.

1. Many retail stores take advantage of holidays to boost sales.

   a. Supermarkets promote picnic supplies around the Fourth of July.

   b. Stores put up huge candy displays at Halloween.

   c. Many department stores have clearance sales in early August.

   d. Supermarkets sell lots of Thanksgiving supplies in November.

   e. _____

   _____

   _____

   _____

   _____

   _____

2. American food is enriched by traditional foods from many different countries.

   a. In summer, people enjoy sweet corn from Illinois and Iowa.

   b. Many Americans enjoy different kinds of sausages imported from Germany.

   c. People love to eat Japanese foods, such as sushi.

   d. Many Mexican foods are popular these days.

   e. _____

   _____

   _____

   _____

   _____

3. You should always examine a used car carefully before you buy it.

   a. You can buy a used car from a used-car dealer or an individual.

   b. You should check the number of miles on the odometer.

   c. Always check the tires for even wear.

   d. Have a mechanic check the engine.

   e. _____

   _____

   _____

   _____

   _____

   _____

4. There are many ways to get exercise.

   a. You can go for a walk in your neighborhood.

   b. You can see the flowers at the Botanic Garden.

   c. You can swim at Lakeside Park.

   d. You can ride your bicycle on the bike trail.

   e. _____

   _____

   _____

   _____

   _____

   _____

Answers are on page 384.

Writing the Concluding Paragraph

Now that the introduction and body of the essay are written, it is time to draw your writing to a close with the conclusion. You do not need any new ideas to write a concluding paragraph. This paragraph serves two main purposes—to give the essay a sense of completeness and to help the reader remember your main point. A good concluding paragraph goes from specific (reviewing the main points of your essay) to general (stating the broader importance of the subject).

To accomplish this, you can use a reworded version of your thesis statement as the first sentence of the concluding paragraph. Then add one or two sentences that relate your ideas to broader issues. Look at the following example:

> Clearly, TV has improved my life in three ways: it has provided education, news and other information, and hundreds of hours of wonderful entertainment. My favorable impression is not unique. Over the years, billions of people around the world have had their lives enriched by this magic box. By watching it, we can accomplish wonderful things from the comfort of our homes.

When you are writing your concluding paragraph, keep these three points in mind:

1. **Do not announce your plans.** Avoid concluding sentences like this:

   I would like to end this essay by saying that I prize my television set.

2. **Do not apologize for your essay.** Avoid sentences like this:

   I am sorry that I did not have much to say on this topic. I don't watch TV a lot, so I don't have much to say about it.

3. **Do not bring up new topics.** Stick to what you already wrote about in the body paragraphs. Avoid sentences like this:

   For these reasons, my television set is my most important possession. Only my car comes close in importance. It takes me to work, to the supermarket and mall, and everywhere else I want to go.

EXERCISE 4

Directions: Read each pair of paragraphs below. Circle the letter of the paragraph that is a better conclusion.

1. a.   As you can see, I really love my walks, my books, and my movies. In fact, no weekend is complete without a walk in the park, a trip to the library, and a night at the movies. After a weekend like this, I am relaxed, happy, and ready to go back to work.

    b.   The last movie I saw was really fun. I walked to the theater and after that I went to a café for a cup of coffee. It was really great, and I wish I could do it every weekend.

2. a.   People who obtain their GED often say that it was the most important thing they ever did. Other important things that I have done include getting married and having my children. I do not regret any of these decisions.

    b.   I just know that when I obtain my GED I will get a better job, my husband will feel really proud of me, and I will feel good about myself. In fact, just the fact that I study every night makes me feel happy and proud. I think that everybody who did not finish high school needs to seriously consider going back for his or her GED.

3. a.   A small town is safe and clean. Big cities are dirty and noisy. Some cities are worse than others. Some cities are much cleaner and safer than others. But even so, I would stay in my village in New England.

    b.   The simplicity, friendliness, and safety of life in a small town make living there an attractive option. I would never give up life in my town and move to a city anywhere. And it seems like a lot of people are beginning to agree with me. Last year, about 20 families moved to my town from several different big cities. If my town keeps growing, I think I will have to move to a smaller one!

4. a.   Using the three tips of sales, coupons, and cooking at home will save you hundreds of dollars every year. In fact, if you follow this advice, your biggest problem will be spending the money you save. What would you do with an extra $50 or $60 a month?

    b.   Even though I know lots of ways to save money, I never use them. I like to spend money, and I hate worrying about it. So I just buy what I want and hope I don't run out of money before the end of the month.

Answers are on page 385.

The following graphic organizer helps illustrate the five-paragraph essay format:

A good introductory paragraph
- is organized from general to specific.
- states the main idea of the essay.
- ends with a specific thesis statement that tells the reader what to expect in each body paragraph.

Good body paragraphs

- are each about one main idea that supports the main idea of the essay.

- are in the same order as they are mentioned in the thesis statement.
- begin with the topic sentence that states the main idea of the paragraph.

- contain detailed supporting sentences that back up the paragraph's topic sentence.

A good concluding paragraph
- is organized from specific to general.
- begins with a restatement of the thesis statement.
- ends with a general statement that relates the topic of the essay to broader ideas.

Writing a GED Essay

Directions: Look at the idea list that you organized for the GED essay at the end of Chapter 10 (page 251). Use it to write a complete five-paragraph essay. The steps below will guide you through the writing process.

1. Look at the topic, main idea, and names of your groups. Use them to write an introductory paragraph on the lines below. Make sure that your introductory paragraph meets these characteristics:

   ☐ The paragraph is indented.

   ☐ The paragraph identifies the topic and main idea of the essay.

   ☐ The paragraph captures the reader's interest.

   ☐ The paragraph indicates the organization of the essay in the thesis statement.

   _____

   _____

   _____

   _____

2. Look at the three groups of ideas. Use them to write three body paragraphs on the lines below. Make sure that your body paragraphs meet these characteristics:

   ☐ The paragraphs are indented.

   ☐ The body paragraphs support, or back up, the thesis statement in the same order that they are mentioned in the thesis statement.

   ☐ Each body paragraph begins with a topic sentence that is a complete sentence and indicates the main idea of that paragraph.

   ☐ The support sentences back up the topic sentence with more detailed information.

   Body Paragraph 1:

   _____

   _____

   _____

   _____

Body Paragraph 2:

_____

_____

_____

_____

_____

Body Paragraph 3:

_____

_____

_____

_____

_____

3. Review your idea list and completed body paragraphs. Use them to write a concluding paragraph on the lines below. Make sure that your concluding paragraph meets these characteristics:

☐ The paragraph is indented.

☐ The concluding paragraph summarizes the information in the body paragraphs.

☐ The first sentence of the concluding paragraph rephrases the thesis statement.

☐ The other sentences relate the thesis statement to broader ideas.

_____

_____

_____

_____

_____

Answers are on page 385.

RAISING YOUR SCORE

Look at the essay you wrote in the GED Practice Exercise. Now look at the criteria on development from the GED Essay Scoring Guide. Circle the number that best describes your introduction, body paragraphs, and conclusion.

LEVEL 4 writing achieves coherent development with specific and relevant details and examples.

LEVEL 3 writing has focused but occasionally uneven development.

LEVEL 2 writing has some development, but it may be limited to a listing, repetition, or generalizations.

LEVEL 1 writing demonstrates little or no development.

Now look at your essay again. What can you do to improve your score? Write one or two ideas on the lines below.

_____

_____

_____

_____

Chapter 11 Highlights: Writing Your GED Essay

- A paragraph is a set of sentences that develops a central point or main idea.

- Indicate the beginning of a paragraph by indenting the first line.

- The introductory paragraph identifies the topic and main idea of the essay, captures the reader's interest, and indicates the pattern of organization.

- Use your notes on the topic and main idea to write your introductory paragraph. Use the group names to write the thesis statement.

- The body paragraphs support, or back up, the thesis statement.

- Each body paragraph begins with a topic sentence. The topic sentence indicates the main idea of each body paragraph. The rest of the sentences support the topic sentence with more detailed information.

- The concluding paragraph summarizes the information in the body paragraphs.

- The first sentence of the concluding paragraph should rephrase the thesis statement. The other sentences should relate the thesis statement to broader ideas.

CHAPTER 12

Revising Your GED Essay

> In this chapter you will learn ways to revise your GED essay in order to get a high score.
>
> ☐ Gathering Ideas
>
> ☐ Organizing
>
> ☐ Writing
>
> ☑ Revising

When you finish writing an essay, does an enormous sense of relief sweep over you—a "Whew! That's done!" sort of feeling? Writing an essay should give you a sense of accomplishment. Gathering ideas, organizing those ideas, and writing the essay can take an enormous amount of mental effort.

But before you turn in your essay as a finished product, remember that the final stage of the writing process is revising. Like the difference between a rough-cut gem and a diamond gleaming in the window of a fancy jewelry store, the difference between a promising piece of writing and a high-scoring GED essay lies in revising.

When you revise, you do two things. First, you examine the essay in order to strengthen its content, organization, and wording. In this step, you put yourself in the shoes of the reader in order to decide what changes will sharpen meaning and make your writing clearer and more convincing.

In the second stage of revising, you examine your writing for key features of standard written English. You correct things such as mechanics, spelling, punctuation, and sentence structure. The GED testing service calls this Edited American English.

You should check your GED essay twice because revising content is a very different task from revising mechanics. Also, since content is weighted more heavily, you should spend the bulk of your revising time checking content.

When you are completing the essay portion of the test, you have only 45 minutes for all four steps of the writing process. There is not enough time to recopy your entire essay when you are ready to revise. Instead, you should write your corrections directly on your first draft.

In this chapter, we will review the entire GED Essay Scoring Guide and use it to evaluate your writing. Then we will examine specific techniques and tools you can use to revise your essay in order to raise your score.

Essay Scoring Guide

	1	2	3	4
	Inadequate	Marginal	Adequate	Effective
Response to the Prompt	**Reader has difficulty identifying or following the writer's ideas.**	**Reader occasionally has difficulty understanding or following the writer's ideas.**	**Reader understands the writer's ideas.**	**Reader understands and easily follows the writer's expression of ideas.**
	Attempts to address prompt but with little or no success in establishing a focus.	Addresses the prompt, though the focus may shift.	Uses the writing prompt to establish a main idea.	Presents a clearly focused main idea that addresses the prompt.
Organization	Fails to organize ideas.	Shows some evidence of an organizational plan.	Uses an identifiable organizational plan.	Establishes a clear and logical organization.
Development and Details	Demonstrates little or no development; usually lacks details or examples or presents irrelevant information.	Has some development but lacks specific details; may be limited to a listing, repetitions, or generalizations.	Has focused but occasionally uneven development; incorporates some specific detail.	Achieves coherent development with specific and relevant details and examples.
Conventions of EAE	Exhibits minimal or no control of sentence structure and the conventions of Edited American English (EAE).	Demonstrates inconsistent control of sentence structure and the conventions of EAE.	Generally controls sentence structure and the conventions of EAE.	Consistently controls sentence structure and the conventions of EAE.
Word Choice	Exhibits weak and/or inappropriate words.	Exhibits a narrow range of word choice, often including inappropriate selections.	Exhibits appropriate word choice.	Exhibits varied and precise word choice.

Rating Your GED Essay

As you know, two readers will rate your essay holistically using a rating scale. Understanding the rating scale will help you figure out how to revise your essay in order to get a better score. Take a few minutes to review the rating scale on the opposite page.

As you can see, most of the criteria cover content and organization, not Edited American English. Therefore, when you are ready to revise, you should concentrate on content and organization and spend only a few minutes checking spelling, punctuation, and so on.

How do the readers apply the scoring guide to an essay? Read the topic and sample essay below. What score do you think this essay received?

──────────── T O P I C ────────────

Families are much smaller today than they were 50 years ago.

In your essay, explain why most couples are having fewer children.

In the passed, people used to have three, four, or even five children, but not today. Nowadays, smaller families are much more common. In fact, most couples now want to have only one or two kids. Many reasons for this change. These days, people have smaller families because of the expense, time, and energy required for having kids.

These days, people don't have time to raise several kids. Many mothers work outside the home, so they do not have time to raise several children. They may stay home for a few months after their first two children are born. After their first children are born, they do not have time to have more children. They also do not have time to do other important things like going back to school for more education.

Parents need money to pay for food, clothing, and shoes. While kids are in elementary school, parents are always paying for field trips, class projects, and other school activities. Parents also need to come up with tuition money if their children want to go to college. College tuition can cost thousands of dollars.

Raising children also takes a lot of energy, which most people do not have these days. Because parents are under so much pressure at work, they do not have energy for all of the activities involved in raising a child. Raising a child requires a lot of energy, too.

If you answered 3, you are correct. This essay received a 3 because it is focused on a single main idea and for the most part controls language and sentence structure. However, there are a few fragments *(Many reasons for this change)* and misspelled words *(passed* instead of *past)*. The writer has a clear organizational plan, but the thesis statement and the body paragraphs are in different orders. In addition, the second body paragraph lacks a topic sentence, and there is no concluding paragraph. There is some detail in the first two body paragraphs but not in the paragraph about energy. The first body paragraph also contains a sentence that is not about the main idea: *They also do not have time to do other important things like going back to school for more education.* Generally, the reader can understand the writer's ideas.

How could the writer improve this score? The writer should carefully revise in order to adjust the order of the thesis statement to reflect the organization of the essay. He or she should also add a concluding paragraph. The writer needs to add a topic sentence to the paragraph on the cost of raising children and delete the irrelevant sentence about going back to school. Finally, the writer should eliminate fragments such as *Many reasons for this change* and correct misspelled words like *passed,* which should be *past.*

EXERCISE 1

Directions: Read the sample topic below and rate the following GED essays using the scoring guide on page 272. Write the scores on the lines below.

— T O P I C —

How do you like to spend your free time?

In your essay, describe what you like to do in your free time. Explain the reasons for your choices.

Essay 1: _____

In my free time I like to wathc TV. There be a lot of good shows. Drama's are very interested. I like comedies, too, comedies make me laugh. After dinner I watch TV every night. Until bedtime every night. Usually I stay up until about midnight. Most people are like me, I think. We prefer TV because it's not very expensive and its fun.

Essay 2: _____

In my free time, I like to watch TV, play with my kids, and take care of my house. Usually, after work I pick up my kids from day care and play with them for an hour or so before I cook dinner. Sometimes, we play hide-and-seek or play a simple board game for kids.

After dinner, I put my kids to bed. and then watch TV for one or two hours. Maybe more. I really like to watch documentaries and news programs, like biographies a lot.

On weekends, I like to work in my yard. I cut the grass and weed the garden. Then water the garden. I love taking care of all of my different plant's.

So I usually am busy during my free time.

Answers are on page 385.

Revising the Organization and Content

When you revise the organization and content of your essay, you should do several things to make sure that your ideas are expressed clearly and well. Check to ensure that you have employed the skills you learned in Chapters 9, 10, and 11 in order to meet specific criteria required on the GED Essay Scoring Guide.

- Relevance to the topic of the essay
- Clearly written introduction with thesis statement
- Three body paragraphs with topic sentences
- Sufficient supporting details in the body paragraphs

You should use the following techniques and tools to polish your writing:

- Specific reasons to support the thesis
- Specific examples
- Specific details
- Showing rather than telling
- Transitions between sentences and paragraphs
- Smooth wording with no repetition

Relevance

You should check to make sure that all of your ideas are about the essay topic and support the main idea of the paragraph and the essay. This step is necessary because, as you learned in Chapter 11, as you write, you may add an idea that is not in your idea list. It might turn out that this idea is not about the topic of the essay. Look at the following paragraph. Cross off any sentences that do not belong.

> Though many people prefer to fly, I like to travel by car. When you drive, you are free. You can stop when you want, take a side trip, or pull over for a rest. When you fly, you are on a fixed schedule and miss all of the scenery you can see from your car window. When you take the bus you are also on a fixed schedule, but at least you can see the scenery if you get a window seat.

If you crossed off the last sentence, you are correct. The paragraph is about comparing and contrasting air travel with travel by car. The last sentence is off topic—it is about bus travel.

Check your essay to make sure that the introductory paragraph goes from general to specific and has a thesis statement. You should also make sure that each of the body paragraphs supports one of the topics in the thesis statement and that each body paragraph begins with a topic sentence. Make sure that the thesis statement and the body paragraphs are in the same order.

Look at how the writer fixed the organization of the essay on smaller families:

In the passed, people used to have three, four, or even five children, but not today. Nowadays, smaller families are much more common. In fact, most couples now want to have only one or two kids. Many reasons for this change. These days, people have smaller families because of the time, expense, ~~time~~ and energy required for having kids.

These days, people don't have time to raise several kids. Many mothers work outside the home, so they do not have time to raise several children. They may stay home for a few months after their first two children are born. After their first children are born, they do not have time to have more children. They also do not have time to do other important things like going back to school for more education.

Nowadays, raising a child can be very expensive. Parents need money to pay for food, clothing, and shoes. While kids are in elementary school, parents are always paying money for field trips, class projects, and other school activities. Parents also need to come up with tuition money if their children want to go to college. College tuition can cost thousands of dollars.

Raising children also takes a lot of energy, which most people do not have these days. Because parents are under so much pressure at work, they do not have energy for all of the activities involved in raising a child. Raising a child requires a lot of energy, too.

As you can see, there are important reasons that motivate people to prefer small families. This is why I am glad I have only two kids.

As you can see, the writer fixed the problems of organization by adjusting the thesis statement, adding a topic sentence to the paragraph on expenses, and adding a conclusion.

EXERCISE 2

Directions: Read the paragraphs below. Cross out any ideas that are not relevant.

1.   There are many reasons that people like to keep dogs as pets. First, dogs have a defensive instinct that makes them good guards of people and property. Even the smallest dog will bark when a stranger comes to the door. Second, dogs are loyal and faithful. A dog always greets each member of the family when they come home. In contrast, cats usually do not pay attention when people come home. Third, dogs are good companions. Dogs love to be around people and will often cuddle up with their owners and keep them company when they are home.

2.   There are many reasons why people collect stamps. Stamps are colorful and visually appealing. For example, a few years ago, the post office printed stamps with the state flowers of all 50 U.S. states. In addition, they carry pictures of interesting people, places, and objects. I really like stamps that carry pictures of famous Americans like Martin Luther King, Jr., Harry Truman, Elvis Presley, and W. C. Fields. I saw a good W. C. Fields movie on TV last night. Third, you can get stamps from countries around the world, for all countries use stamps. Finally, stamps are not very expensive— literally no more than mailing a letter. So you can assemble a beautiful collection at a very low cost.

3.   You should always keep certain supplies in your home medicine cabinet in case of minor illness. First, every medicine cabinet should have some form of pain reliever, such as aspirin, acetaminophen, or ibuprofen. Your medicine cabinet should also have bandages and disinfectant in case anyone gets a cut. Finally, in winter your medicine cabinet should have some cough medicine for people to take when they have a cold. Always keep all your medical supplies away from children so that they cannot accidentally take an overdose.

Answers are on page 385.

Sufficient Support

When you revise, you should make sure that every paragraph has at least two or three strong supporting ideas. If a paragraph lacks supporting ideas, add them. Look at this example from the essay on smaller families. What ideas might the writer add?

> *Raising children also takes a lot of energy, which most people do not have these days. Because parents are under so much pressure at work, they do not have energy for all of the activities involved in raising a child. Raising a child requires a lot of energy, too.*

The writer might add specific activities that require energy, such as attending school plays and parent-teacher conferences, going to scout meetings, and helping the children with homework. Look at the revised paragraph below and notice how much more convincingly this paragraph supports its topic sentence.

> *Raising children also takes a lot of energy, which most people do not have these days. Because parents are under so much pressure at work, they do not have energy for all of the activities involved in raising a child. Raising a child requires a lot of energy, too. For example, parents need to attend school plays and parent-teacher conferences, go to scout meetings, and help their children with their homework. Parents also need to talk to their kids and spend time with them on weekends and after school.*

Specific Reasons

When someone is trying to persuade you, what makes his or her arguments convincing? Usually, you will be willing to consider someone else's point of view if the person offers good reasons to back up his or her opinions. For this reason, when you write, you should always make sure you give specific reasons to support your main idea.

Many writers make the mistake of using **circular reasoning**. That is, rather than providing a specific reason to support their opinion, they restate the opinion in other words. Look at the following example:

Teenagers are too young to drink alcoholic beverages because they aren't mature enough to handle alcohol.

This sentence is basically saying, "Teenagers are too young to drink because they are too young to drink." On the following page, look at a revised version, which states a specific reason.

Teenagers are too young to drink alcoholic beverages because they tend to be daredevils. They are willing to drink to excess because they are still testing their limits.

Here is another example:

Titanic is the most extravagant film I have ever seen. Every other film pales in comparison.

Notice that the second sentence simply restates the same idea of the first sentence without giving a specific reason. Now look at this example. How many specific reasons does it give?

Titanic is the most extravagant film I have ever seen because of the expensive costumes, the elaborate set, and the abundance of computerized special effects.

The revised example gives three good reasons that support the writer's belief that the movie is extravagant. As you revise, you should check the reasons you provide to support your main idea. If your reasoning is circular, revise it by thinking of a specific reason. For example, look at the following sentences. Which sentence uses circular reasoning? Find it and correct it on the lines provided.

Japanese cars are better than American cars because Japanese cars are sturdier and use less gas.

That book is boring because it simply does not interest me.

A tax decrease is needed because people need more buying power to keep up with inflation.

_____

_____

Did you revise the second sentence? *Boring* and *doesn't interest me* are two ways of saying the same thing.

EXERCISE 3

Directions: Read each sentence. If it uses circular reasoning, rewrite the sentence on the line below and try to add at least one specific reason. If a sentence provides a specific reason, write *correct*.

Example: The mandatory retirement age should be raised because age 65 is too low.

The mandatory retirement age should be raised because most 65-year-old people are in better physical and mental health than older people were 35 years ago.

1. City life is more stressful than farm life because city life has more tension.

   _____

2. The telephone has brought the world closer together by allowing people thousands of miles apart to communicate instantly.

   _____

3. In my opinion, the federal government wastes taxpayers' money by spending it needlessly.

   _____

4. The automobile is one of the most useful inventions of the twentieth century. It has provided many benefits.

   _____

5. I believe that water pollution is a serious environmental problem in this country because it is a threat to our surroundings.

   _____

6. America needs tougher gun-control legislation because too many people are killed each year in accidental shootings and shootings related to domestic violence.

   _____

7. Elementary school children should be required to learn a foreign language because learning a foreign language should be a part of everyone's education.

   _____

8. College athletes should be paid for playing because they earn large amounts of money for their schools.

   _____

Answers are on page 385.

Specific Examples

Which of the following passages creates a clearer image in your mind?

> Old people in nursing homes are often neglected. Their relatives ignore them, and the staff is too busy to attend to anything but their basic survival needs.

> Old people in nursing homes are often neglected. Their relatives ignore them, and the staff is too busy to attend to anything but their basic survival needs. Imagine an 86-year-old man strapped in a wheelchair for eight hours every day, staring vacantly as the nurses hurry past without a glance in his direction. In the five years he has been in the nursing home his children have visited him twice.

Without a doubt, the second passage is more vivid. Notice that the writer has added specific examples that illustrate the general ideas in the first two statements. Note the general statements and specific examples summarized in the chart below:

General Statement	Specific Example
old people	an 86-year-old man
neglected	strapped in a wheelchair for eight hours a day
relatives ignore them	his children have visited him twice
staff too busy	the nurses hurry past without a glance

Using detailed examples can help make your writing interesting and convincing to your reader. You can draw examples from your own personal experience and that of your family and friends. You can also draw examples from the newspaper, what you have seen on TV or at the movies, or simply your imagination.

How would you add a specific example to this general statement?

People are obsessed with money.

You can probably think of a lot of examples of how people are obsessed with money. You could write about yourself or someone you know, as in the following statement:

> People are obsessed with money. My friend Carl walks three miles to work and back every day in order to save just three dollars in bus fare.

Or you could use less personal examples, such as these:

> People are obsessed with money. Every day, you hear stories about families feuding over who is going to get Grandpa's money.

> People are obsessed with money. I've read that most marital problems are caused by people arguing about money.

EXERCISE 4

Directions: Add a specific example to each of the following general statements. You can draw on personal experience, general knowledge, or your imagination.

1. High school students drop out for a variety of reasons.

   _____

2. We could learn a lot from older people if only we spent more time with them.

   _____

3. Many workers are dissatisfied with their jobs.

   _____

4. Having a lot of money does not always make people happy.

   _____

5. Big cities can be dangerous.

   _____

Answers are on page 386.

Specific Details

You can add detail and color to your writing in several ways. One easy way to dress up your writing is to use specific nouns and verbs to create a clearer image for your reader. For example, a general sentence such as *A man walked into the room* could be revised in a variety of ways:

A trucker strode into Todd's Diner.

A drunk staggered into the hotel bar.

General Powell marched into the Pentagon.

On the lines below, write two revisions of your own of the sentence *A man walked into the room.*

_____

_____

Use Specific Words and Phrases

You can also add describing words and phrases. Include details that answer questions such as *what kind? which one? how many? where? when? how?* and *why?*

You could rewrite the sentence *A trucker strode into Todd's Diner* in this way:

At 8:00 last night, a burly, 250-pound trucker with a tattoo of a snake on his left forearm strode menacingly into Todd's Diner to confront his ex-girlfriend, Sadie, who's the manager there.

How about the sentence *A drunk staggered into the hotel bar?* You could rewrite it like this:

Nearly tripping on the doorsill, a disheveled drunk in a rumpled business suit staggered into the Starlight Hotel's bar at midnight for one last shot of whiskey before stumbling off to bed.

Don't you get a better picture when the writer uses more describing words and phrases? Revise the two sentences that you wrote on page 285. Add at least three describing words and phrases to each—more if you can.

_____

_____

Show, Don't Tell

Another way to add specifics to your writing is to show your readers what you mean. Don't just tell them what you think. Provide the specific details that allow your readers to reach the same conclusions you have reached.

Telling: My daughter was delighted.

Showing: My three-year-old daughter danced around the room clapping her hands and laughing.

Telling: The garden was beautiful.

Showing: The garden contained beds of multicolored tulips flanked by rows of dark-green juniper hedges.

As you can see, specific observations will make your writing much more convincing and interesting. Try revising the following sentence by showing rather than telling.

The dog was incredibly ugly.

_____

_____

EXERCISE 5

Part A   **Directions:**   Revise the sentences below by using specific nouns and verbs, adding describing words and phrases, and replacing telling statements with showing statements to make the reader see what you see. Use your imagination!

Example: Two vehicles collided at an intersection.

A dump truck smashed into a motorcycle at the intersection of State Street and Tenth Avenue during a pouring rainstorm last night.

1. The victim was upset.

      _____

2. The neighborhood is run-down.

      _____

3. The musician played an instrument.

      _____

4. The teenager asked his parent a question.

      _____

5. The shopping mall was crowded.

      _____

6. Grocery prices have increased.

      _____

Answers are on page 386.

EDITING TIP

To see how specifics can strengthen an essay, study some changes made by the writer of the essay below:

Everyone should have a pet, ^ *such as a furry cat or a fuzzy dog.* ~~Pets keep you company.~~ ^ ~~Pets have helpful roles.~~ *For example, my dog loves to snuggle up on the couch next to me while I study for the GED.* ^ *My cat caught a mouse last week, and my dog always barks when a stranger comes to the door.*

Hints:

1.   Use carets (^) to show where new material will be added rather than recopying the entire essay. This will haelp you save time when you are writing the GED essay.

2.   As you get more practice writing a GED essay, you will begin to use more specifics as you write, and your revision time will go down.

Sentence and Paragraph Links

Transitions

Making the relationships among your ideas clear to the reader is the key to readable writing. You have already worked with patterns of organization and the five-paragraph essay format in Chapters 8–11. In this section, you will look closely at how to help your reader follow the organization of your essay by using transition words and phrases.

Transitions help your reader follow your thoughts from sentence to sentence and from paragraph to paragraph. In the chart below, you will find a few of the most common transition words and their uses.

Transition Words	Uses
first, second, third, then, next, later, finally	to show time order
one, another, also, in addition, the most important, moreover, furthermore, first, second	to join ideas and rank them in order of importance
as a result, consequently, therefore	to show cause and effect
also, both, similar, like, on the other hand, in contrast, different, disadvantage, advantage, however	to compare and contrast
for example, for instance	to give a specific detail to illustrate a general point

Transitions Between Sentences

Let's take a look at how to use transitions between sentences within a paragraph. The writer wants to explain why, with all the problems of city life, she prefers to live there instead of in a small town. She has written the two sentences below, and she wants to use a transition between them that will help her reader see the point that she is trying to make. Think of a transition word she could use.

Small towns may be quiet and peaceful. I prefer the excitement and variety of a big city.

She needs a transition word that shows contrast, such as *however* or *on the other hand*. Read the sentences again with the transition word *however* inserted. Can you see how much easier it is to understand the writer's point?

Small towns may be quiet and peaceful. **However**, I prefer the excitement and variety of a big city.

Commas and Transition Words

Commas usually separate transition words and phrases from the rest of the sentence.

> Candy and soda provide nothing but empty calories to the consumer. **However,** fruits and vegetables provide important vitamins and minerals with fewer calories.

> Candy and soda provide nothing but empty calories to the consumer. Fruits and vegetables, **however,** provide important vitamins and minerals with fewer calories.

Many other transitional words and phrases are probably familiar to you. Circle the transitional words in this example:

> In my opinion, Congress should pass a tax reform bill. The Senate, as a matter of fact, is debating the issue this week. Of course, the chances for passage in an election year are slim at best.

Did you circle *In my opinion*, *as a matter of fact*, and *of course*?

EXERCISE 6

Directions: Insert transition words in the sentences below to show the logical links between the ideas. Be sure to include any necessary punctuation.

Example: Sylvester insisted that everyone call him Rocky.

His parents, *however,* continued to use his given name.

1. Two hundred years ago, settlers needed guns to protect themselves from wild animals. _____ those frontier days are long past.

2. Many immigrants face a language barrier when they try to find jobs in their new country. _____ they must adapt to unfamiliar interviewing practices.

3. The food at Mick's Restaurant is excellent. _____ the prices are very low.

4. If the weather is good, we will go to the park for a picnic. _____ we will go to the movies.

5. First, preheat the oven to 350 degrees. _____ empty the contents of the cake mix package into a large bowl.

6. Tamika is very quiet and serious. Her sister Tonya _____ is quite talkative and vivacious.

Answers are on page 386.

Transitions Between Paragraphs

Here are two paragraphs from the essay on living in a big city. How could the writer use a transition to link the two paragraphs? Think of at least one good transition.

> Small towns may be quiet and peaceful. However, I prefer the excitement and variety of a big city. Urban entertainment ranges from live blues clubs to ethnic street festivals. I can go see old movies for two dollars or go to a dance club. No matter how much or how little money I have in my pocket, I can always find something to do.

> Job opportunities are better in a big city. New businesses are opening all the time here, and the help-wanted ads on Sundays fill three whole sections of the paper. No matter what part of the nation's economy is growing, the growth is likely to happen in a big city.

What relationship do these two paragraphs have? They both give information about the advantages of living in a big city. The writer could revise the topic sentence of the second paragraph in any number of ways so that the relationship between the two paragraphs is clear to the reader. Look at the following examples:

Furthermore, job opportunities are better in a big city.

In addition, job opportunities are better in a big city.

Another advantage of life in a big city is that job opportunities are better there.

The following three paragraphs of the sample essay on smaller families have been revised to include transition words and phrases to emphasize overall organization and to link paragraphs and sentences effectively.

First, these days, people don't have time to raise several kids. Many mothers work outside of the home, so they do not have time to raise several children. They may stay home for a few months after their first two children are born. After their first children are born, they do not have time to have more children. They also do not have time to do other important things like going back to school for more education.

Moreover, nNowadays, raising a child can be very expensive. Parents need money to pay for food, clothing, and shoes. While kids are in elementary school, parents are always paying money for field trips, class projects, and other school activities. Parents also need to come up with tuition money if their children want to go to college. College tuition can cost thousands of dollars.

Finally, rRaising children also takes a lot of energy, which most people do not have these days. Because parents are under so much pressure at work, they do not have energy for all of the activities involved in raising a child. Raising a child requires a lot of energy, too. For example, parents need to attend school plays and parent-teacher conferences, go to scout meetings, and help their children with their homework. Parents also need to talk to their kids and spend time with them on weekends and after school.

EXERCISE 7

Directions: Revise the following passage, adding transition words and phrases to make the relationship among ideas clearer to the reader. Use carets (^) to show where new material is inserted.

High school students should not be allowed to drive for several reasons. They are not mature enough to handle the responsibility. Every Friday night, one teenager I know downs a six-pack of beer and then challenges his classmates to drag race down Main Street.

Cars detract from schoolwork. Most students who own cars work to pay for gas and insurance. They spend less time on schoolwork, which should be their primary concern.

Cars give high school students too much freedom. Instead of cruising the streets looking for parties to crash or someone to pick up, they should be with their families, where more adult supervision is provided.

Answers are on page **386.**

Smooth Wording

Avoid Repetition

Does your writing seem to repeat itself? Perhaps you have overused a word or a phrase. Read the paragraph below and circle the repetitive words and phrases.

> Misha is one of the most versatile people I know. Misha teaches math, chemistry, and electronics for a living. Misha plays the banjo and sings in a bluegrass band on the side. Misha also writes his own computer programs as a hobby. Misha also paints as a hobby.

Each sentence in the paragraph begins with the same word: *Misha*. In addition, the word *also* and the phrase *as a hobby* are both used twice.

If repetition is a problem, look for ways to rephrase the writing. For example, you can use a pronoun such as *he, they,* or *our* to take the place of a noun. For more information on pronouns, see Chapter 1, pages 38–42. Another way to avoid repetition is to use **synonyms**, words or phrases that have the same meaning.

Here is a revised version of the repetitive paragraph, with synonyms and pronouns:

> Misha is one of the most versatile people I know. **He** teaches math, chemistry, and electronics for a living, **and he** plays the banjo and sings in a bluegrass band on the side. **This multitalented person** also writes his own computer programs as a hobby. **Another of his pastimes** is painting.

EXERCISE 8

Directions: Revise the following paragraph to eliminate repetition. Use synonyms and pronouns. The first change has been made as an example.

Frank was annoyed with Lisa because ~~Lisa~~ *she* never became angry with him. Whenever Frank complained to Lisa about anything, Lisa apologized to Frank instead of becoming angry in return. Frank found it impossible to have a good argument with Lisa because Lisa refused to argue. Lisa's refusal to argue simply made Frank even angrier than Frank was to begin with.

Answers are on page 386.

Eliminate Wordiness

Even if no words are repeated unnecessarily in a passage, the passage may still suffer from wordiness. What idea is repeated unnecessarily in the following sentence?

A great big huge dog attacked the mail carrier.

Three words *(great, big,* and *huge)* are used to describe the dog, but all of them say basically the same thing. You could revise the sentence like this:

A huge dog attacked the mail carrier.

As you revise, look for ways to reduce the number of words in your essay without losing important ideas. This process, called **tightening**, will make your writing clearer and more forceful. When you cut words, don't cut interesting details or reasons that support your main idea. Just eliminate extra words that say the same thing as other words.

Note the changes made to tighten each of the following sentences:

Wordy:	Ricardo is a man who has great strength.
Tight:	Ricardo is very strong.
Wordy:	The doctor took a look at the patient's leg.
Tight:	The doctor looked at the patient's leg.
Wordy:	In this day and age, computers are a significant part of our daily lives.
Tight:	Computers are now an important part of our lives.
Wordy:	It is a fact that our bodies need vitamin A.
Tight:	Our bodies need vitamin A.

How can this sentence be tightened? Rewrite it on the lines below.

Substances that are hazardous or dangerous shouldn't be dumped or discarded near locations that are residential areas.

_____

_____

You might have rewritten the sentence like this:

Hazardous substances shouldn't be dumped near residential areas.

EXERCISE 9

<u>Part A</u> **Directions:** Revise the following sentences to eliminate wordiness. Change the wording as needed. As you revise, be sure you avoid cutting important details. If a sentence is not wordy, write *correct*.

Example: The house that was old and rickety was on the market for sale. *The old, rickety house was for sale.*

1. The dress is blue in color and cotton in fabric.

   _____

2. At last we finally found an apartment that is large in size but inexpensive in cost.

   _____

3. I'm going to go ahead and order a large pizza.

   _____

4. The valuable silver dollars were worth a minimum of $50 each, at least.

   _____

5. We are going to the store for the purpose of buying some milk, eggs, and cheese.

   _____

<u>Part B</u> **Directions:** Revise the following paragraph to eliminate wordiness. Change the wording as necessary.

   At this particular point in time, heating costs are dangerously high for people living near or below the poverty level. Retired people who aren't working anymore must rely on fixed incomes that don't change from month to month or year to year. As a rule, their Social Security checks are not large enough in amount to cover higher utility bills when the weather is cold in the winter months. Congress should pass a law or bill that would offer some relief, assistance, or help for such people who find themselves in this sort of situation.

   _____

   _____

   _____

   _____

Answers are on page 386.

Checking for Edited American English

Now that you have revised the content, organization, and language of your essay, you can turn to checking for mistakes in grammar, punctuation, capitalization, and spelling. Reread your essay to check for all of the following:

1. **Capitalization.** Make sure that every sentence begins with a capital letter. Make sure that all proper nouns (names of people, places, and things) are capitalized.

   Which words should be capitalized in the following sentence?

   > next week John and mary are going to visit us in chicago.

   If you said *Next, Mary,* and *Chicago,* you were correct.

2. **Complete sentences.** Make sure that all your sentences have a subject and a verb. Look at the following sentences. Which ones need a subject? a verb?

   > A small sports car with a high-powered engine.

   > Suddenly appeared on the stage when the magician waved his wand.

   You should have said that the first sentence needs a verb and the second sentence needs a subject. The sentences can be completed in any number of ways.

   > A small sports car with a high-powered engine drove down the highway at 80 miles per hour.

   > An elephant suddenly appeared on the stage when the magician waved his wand.

3. **Subject-verb agreement.** Make sure that subjects and verbs agree. How would you correct these sentences?

   > I likes collecting stamps.

   > They was getting ready to leave when the phone rang.

   If you said change *likes* to *like* and *was* to *were,* you were correct.

4. **Correct punctuation.** Make sure that every sentence ends with a period. Also make sure that you have used commas correctly.

5. **Spelling.** Review your work carefully to make sure all the words are spelled correctly. While spelling is not specifically graded, it will affect the reader's overall impression of your essay.

EXERCISE 10

Directions: Read the sentences below. Check for capitalization errors, complete sentences, subject-verb agreement, punctuation, and spelling. Make any necessary corrections.

Example: *M*~~most~~ people like donuts, candy, and other sweets.

1. She past the GED test in 2001.

2. Mary Elizabeth were late today.

3. I do not like cheese. However I love yogurt.

4. Ms. greene is going to the supply room to get some paper.

5. I went to the store to by some supplies.

6. jerome is my best friend.

7. My uncle is going to visit me in Chicago next year

8. Don't like to go swimming in the morning.

9. The girl that was hit by a car.

10. The painters cleaned they're equipment after they finished painting the house.

Answers are on page 387.

Writing a GED Essay

Part A   **Directions:**   Look at the essay you wrote at the end of Chapter 11 (page 268). Use the rating scale on page 272 to give it a score. If possible, show your essay to your instructor or another student and have him or her score your essay too.

Your score: _____   Other reader's score: _____

Part B   **Directions:**   Review your essay a second time. Use the checklist below as a revision guide.

Checklist: Revising for Content and Organization

☐ Is there an introductory paragraph? Does it have a thesis statement?

☐ Are all the ideas relevant?

☐ Does each body paragraph have a topic sentence?

☐ Are the thesis statement and the body paragraphs in the same order?

☐ Does every body paragraph have two to three supporting ideas?

☐ Does the essay have specific reasons and examples?

☐ Does the essay show rather than tell, using specific details?

☐ Does the essay use sentence and paragraph transitions?

☐ Does the essay avoid repetition and wordiness?

Part C   **Directions:**   Review your essay one more time. Use the following list to check for Edited American English.

Checklist: Checking for Edited American English

☐ Is the first word of every sentence capitalized?

☐ Are proper nouns capitalized?

☐ Are the sentences complete?

☐ Do subjects and verbs agree?

☐ Does every sentence end in a period?

☐ Are commas used correctly?

☐ Are all the words spelled correctly?

Answers are on page 387.

RAISING YOUR SCORE

Look at the corrected essay you completed in the GED Practice Exercise. Now look at the criteria on conventions of Edited American English (EAE) and word choice from the GED Essay Scoring Guide. Circle the number that best describes your writing.

LEVEL **4** writing consistently controls sentence structure and the conventions of EAE. Word choice is varied and precise.

LEVEL **3** writing generally controls sentence structure and the conventions of EAE. Word choice is appropriate.

LEVEL **2** writing demonstates inconsistent control of sentence structure and the convntions of EAE. There is a narrow range of word choice, often including inappropriate selections.

LEVEL **1** writing exhibits minimal or no control of sentence structure and the conventions of EAE. Word choice is weak and inappropriate.

Now look at your essay again. What can you do to improve your score as you revise? Write one or two ideas on the lines below.

_____

_____

_____

Chapter 12 Highlights: Revising Your GED Essay

• The last stage of the writing process is revising your GED essay.

• You revise in two steps. First examine the essay in order to strengthen its content, organization, and wording. Then check for mistakes in Edited American English (spelling, punctuation, sentence structure, and so on).

• There is not enough time to recopy your entire essay. Therefore, you should write your revisions on the draft you prepared when you were writing.

• When you revise, you should spend most of your time on content and organization, since these areas count more on the GED Essay Scoring Guide.

• Use the checklists on pages 295 to help you revise.

CHAPTER 13

Review of the Writing Process

> In this chapter, you will review the steps in the writing process.
> - ☑ Gathering Ideas
> - ☑ Organizing
> - ☑ Writing
> - ☑ Revising

Congratulations! So far in this section of the book, you have learned a simple, four-step process for writing a good five-paragraph GED essay. In addition, you have learned to use the GED Essay Scoring Guide to raise your score. As you did this, you used the information you were learning to write a good GED essay on the topic of public transportation.

In this chapter, we will review every skill and tool you need to write a good GED essay:

- the five-paragraph essay
- the four steps of the writing process
- time organization
- the GED Essay Scoring Guide

We will then use these skills and tools to create two more GED essays.

The Five-Paragraph Essay

As you remember, one of the main criteria of the GED Essay Scoring Guide is organization. In order to score a 4 (*effective*) an essay must have a "clear and logical organization." The five-paragraph format is a good way to organize an essay on any subject. Can you remember the components of a five-paragraph essay? Write them on the lines below.

_____

_____

If you answered *introductory paragraph, three body paragraphs,* and *concluding paragraph*, you are correct. Here is more detailed information on each component:

· **An introductory paragraph** introduces the topic of your essay, states the main idea, and gives the thesis statement. The thesis statement tells the reader your main idea and gives an indication of how the rest of the essay will be organized. Usually, an introductory paragraph is organized from general to specific.

· **Three body paragraphs** give specific information to support, or back up, the thesis statement. Each body paragraph should begin with a topic sentence, which gives the main idea of the paragraph.

· **A concluding paragraph** restates the main idea of your essay and relates your main idea to broader ideas. Usually, a good concluding paragraph is organized from specific to general, beginning with a restatement of the thesis statement and ending with a broader statement that gives a sense of completeness to the essay.

EXERCISE 1

Directions: Match the parts of a five-paragraph essay with the items listed below.

a. introductory paragraph

b. body paragraphs

c. concluding paragraph

_____**1.**   thesis statement

_____**2.**   restatement of thesis statement

_____**3.**   topic sentence

_____**4.**   support sentences

Answers are on page 387.

The Writing Process

As you remember, the writing process has four steps. Can you name the steps? Write them on the lines below.

1. _____

2. _____

3. _____

4. _____

If you wrote *gathering ideas, organizing, writing,* and *revising,* you are correct. Each of the four steps has several substeps.

Gathering Ideas

When you gather ideas, follow these three steps:

1. **Analyze the GED essay question.** Read over the question to discover the topic and the way you should respond. Usually, the essay assignment will ask you to give reasons to explain a belief, state causes and effects, or compare and contrast two items. You can use key words to figure out the pattern of organization required. Look at the following chart:

Pattern of Organization	Key Words in the Essay Assignment
Give reasons to explain your belief.	• give your views • present your opinion • say whether you believe • state whether you agree
State causes and effects.	• state the effect of • tell the causes of • explain what happens when • tell why • explain how • explain why
Compare and contrast two items.	• compare • explain the similarities and differences

2. **Decide on your main idea.** Once you know the topic and the way in which you will respond, you can figure out your main idea. You can decide whether you agree or disagree with the essay topic. You can also decide what you believe to be the cause or the effect of the situation. You may consider how two items relate to one another. The main idea is your belief about the essay topic.

    Once you know the essay topic, the way to respond, and your main idea, write them down on scratch paper.

3. **Think of ideas and supporting details that support your main idea.** You can use brainstorming or an idea map to gather your ideas. Write down all the ideas that occur to you .

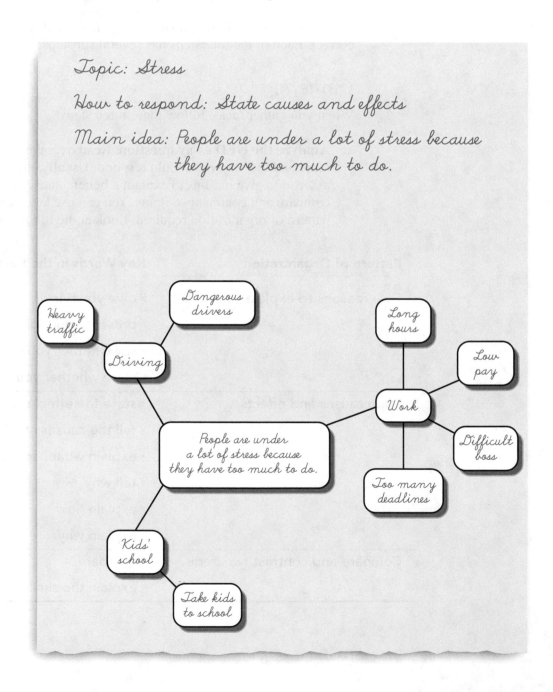

Topic: Stress

How to respond: State causes and effects

Main idea: People are under a lot of stress because they have too much to do.

Dangerous drivers

Heavy traffic

Driving

Long hours

Low pay

Work

People are under a lot of stress because they have too much to do.

Difficult boss

Too many deadlines

Kids' school

Take kids to school

Organizing Your Ideas

Once you have plenty of good ideas on your scratch paper, organize them into three body paragraphs. Follow these steps:

1. **Consider the pattern of organization you selected**—reasons why (which includes time order and order of importance), cause and effect, or comparison and contrast.

2. **Use circling or outlining to organize your ideas** (for reasons why or cause and effect).

Ideas/ Supporting details:

game shows
movies
comedies
football, baseball, and basketball games
dramas

Entertainment 3

news shows
biographies
documentaries
health programs

Information 2

GED preparation program
Sesame Street— for kids

Education 1

Benefits of TV

I. A few educational programs
    A. GED preparation program
    B. Sesame Street—for kids

II. Several kinds of information programs
    A. News
    B. Biographies
    C. Documentaries
    D. Health programs

III. Many entertainment programs
    A. Game shows
    B. Movies
    C. Comedies
    D. Football, baseball, and basketball games
    E. Dramas

Use a chart to organize your ideas for comparison/contrast essays.
Below is a chart for organizing an essay comparing driving a car and using public transportation.

Items to Discuss	Driving	Using Public Transportation
Cost		
Speed		
Convenience		

If you made an idea map, your ideas are probably already organized into groups. You just need to make sure that you have three groups.

3. **Cross off any ideas that are not about your main idea.** As you organize, you should make sure that all of your ideas support your main idea.

4. **Make sure you have enough ideas.** Each group should have two to three strong ideas. If you do not have enough ideas in a group, use brainstorming, questions, or the ideas you already gathered to think of more supporting details.

5. **Name and number your groups.** Make sure that your groups have names, as these names will be used to formulate the main ideas for your body paragraphs. Then number the groups in the order you will use them in your essay.

Writing Your Essay

When you write your essay, you should write quickly and not worry a lot about spelling, punctuation, and so on. In the writing phase, focus on getting your ideas down in complete sentences in the five-paragraph format. Follow these steps:

1. **Write the introductory paragraph.** Use the information you gathered on the topic to write the first few sentences, which should be organized from general to specific. Use the main idea you wrote on scratch paper to develop your thesis statement, which will introduce the main ideas of your body paragraphs.

2. **Write the body paragraphs.** Use your organized ideas to write each paragraph. Use the group names to create the topic sentence of each paragraph. Then write the supporting sentences using the ideas you gathered. Sometimes a new idea will occur to you as you write. If this happens, include the idea.

3. **Write your concluding paragraph.** Make sure that it begins with a restatement of the thesis statement and that it relates your main idea to broader issues.

4. **Make sure you indent and leave wide side margins.** You need to leave room so that you can add words or sentences when you revise.

5. **Write quickly but neatly.** Remember, you have only 45 minutes, so you will not have time to rewrite your essay. It's okay to print, but make sure that you use both capital letters and small letters. When you take the GED Test, be sure to write your essay in ink.

Revising Your Essay

When you revise your essay, you should check it twice—once for content and organization and once for Edited American English. Since content and organization are more important on the GED Essay Scoring Guide, focus on them as you revise. Follow these steps:

1. **Revise for content and organization.** Use the checklist below.

Checklist: Revising for Content and Organization

- ☐ Is there an introductory paragraph? Does it have a thesis statement?

- ☐ Are all the ideas relevant?

- ☐ Does each body paragraph have a topic sentence?

- ☐ Are the thesis statement and the body paragraphs in the same order?

- ☐ Does every body paragraph have two to three supporting ideas?

- ☐ Does the essay have specific reasons and examples?

- ☐ Does the essay show rather than tell, using specific details?

- ☐ Does the essay use sentence and paragraph transitions?

- ☐ Does the essay avoid repetition and wordiness?

2. **Revise for Edited American English.** Use the following checklist.

> **Checklist: Checking for Edited American English**
> ☐ Is the first word of every sentence capitalized?
> ☐ Are proper nouns capitalized?
> ☐ Are the sentences complete?
> ☐ Do subjects and verbs agree?
> ☐ Does every sentence end in a period?
> ☐ Are commas used correctly?
> ☐ Are all the words spelled correctly?

Whenever you make a change, cross off what you do not want the reader to read. Use a caret (^) to indicate material that you want to add.

EXERCISE 2

Directions: Read the writing tasks numbered below. Which step in the writing process do they belong to? Write the letter of each response on the appropriate line below.

a. Gathering ideas

b. Organizing ideas

c. Writing

d. Revising

_____ 1. Check for Edited American English.

_____ 2. Use your statement of the main idea to create the thesis statement.

_____ 3. Figure out the topic of your essay.

_____ 4. Make sure the essay is not wordy.

_____ 5. Brainstorm or use an idea map.

_____ 6. Group your ideas using circling or outlining.

_____ 7. Figure out the pattern of organization you will use.

_____ 8. Use your organized idea list to create the body paragraphs.

Answers are on page 387.

Following the Steps in 45 Minutes

As you know, when you take the Language Arts, Writing Test you will have only 45 minutes to complete your essay. In order to complete all four steps of the writing process, you need to watch the time carefully. Here is one way to allocate your time:

Gathering ideas: **10 minutes**

Organizing: **5 to 10 minutes**

Writing **15 to 20 minutes**

Revising **10 minutes**

As you work, keep your eye on the time. If you find yourself taking too much time on any one step, figure out a way to finish that step in a few minutes and go on to the next step. Before you start working, you might want to write down the time you will spend on each step of the writing process. This writer began working at 10:00 A.M. Before doing anything else, the writer wrote the following notes:

Gather ideas: 10:00 to 10:10
Organize: 10:10 to 10:15
Write: 10:15 to 10:35
Revise: 10:35 to 10:45

EXERCISE 3

Directions: Follow the steps of the writing process to write a good GED essay on the topic below.

── TOPIC ──

People often dream of what would happen if they suddenly became rich. What would you do if you suddenly became a millionaire?

In your essay, state what you would do if you suddenly became rich. Explain the reasons for your answer.

<u>Part A</u> **Directions:** Plan your time.

Gather ideas:	_____ to _____
Organize:	_____ to _____
Write:	_____ to _____
Revise:	_____ to _____

<u>Part B</u> **Directions:** Now follow the steps of the writing process. Try to stick to your plan for using your time. If you take more than 45 minutes, mark the step you are working on when you run out of time. Then continue working as quickly as possible and complete your essay. When you finish, take note of the time again. This will help you figure out how much more quickly you will have to work to complete your essay in 45 minutes during the GED Test.

Step 1: Gather Your Ideas

Figure out the essay topic, pattern of organization, and the main idea.

Topic: _____

How to respond: _____

Main idea: _____

Gather ideas—brainstorm or use an idea map.

Ideas/Supporting details:

Step 2: Organize Your Ideas

Figure out how you will arrange your ideas using the pattern of organization you chose in Step 1. Organize your ideas into three groups and name the groups. Use circling or outlining to organize your ideas. If you used an idea map to gather your ideas, then you just need to make sure that you have three groups and give them names. Make sure that all of your ideas are relevant and that you have two to three good ideas in each group.

Step 3: Write

Use your notes on the essay topic and main idea to write the introductory paragraph and thesis statement. Use your organized groups of ideas to write the three body paragraphs. Restate the thesis statement in the concluding paragraph. Relate the ideas in your essay to broader issues. Write your essay on a separate sheet of paper.

Step 4: Revise

Revise the content and organization of your essay.

Checklist: Revising for Content and Organization

☐ Is there an introductory paragraph? Does it have a thesis statement?

☐ Are all the ideas relevant?

☐ Does each body paragraph have a topic sentence?

☐ Are the thesis statement and the body paragraphs in the same order?

☐ Does every body paragraph have two to three supporting ideas?

☐ Does the essay have specific reasons and examples?

☐ Does the essay show rather than tell, using specific details?

☐ Does the essay use sentence and paragraph transitions?

☐ Does the essay avoid repetition and wordiness?

Revise for Edited American English.

Checklist: Checking for Edited American English

☐ Is the first word of every sentence capitalized?

☐ Are proper nouns capitalized?

☐ Are the sentences complete?

☐ Do subjects and verbs agree?

☐ Does every sentence end in a period?

☐ Are commas used correctly?

☐ Are all the words spelled correctly?

Whenever you make a change, cross off what you do not want the reader to read. Use a caret (^) to indicate material that you want to add.

Part C   **Directions:** Look at your final corrected essay. Now look at the GED Essay Scoring Guide. Circle the number that best describes your writing.

Answers are on page 387.

LANGUAGE ARTS, WRITING, PART II

Essay Scoring Guide

	1 Inadequate	2 Marginal	3 Adequate	4 Effective
Response to the Prompt	Reader has difficulty identifying or following the writer's ideas.	Reader occasionally has difficulty understanding or following the writer's ideas.	Reader understands the writer's ideas.	Reader understands and easily follows the writer's expression of ideas.
	Attempts to address prompt but with little or no success in establishing a focus.	Addresses the prompt, though the focus may shift.	Uses the writing prompt to establish a main idea.	Presents a clearly focused main idea that addresses the prompt.
Organization	Fails to organize ideas.	Shows some evidence of an organizational plan.	Uses an identifiable organizational plan.	Establishes a clear and logical organization.
Development and Details	Demonstrates little or no development; usually lacks details or examples or presents irrelevant information.	Has some development but lacks specific details; may be limited to a listing, repetitions, or generalizations.	Has focused but occasionally uneven development; incorporates some specific detail.	Achieves coherent development with specific and relevant details and examples.
Conventions of EAE	Exhibits minimal or no control of sentence structure and the conventions of Edited American English (EAE).	Demonstrates inconsistent control of sentence structure and the conventions of EAE.	Generally controls sentence structure and the conventions of EAE.	Consistently controls sentence structure and the conventions of EAE.
Word Choice	Exhibits weak and/or inappropriate words.	Exhibits a narrow range of word choice, often including inappropriate selections.	Exhibits appropriate word choice.	Exhibits varied and precise word choice.

Writing a GED Essay

Directions: Read the GED essay topic below. Plan your essay before you write. Use your own scratch paper to make any notes. Follow all four steps of the writing process and write a well-developed essay on a separate sheet of paper.

―――――――― T O P I C ――――――――

Fifty years ago computers were almost completely unknown, but today we see them everywhere. What are the effects of computers on everyday life?

In your essay, explain the effects of computers on everyday life. Give reasons to explain your beliefs.

Answers are on page 387.

RAISING YOUR SCORE

Look at your final corrected essay. Look at the GED Essay Scoring Guide from Exercise 3. Circle the number that best describes your writing.

Now look at your essay again. What can you do to improve your score as you revise? Write one or two ideas on the lines below.

_____

_____

_____

_____

Chapter 13 Highlights: Review of the Writing Process

- The five-paragraph format is a good way to organize a GED essay.

- A five-paragraph essay has an introductory paragraph, three body paragraphs, and a concluding paragraph.

- Follow the four steps of the writing process to write a good GED essay: gathering ideas, organizing, writing, and revising.

- To complete your GED essay in the allocated 45 minutes, you need to watch your time carefully. Allow a certain amount of time for each part of the writing process.

- Before you begin working, write down the time you will spend on each step of the writing process.

- Once you start writing, write quickly and neatly. Don't worry if you make a few mistakes as you write. You can go back and correct them when you revise.

- First revise for content and organization, since these factor more heavily in the GED Essay Scoring Guide. Then revise for Edited American English.

Language Arts Writing, Part I

This posttest will give you the opportunity to evaluate your readiness for the actual GED Language Arts, Writing Test.

Directions: Choose the <u>one best answer</u> to each question. Some of the sentences may contain errors in organization, sentence structure, usage, or mechanics. A few sentences, however, may be correct as written. Read the sentences carefully and then answer the questions based on them. For each question, choose the answer that would result in the most effective writing of the sentence or sentences. You should take approximately 75 minutes to complete Part I.

Posttest Answer Grid

1 ① ② ③ ④ ⑤	18 ① ② ③ ④ ⑤	35 ① ② ③ ④ ⑤
2 ① ② ③ ④ ⑤	19 ① ② ③ ④ ⑤	36 ① ② ③ ④ ⑤
3 ① ② ③ ④ ⑤	20 ① ② ③ ④ ⑤	37 ① ② ③ ④ ⑤
4 ① ② ③ ④ ⑤	21 ① ② ③ ④ ⑤	38 ① ② ③ ④ ⑤
5 ① ② ③ ④ ⑤	22 ① ② ③ ④ ⑤	39 ① ② ③ ④ ⑤
6 ① ② ③ ④ ⑤	23 ① ② ③ ④ ⑤	40 ① ② ③ ④ ⑤
7 ① ② ③ ④ ⑤	24 ① ② ③ ④ ⑤	41 ① ② ③ ④ ⑤
8 ① ② ③ ④ ⑤	25 ① ② ③ ④ ⑤	42 ① ② ③ ④ ⑤
9 ① ② ③ ④ ⑤	26 ① ② ③ ④ ⑤	43 ① ② ③ ④ ⑤
10 ① ② ③ ④ ⑤	27 ① ② ③ ④ ⑤	44 ① ② ③ ④ ⑤
11 ① ② ③ ④ ⑤	28 ① ② ③ ④ ⑤	45 ① ② ③ ④ ⑤
12 ① ② ③ ④ ⑤	29 ① ② ③ ④ ⑤	46 ① ② ③ ④ ⑤
13 ① ② ③ ④ ⑤	30 ① ② ③ ④ ⑤	47 ① ② ③ ④ ⑤
14 ① ② ③ ④ ⑤	31 ① ② ③ ④ ⑤	48 ① ② ③ ④ ⑤
15 ① ② ③ ④ ⑤	32 ① ② ③ ④ ⑤	49 ① ② ③ ④ ⑤
16 ① ② ③ ④ ⑤	33 ① ② ③ ④ ⑤	50 ① ② ③ ④ ⑤
17 ① ② ③ ④ ⑤	34 ① ② ③ ④ ⑤	

Questions 1–7 refer to the following article.

Take Steps Toward Healthy Eating

(A)

(1) It's a good idea to remember that what we put into our bodies directly effects how our bodies work for us. (2) The foods we eat give us the vitamins, minerals, and they give us fiber we need to be healthy human beings. (3) Although we eat only junk food, such as french fries and cookies, our bodies will work like an old run-down jalopy. (4) If we eat a variety of healthy foods, such as fruits, vegetables, fiber-rich products, and lean meats, our muscles, heart, and bones will work together like a well-oiled sports car. (5) Here are some healthy eating tips that will help keep your body engine running smoothly.

(B)

(6) Choose whole-grain bread, pasta, and rice instead of processed white-flour products. (7) Whole-grain products contain the fiber, vitamins, and minerals that the United States Department of Agriculture (USDA) recommend for good digestion and nutrient absorption. (8) Even choosing a whole-wheat roll for your ham sandwich is a step in the right direction.

(C)

(9) The USDA also recommends getting three to five daily servings of vegetables and two to four daily servings of fruit. (10) If you don't already eat lots of these foods, try to work gradually toward these goals, and you were probably more successful than if you tried to achieve the ideal overnight. (11) Each day, add a new fruit or vegetable to you're daily routine. (12) You may discover that you enjoy these foods much more than you thought you would.

(D)

(13) Another suggestion for a more healthful diet is to watch out for excess fat while you strive to include enough protein, high protein does not have to mean high fat! (14) If you're cooking, choose the leanest cut of meat you can find and trim excess fat before you cook it. (15) Try broiling or baking instead of frying. (16) And remember that tofu and beans are delicious, high-protein substitutes to use in many meat-oriented recipes.

---

1. Sentence 1: **It's a good idea to remember that what we put into our bodies directly effects how our bodies work for us.**

   What correction should be made to sentence 1?

   (1) change *It's* to *Its*
   (2) insert a comma after *remember*
   (3) replace *we* with *they*
   (4) replace *effects* with *affects*
   (5) no correction is necessary

2. Sentence 2: **The foods we eat give us the <u>vitamins, minerals, and they give us fiber</u> we need to be healthy human beings.**

   Which is the best way to write the underlined portion of the text? If the original is the best way, choose option (1).

   (1) vitamins, minerals, and they give us fiber
   (2) vitamins minerals and they give us fiber
   (3) vitamins, minerals, and fiber
   (4) Vitamins, Minerals, and they give us Fiber
   (5) vitamins, minerals, and it gives us fiber

POSTTEST

3. **Sentence 3: Although we eat only junk food, such as french fries and cookies, our bodies will work like an old run-down jalopy.**

   The most effective revision of sentence 3 would begin with which group of words?

   (1) If we eat only junk food
   (2) Because we eat only junk food
   (3) The fact that we eat junk food
   (4) We eat only junk food
   (5) Only eating junk food

4. **Sentence 7: Whole-grain products contain the fiber, vitamins, and minerals that the United States Department of Agriculture (USDA) recommend for good digestion and nutrient absorption.**

   What correction should be made to sentence 7?

   (1) remove the comma after *fiber*
   (2) change *United States* to *united states*
   (3) insert a comma after *United States*
   (4) change *recommend* to *recommends*
   (5) insert a comma after *recommend*

5. **Sentence 10: If you don't already eat lots of these foods, try to work gradually toward these goals, and you were probably more successful than if you tried to achieve the ideal overnight.**

   Which is the best way to write the underlined portion of the text? If the original is the best way, choose option (1).

   (1) goals, and you were probably
   (2) goals and you were probably
   (3) goals, and he was probably
   (4) goals, but you were probably
   (5) goals, and you will probably be

6. **Sentence 11: Each day, add a new fruit or vegetable to you're daily routine.**

   What correction should be made to sentence 11?

   (1) remove the comma after *day*
   (2) change *add* to *added*
   (3) insert a comma after *fruit*
   (4) replace *you're* with *your*
   (5) no correction is necessary

7. **Sentence 13: Another suggestion for a more healthful diet is to watch out for excess fat while you strive to include enough protein, high protein does not have to mean high fat!**

   Which is the best way to write the underlined portion of the text? If the original is the best way, choose option (1).

   (1) enough protein, high protein does
   (2) enough protein. High protein does
   (3) enough protein, high protein do
   (4) enough protein so high protein
   (5) enough protein but high protein

Questions 8–14 refer to the following information.

Do You Need Assistance Heating Your Home This Winter?

(A)

(1) If you think you may not be able to afford to heat your home or apartment adequately this Winter, there is help for you. (2) The Federal Emergency Fuel Program (FEFP) has been established to ensure that no homeowner or renter go without adequate heat this year. (3) Eligibility for this assistance is determined by a nonprofit organization under contract by the State Department of Housing. (4) If you think you might be interested in this fuel program, read the information below.

(B)

(5) Eligibility for the Federal Emergency Fuel Program is based on the annualized household income and the number of members in the household. (6) If you have an annual income below $30,000 and you have four or more people living in your home, you will probably qualify for fuel assistance. (7) You have been approved for the program, a local agency will make payments toward your heating bills to the primary heat-source vendor (oil, propane, wood, or coal dealer; gas or electric utility).

(C)

(8) Preliminary application forms for the Federal Emergency Fuel Program is included in this envelope. (9) When you have completed an application, send it to FEFP at the address given on the form. (10) Completing applications can be so time consuming, can't it? (11) You will be called within two weeks and told whether or not you qualify for the program. (12) If you do qualify, you be asked to submit a recent pay stub or letter from your employer as well as a recent heating bill. (13) It is a good idea to secure these documents now, avoid any delays later in the process.

8. **Sentence 1: If you think you may not be able to afford to heat your home or apartment adequately this Winter, there is help for you.**

   What correction should be made to sentence 1?

   (1) replace *your* with *you're*
   (2) insert a comma after *home*
   (3) change *Winter* to *winter*
   (4) remove the comma after *Winter*
   (5) replace *there* with *their*

9. **Sentence 2: The Federal Emergency Fuel Program (FEFP) has been established to ensure that no homeowner or renter go without adequate heat this year.**

   Which is the best way to write the underlined portion of the text? If the original is the best way, choose option (1).

   (1) homeowner or renter go without
   (2) homeowner, or renter go without
   (3) homeowner or renter to go without
   (4) homeowner or renter going without
   (5) homeowner or renter goes without

POSTTEST

10. **Sentence 7: You have been approved for the program, a local agency will make payments toward your heating bills to the primary heat-source vendor (oil, propane, wood, or coal dealer; gas or electric utility).**

The most effective revision of sentence 7 would include which group of words?

(1) approved for the program, so that
(2) approved for the program, when
(3) approved for the program when
(4) When you have been approved
(5) To be approved for the program

11. **Sentence 8: Preliminary application forms for the Federal Emergency Fuel Program is included in this envelope.**

The most effective revision of sentence 8 would include which group of words?

(1) Preliminary application form by
(2) Preliminary application forms,
(3) are included in this envelope
(4) May be included in this envelope
(5) are folded and enclosed within this envelope.

12. **Sentence 10: Completing applications can be so time consuming, can't it?**

Which revision should be made to sentence 10 to improve paragraph C?

(1) move sentence 10 to the end of paragraph A
(2) move sentence 10 to the end of paragraph B
(3) move sentence 10 to the beginning of paragraph C
(4) move sentence 10 to the end of paragraph C
(5) remove sentence 10

13. **Sentence 12: <u>If you do qualify, you be asked</u> to submit a recent pay stub or letter from your employer as well as a recent heating bill.**

Which is the best way to write the underlined portion of the text? If the original is the best way, choose option (1).

(1) If you do qualify, you be asked
(2) If you do qualify you be asked
(3) If you do qualify, you will be asked
(4) If you do qualify, you were asked
(5) If you do qualify, you was asked

14. **Sentence 13: It is a good idea to secure these documents now, avoid any delays later in the process.**

The most effective revision of sentence 13 would include which group of words?

(1) secure these documents because of avoiding
(2) secure these documents in order to avoiding
(3) secure these documents now so that you can
(4) and later in the process, avoid delays
(5) and delays may be later provided

POSTTEST

Questions 15–21 refer to the following letter.

Dear Marketing Representative:

(A)

(1) I am writing to request some information about a product the Preview 2003 your company manufactures and sells. (2) Specifically, I would like to know if the Preview 2003 computer, model X47, is appropriate for my needs. (3) I would appreciate it if you would answer my questions and provide some information. (4) I hope to make a decision on which software printer and computer to buy at the end of the month.

(B)

(5) I will primarily use it for household record-keeping, including budgets, investments, and maintenance records. (6) I use the latest version of Lotus for these tasks. (7) I also do a fair amount of writing each day using Word software. (8) In addition, I am on the Internet quite often to do research, and my children use the Internet for research too.

(C)

(9) Finally, my children and husband play lots of games on our current computer. (10) I would like to know if the Preview 2003 will accommodate all of these applications and still leave room for other needs as they arise. (11) Also, how much memory do you recommend for users like my family? (12) Any help you can offer me was greatly appreciated. (13) Buying a computer these days seem like an overwhelming task, and I do not want to make a foolish purchase. (14) Thank you for your time.

Sincerely,

Linda Williams

15. Sentence 1: **I am writing to request some information about a <u>product the Preview 2003 your company manufactures and sells</u>.**

Which is the best way to write the underlined portion of the text? If the original is the best way, choose option (1).

(1) product the Preview 2003 your company manufactures and sells
(2) product, the Preview 2003, your company manufactures and sells
(3) product the Preview 2003 your Company manufactures and sells
(4) product the Preview 2003 your company manufacture and sell
(5) product the Preview 2003 your company manufactures, and sells

16. Sentence 4: **I hope to make a decision on which <u>software printer and computer to buy at the end of the month</u>.**

Which is the best way to write the underlined portion of the text? If the original is the best way, choose option (1).

(1) software printer and computer to buy at the end of the month.
(2) software printer and computer to by at the end of the month.
(3) software printer and computer to buy at the end of the Month.
(4) software printer and, computer to buy at the end of the month.
(5) software, printer, and computer to buy at the end of the month.

POSTTEST

17. Which sentence would be most effective at the beginning of paragraph B?

(1) First, this is what I plan to do with my computer.
(2) Computers are so useful.
(3) Most often, I will use this new computer at my workplace.
(4) I have used my computer for many things in the past.
(5) Does your company manufacture other models that I might be interested in?

18. Sentence 8: In addition, I am on the Internet quite often to do research, and my children use the Internet for research too.

If you rewrote sentence 8 beginning with

In addition, both my children and I

the next words should be

(1) , on the Internet, quite often do
(2) study the Internet
(3) are on the Internet
(4) were on the Internet
(5) will be on the Internet

19. Sentence 9: Finally, my children and husband play lots of games on our current computer.

Which revision should be made to sentence 9?

(1) move sentence 9 to the end of paragraph A
(2) move sentence 9 to follow sentence 11
(3) move sentence 9 to the end of paragraph B
(4) move sentence 9 to the end of paragraph C
(5) remove sentence 9

20. Sentence 12: Any help you can offer me was greatly appreciated.

What correction should be made to sentence 12?

(1) replace *you* with *they*
(2) replace *me* with *them*
(3) replace *was* with *were*
(4) replace *was* with *will be*
(5) no correction is necessary

21. Sentence 13: Buying a computer these days seem like an overwhelming task, and I do not want to make a foolish purchase.

Which is the best way to write the underlined portion of the text? If the original is the best way, choose option (1).

(1) days seem like an overwhelming task, and
(2) days seems like an overwhelming task, and
(3) Days seem like an overwhelming task, and
(4) days seem like an overwhelming task, even though
(5) days seem like an overwhelming task and

Questions 22–29 refer to the following article.

Saving for Retirement

(A)

(1) Saving money for retirement should be a crucial financial goal for almost everybody, yet financial analysts say that most people neglect to plan for their golden years. (2) If a person saves just $25 per week for 25 years at an annual interest rate of 7 percent, you'll have more than $100,000 to put toward retirement. (3) Because it seems fairly easy for most people to put aside $25 per week, almost one-third of the respondents in a recent survey said that they have saved nothing.
(4) Considered safe and dependable, many retirees rely solely on Social Security for income. (5) They say that's not a good idea.

(B)

(6) One factor in people's failure to save, according to Charles S. Perkins Senior Employee Benefit Researcher at InvestCo is the perceived enormity and complexity of retirement issues. (7) People fall into the trap of thinking that large retirement funds are only for the wealthy, says Perkins. (8) Perkins advises people not to be overwhelmed by topics such as annuities, IRAs, trusts, and long-term care insurance. (9) The most important first step, he says, is to start a savings account, put some money in it each week, and you do not withdraw it.

(C)

(10) Mr. Perkins's company encourages people to take this first step by completing a "Retirement Estimate Worksheet," which allows people to estimate their annual retirement income needs. (11) The worksheet also helps determine how much money should be set aside each week to achieve that goal. (12) People who take the time to complete this kind of worksheet are usually well prepared to face whatever the future holds for them. (13) In summary the saying "every little bit helps" is absolutely true when one thinks about long-term savings.

22. **Sentence 2: If a person saves just $25 per week for 25 years at an annual interest rate of 7 percent, you'll have more than $100,000 to put toward retirement.**

The most effective revision of sentence 2 would include which group of words?

(1) Although a person saves just
(2) If a person save just
(3) they'll have more than
(4) he or she will have more than
(5) no correction is necessary

23. **Sentence 3: Because it seems fairly easy for most people to put aside $25 per week, almost one-third of the respondents in a recent survey said that they have saved nothing.**

What correction should be made to sentence 3?

(1) replace *Because* with *Although*
(2) replace *Because* with *If*
(3) change *seems* to *seem*
(4) remove the comma after *week*
(5) replace *they* with *them*

POSTTEST

24. Sentence 4: <u>**Considered safe and dependable, many retirees rely solely on Social Security**</u> **for income.**

Which is the best way to write the underlined portion of the text? If the original is the best way, choose option (1).

(1) Considered safe and dependable, many retirees rely solely on Social Security
(2) Considered safe and dependable many retirees rely solely on Social Security
(3) Considered safe and dependable, many retirees relies solely on Social Security
(4) Considered safe and dependable, many retirees relies souly on Social Security
(5) Many retiree's rely solely on Social Security, considered safe and dependable,

25. Sentence 5: **They say that's not a good idea.**

What correction should be made to sentence 5?

(1) replace *They* with *Experts*
(2) replace *They* with *He*
(3) replace *that's* with *that was*
(4) insert a comma after *good*
(5) no correction is necessary

26. Sentence 6: **One factor in people's failure to save, according to Charles S.** <u>**Perkins Senior Employee Benefit Researcher at InvestCo is**</u> **the perceived enormity and complexity of retirement issues.**

Which is the best way to write the underlined portion of the text? If the original is the best way, choose option (1).

(1) Perkins Senior Employee Benefit Researcher at InvestCo is
(2) Perkins, Senior Employee Benefit Researcher at InvestCo, is
(3) Perkins Senior Employee Benefit Researcher, at InvestCo is
(4) Perkins Senior Employee Benefit Researcher at InvestCo are
(5) Perkins Senior Employee Benefit Researcher at InvestCo was

27. Sentence 9: **The most important first step, he says, is to start a savings account, put some money in it each week, and you do not withdraw it.**

What correction should be made to sentence 9?

(1) replace *is* with *are*
(2) remove the comma after *account*
(3) change *put* to *putting*
(4) replace *you do not* with *not*
(5) no correction is necessary

28. Sentence 12: **People who take the time to complete this kind of worksheet are usually well prepared to face whatever the future holds for them.**

What correction should be made to sentence 12?

(1) replace *worksheet* with *Worksheet*
(2) insert a comma after *worksheet*
(3) insert a comma after *face*
(4) replace *them* with *him*
(5) no correction is necessary

29. Sentence 13: **In summary the saying "every little bit helps" is absolutely true when one thinks about long-term savings.**

What correction should be made to sentence 13?

(1) insert a comma after *summary*
(2) replace *one* with *you*
(3) replace *is* with *was*
(4) insert a comma after *true*
(5) change *thinks* to *think*

POSTTEST

Questions 30–37 refer to the following guidelines.

Ergonomic Guidelines for Computer Users

(A)

(1) Believe it or not, their are health risks associated with continued computer use. (2) As the number of people who use computers for work and at home increase, doctors are reporting that their patients have growing problems with wrists, backs, eyes, and heads. (3) For your own comfort, health, and efficiency, observe the following ergonomic guidelines when setting up and using your computer.

(B)

(4) First, setting up your computer so that the monitor is easy to see. (5) Put the computer on a level surface and position it directly in front of you as you work. (6) Adjust the tilt of the display screen and the lighting in the room so that there are no glare or reflection that will make the screen difficult to read. (7) Make sure that the monitor, or screen, is at eye level or slightly lower when you sit in front of them. (8) A comfortable viewing distance is usually approximately 22 inches from eyes to screen.

(C)

(9) Next, choose an excellent quality chair that provides good lower-back support. (10) When sitting in the chair, your feet should rest gently on the floor and your thighs should be parallel to the floor. (11) Make sure that the weight of your legs is on your feet and not on the front of the chair seat. (12) Adjust the height of the chair if necessary or use a footrest. (13) The last aspect of good ergonomics in computer use is the placement of your hands, wrists, and fingers. (14) Keeping your forearms horizontal and your wrists in a neutral, comfortable position is essential for the health of your bones, muscles, and ligaments. (15) Your upper arms should hang naturally at your sides, not stretched outward or cramped at the elbows.

---

30. Sentence 1: <u>Believe it or not, their are</u> health risks associated with continued computer use.

Which is the best way to write the underlined portion of the text? If the original is the best way, choose option (1).

(1) Believe it or not, their are
(2) Believe it or not their are
(3) Believing it or not, their are
(4) Believe it or not, there are
(5) Believe it or not, they're are

31. Sentence 2: As the number of people who use computers for work and at home increase, doctors are reporting that their patients have growing problems with wrists, backs, eyes, and heads.

The most effective revision of sentence 2 would include which group of words?

(1) who use computers for work, and at home
(2) for work and at home increases
(3) for work and at home increase doctors are reporting
(4) growing problems with wrists back, eyes
(5) no revision is necessary

32. **Sentence 4: First, setting up your computer so that the monitor is easy to see.**

What correction should be made to sentence 4?

(1) remove the comma after *First*
(2) change *setting* to *set*
(3) replace *your* with *their*
(4) insert a comma after *computer*
(5) replace *is* with *was*

33. **Sentence 6: Adjust the tilt of the display screen and the lighting in the<u> room so that there are no glare or reflection that will make</u> the screen difficult to read.**

Which is the best way to write the underlined portion of the text? If the original is the best way, choose option (1).

(1) room so that there are no glare or reflection that will make
(2) room, so that there are no glare or reflection that will make
(3) room so that there are no glare or reflection that made
(4) room so that there is no glare or reflection that will make
(5) room so that there were no glare or reflection that will make

34. **Sentence 7: Make sure that the monitor, or screen, is at eye level or slightly lower when you sit in front of them.**

What correction should be made to sentence 7?

(1) remove the comma after *monitor*
(2) replace *is* with *are*
(3) insert a comma after *lower*
(4) replace *them* with *it*
(5) no correction is necessary

35. **Sentence 10: <u>When sitting in the chair,</u> your feet should rest gently on the floor and your thighs should be parallel to the floor.**

Which is the best way to write the underlined portion of the text? If the original is the best way, choose option (1).

(1) When sitting in the chair,
(2) When sitting in the chair
(3) While sitting in the chair,
(4) Although sitting in the chair,
(5) When you are sitting in the chair,

36. **Which revision would make paragraph C more effective?**

Begin a new paragraph

(1) with sentence 10
(2) with sentence 11
(3) with sentence 12
(4) with sentence 13
(5) with sentence 14

37. **Sentence 14: Keeping your forearms horizontal and your wrists in a neutral, comfortable position <u>is essential for the health of your bones, muscles, and ligaments.</u>**

Which is the best way to write the underlined portion of the text? If the original is the best way, choose option (1).

(1) is essential for the health of your bones, muscles, and ligaments
(2) are essential for the health of your bones, muscles, and ligaments
(3) is essential for the health of you're bones, muscles, and ligaments
(4) is essential for the health of your bones muscles, and ligaments
(5) was essential for the health of your bones, muscles, and ligaments

POSTTEST

Questions 38–43 refer to the following promotional piece.

Sick Building Syndrome: Its Causes, Its Cures, and What Systems Surplus Is Doing About It

(A)

(1) Called Sick Building Syndrome (SBS), scientists have recently discovered a new problem caused by indoor pollution. (2) Someone who gets headaches and sniffles when they are cooped up inside all day may not have a cold at all. (3) That person may be suffering from SBS. (4) Colds can be treated by bed rest, lots of fluids, and an over-the-counter medicine. (5) Inadequate ventilation is one of the primary causes of SBS. (6) Harmful chemical fumes come from unexpected places such as carpets, curtains, and paneling. (7) Harmful chemical fumes can build up. (8) The very products used to keep these places clean may be making inhabitants sick. (9) Animal dander is a possible cause of indoor pollution, and dust mites can cause indoor pollution, and molds cause indoor pollution too.

(B)

(10) We here at Systems Surplus Company are serious about preventing SBS from affecting workers. (11) We know that the best cure for SBS is proper ventilation of all areas of our buildings—including storage, warehouses, and offices. (12) By allowing adequate amounts of air to circulate from outdoors, we keep our work areas free of harmful fume buildup. (13) In addition, we have hired an outside Consultant to test our worksite periodically to ensure that we have clean, healthy air throughout our buildings. (14) If you have any questions about SBS, please contact Jim Loring, Plant Manager, at extension 4546.

38. Sentence 1: <u>Called Sick Building Syndrome (SBS), scientists have recently discovered a new problem</u> caused by indoor pollution.

Which is the best way to write the underlined portion of the text? If the original is the best way, choose option (1).

(1) Called Sick Building Syndrome (SBS), scientists have recently discovered a new problem
(2) Called Sick Building Syndrome (SBS) scientists have recently discovered a new problem
(3) Scientists, called Sick Building Syndrome (SBS), have recently discovered a new problem
(4) Scientists have recently discovered a new problem, called Sick Building Syndrome (SBS),
(5) Scientists have recently discovered a new problem

39. Sentence 2: Someone who gets headaches and sniffles when they are cooped up inside all day may not have a cold at all.

What correction should be made to sentence 2?

(1) change *gets* to *get*
(2) replace *when* with *but*
(3) replace *they are* with *he or she is*
(4) insert a comma after *day*
(5) no correction is necessary

POSTTEST

40. Sentence 4: Colds can be treated by bed rest, lots of fluids, and an over-the-counter medicine.

Which revision should be made to sentence 4 to improve paragraph A?

(1) move sentence 4 to the beginning of paragraph A
(2) move sentence 4 to follow sentence 1
(3) move sentence 4 to follow sentence 2
(4) remove sentence 4
(5) move sentence 4 to the end of paragraph A

41. Sentences 6 and 7: Harmful chemical fumes come from unexpected places such as carpets, curtains, and paneling. Harmful chemical fumes can build up.

The most effective combination of sentences 6 and 7 would include which group of words?

(1) To come from unexpected places such as carpets, curtains, and paneling, harmful chemical fumes
(2) Coming from unexpected places such as carpets, curtains, and paneling, harmful chemical fumes
(3) Harmful chemical fumes build up, and come from unexpected places such as carpets, curtains, and paneling.
(4) Although they come from unexpected places such as carpets, curtains, and paneling, harmful chemical fumes
(5) Unexpected places such as carpets, curtains, and paneling can come

42. Sentence 9: Animal dander is a possible cause of indoor pollution, and dust mites can cause indoor pollution, and molds cause indoor pollution too.

The most effective revision of sentence 9 would begin with which group of words?

(1) Animal dander is a possible
(2) Animal dander and dust mites
(3) Animal dander and dust mites and pollution
(4) Animal dander, dust mites, and molds
(5) Animal dander can cause indoor

43. Sentence 13: In addition, we have hired an outside Consultant to test our worksite periodically to ensure that we have clean, healthy air throughout our buildings.

What correction should be made to sentence 13?

(1) remove the comma after *addition*
(2) change *have* to *has*
(3) change *Consultant* to *consultant*
(4) remove the comma after *clean*
(5) change *buildings* to *Buildings*

POSTTEST

Questions 44–50 refer to the following letter.

November 7, 2001
Ms. Tamara Jones
Personnel Manager
Payson Department Store
111 Darcelle Circle
Scranton, PA 18501

Dear Ms. Jones:

(A)

(1) It is with great pleasure that I recommend Michael Alvarez to you for a management position at your department store. (2) Honesty is a quality that Michael has, and responsibility and intelligence are also his qualities that he has as a person. (3) Michael Alvarez has all of these things and more. (4) In this letter I will tell you what I know about him.

(B)

(5) Michael has been an assistant manager here at Computer Connect for two years. (6) He learned store systems and policies very quickly, he was always eager to learn more. (7) He is also extremely good with both coworkers and customers. (8) For example, one day me and another manager were having trouble filling shifts on the next week's schedule.

(C)

(9) Michael came along and offered to work the shift of a woman who needed time off to care for her sick father. (10) That's the kind of person Michael is—one hundred percent of the time.

(D)

(11) In summary, I would love it if he would stay and be a manager at our store. (12) However, Michael has told us he needs new challenges. (13) Although he has enjoyed working with computers, he would like greater variety in the kinds of products he works with. (14) I wish Michael the best and I think he would do a terrific job as a manager in your store. (15) In the event of wishing for me to provide further information and so that I may offer you more information about Michael, you may call me at any time for additional information.

Sincerely,
Yolanda Martin
Senior Vice-President, Computer Connect

44. Sentence 2: **Honesty is a quality that Michael has, and responsibility and intelligence are also his qualities that he has as a person.**

If you rewrote sentence 2 beginning with *Honesty, responsibility, and* the next words should be

(1) qualities such as these are
(2) intelligence are all qualities
(3) being intelligent are all
(4) Michael is intelligent
(5) being an intelligent person, Michael

45. Sentence 6: **He learned store systems and policies <u>very quickly, he was</u> always eager to learn more.**

Which is the best way to write the underlined portion of the text? If the original is the best way, choose option (1).

(1) very quickly, he was
(2) very quick, he was
(3) very quickly, and he was
(4) very quickly, but he was
(5) very quickly, even though he was

46. Sentence 8: **For example, one day me and another manager were having trouble filling shifts on the next week's schedule.**

What correction should be made to sentence 8?

(1) remove the comma after *example*
(2) replace *me and another manager* with *another manager and I*
(3) replace *were* with *are*
(4) change *manager* to *Manager*
(5) no correction is necessary

47. **Which revision would make paragraph B more effective?**

(1) move sentences 9 and 10 to the end of paragraph B
(2) begin a new paragraph with sentence 7
(3) move sentence 5 to the end of paragraph B
(4) move sentence 5 to follow sentence 8
(5) move sentence 6 to follow sentence 8

48. Sentence 13: **<u>Although he has enjoyed working with computers, he</u> would like greater variety in the kinds of products he works with.**

Which is the best way to write the underlined portion of the text? If the original is the best way, choose option (1).

(1) Although he has enjoyed working with computers, he
(2) Because he has enjoyed working with computers, he
(3) Although he have enjoyed working with computers, he
(4) Although he will enjoy working with computers, he
(5) Although he has enjoyed working with computers he

49. Sentence 14: **I wish Michael the best and I think he would do a terrific job as a manager in your store.**

What correction should be made to sentence 14?

(1) insert a comma before *best*
(2) insert a comma before *and*
(3) replace *think* with *thought*
(4) replace *he* with *they*
(5) replace *your* with *you're*

50. Sentence 15: In the event of wishing for me to provide further information and so that I may offer you more information about Michael, you may call me at anytime for additional information.

The most effective revision of sentence 15 would begin with which group of words?

(1) For further information and so that I can give you more information,
(2) Call Michael for more information,
(3) Information about Michael can be offered
(4) You may call me any time for more information
(5) Wishing to give more information, I

Answers are on page 331.

POSTTEST
Language Arts Writing, Part II

Essay Directions and Topic

Look at the box on the following page. In the box is your assigned topic.

You must write on the assigned topic ONLY.

You will have 45 minutes to write on your assigned essay topic. You may return to the multiple-choice section after you complete your essay if you have time remaining in this test period.

Pay attention to the following features as you write:

- Well-focused main points
- Clear organization
- Specific development of your ideas
- Control of sentence structure, punctuation, grammar, word choice, and spelling

As you work, be sure to do the following:

- Do not leave pages blank.
- Write legibly **in ink**.
- Write on the assigned topic.
- Write your essay on a separate sheet of paper.

--- TOPIC ---

We all play many roles in life. For instance, you might be a parent, a construction worker, a political party member, and a student, among others. What are some of the roles you play in your life?

In your essay, tell about three of the roles you play in your life. Give specific examples to illustrate your ideas.

Part II is a test to determine how well you can use written language to explain your ideas.

In preparing your essay, you should take the following steps:

- Read the **DIRECTIONS** and the **TOPIC** carefully.

- Plan your essay before you write. Use scratch paper to make any notes.

- After you finish writing your essay, reread what you have written and make any changes that will improve your essay.

Your essay should be long enough to develop the topic adequately.

Evaluation guidelines are on page 334.

POSTTEST

Part 1: Answer Key

1. (4) The correct homonym is *affects*, not *effects*.

2. (3) The series in the original sentence is not parallel in structure. Changing *they give us fiber* to simply *fiber* makes the sentence parallel.

3. (1) The sentence should express a cause-effect relationship, not a contrasting one. Using *If* instead of *Although* correctly expresses this relationship.

4. (4) The subject of the sentence is *United States Department of Agriculture*, a singular noun. Therefore, the present-tense verb should end in *s*—*recommends*.

5. (5) The correct tense is future—*you will probably be*. The past tense makes no sense here.

6. (4) The possessive pronoun *your* is correct. The homonym *you're* is a contraction meaning *you are*.

7. (2) The original sentence is a comma splice. Dividing it into two complete sentences corrects the error.

8. (3) Seasons, such as *winter*, are not proper nouns and should not be capitalized.

9. (5) The conjunction *or* in a compound subject requires that the verb agree with the noun closer to the verb, not with both nouns added together. In this case, *goes* agrees with *renter*.

10. (4) The adverb *When* corrects the comma splice of the original sentence and expresses the cause-effect relationship of the two clauses.

11. (3) The subject of the sentence is plural—*forms*. Therefore, the verb *are* is correct, not *is*, which agrees with a singular subject. Watch out for the interrupting phrase.

12. (5) A sentence about how applications are time consuming does not belong in this paragraph or in this piece of writing.

13. (3) The correct form of the verb is in the future tense—*will be*.

14. (3) The original sentence is a comma splice. Add the phrase *so that you can* to correct the error.

15. (2) The appositive *the Preview 2003* should be set off from the rest of the sentence with commas.

16. (5) Use commas to separate the three items in this series—*software, printer,* and *computer*.

17. (1) The sentences of paragraph B give details about what the customer does with her computer. This answer makes the best topic sentence.

18. (3) This answer uses the present tense and the plural form of the verb, which corresponds to the compound subject of the revised sentence—*my children and I*.

19. (3) This sentence gives an example of what the family does with its computer. It belongs in paragraph B.

20. (4) The past tense *was* makes no sense here. The customer is asking for help in the future, so *will be* is the correct form of the verb.

21. (2) The subject of the sentence *Buying a computer* agrees with the singular verb *seems*, not *seem*.

22. (4) This passage is written in the third person. The pronoun *you* shifts to the second person, which is incorrect. *He or she* is the correct pronoun choice to match the subject, *person*.

23. (1) The conjunction *because* incorrectly indicates a cause-effect relationship. The correct relationship between the two clauses is contrast, so *Although* is a better choice.

24. (5) This answer correctly moves the modifying phrase *considered safe and dependable* closer to the noun it describes, *Social Security*.

POSTTEST

25. (1) The pronoun *They* is vague. Who are *They*? The noun *Experts* is a better choice.

26. (2) The appositive, *Senior Employee Benefit Researcher at InvestCo*, should be set off with commas.

27. (4) In the original sentence, the three items in the series are not parallel in structure. This answer corrects the error.

28. (5) This sentence is correct as written.

29. (1) Use a comma to set off the introductory phrase *In summary.*

30. (4) The homonym *their* indicates possession. The correct spelling in this sentence is *there.*

31. (2) The subject of the sentence is *number*, a singular noun not *people*, the object of the preposition. The correct present-tense verb form is *increases.*

32. (2) The original sentence is actually a fragment. If you replace *setting* with *set*, you correct this error.

33. (4) The subject of the clause is *glare or reflection*, not *glare and reflection*, which means you need to use the verb that agrees with a singular noun. The verb *is* is correct, not *are.*

34. (4) The antecedent of the pronoun is *monitor*, a singular noun. The pronoun that agrees with a singular noun is *it*, not *them.*

35. (5) The sentence as written contains a dangling modifier—*When sitting in the chair.* This answer corrects the error.

36. (4) The second half of paragraph C deals with the correct placement of hands, not the correct chair placement. Starting a new paragraph with sentence 13 separates these two main ideas.

37. (1) This sentence is correct as written.

38. (4) The modifier *called Sick Building Syndrome* is misplaced in the original sentence. It should describe *problem*, not *scientists.*

39. (3) The pronoun and verb should agree with the singular noun *Someone.*

40. (4) The treatment of colds is not the subject of this passage. The sentence should be removed.

41. (2) This answer is the best way to combine these two sentences with a minimum of repetition while still keeping the same meaning.

42. (4) Combining the common elements of the sentence makes a smoother, less repetitive sentence.

43. (3) The noun *consultant* should not be capitalized since it does not name a specific person.

44. (2) The original sentence is awkward and repetitive. This answer gets rid of the problems without sacrificing meaning.

45. (3) The original sentence contains a comma splice. This answer corrects the error by adding the conjunction *and.*

46. (2) The subject pronoun *I* is correct, not the object pronoun *me.*

47. (1) Sentences 9 and 10 tell how Michael has performed on his job. These sentences belong in paragraph B.

48. (1) This sentence is correct as written.

49. (2) This is a compound sentence, so a comma is needed before the conjunction *and.*

50. (4) This answer corrects the awkward and repetitive problems in the original sentence.

Part 1: Evaluation Chart

On the following chart, circle the number of any item you answered incorrectly. Next to each group of item numbers, you will see the pages you can review to learn how to answer the items correctly. Pay particular attention to reviewing skill areas in which you missed half or more of the questions.

Skill Area	Item Number	Review Pages
ORGANIZATION		
Text divisions	19, 36	120–126
Topic sentences	17	115–119
Unity/coherence	12, 40, 47	127–133
SENTENCE STRUCTURE		
Complete sentences, fragments, and sentence combining	32, 41	19–24, 83–104
Run-on sentences/comma splices	7, 10, 14, 45	86–88, 96
Wordiness/repetition	42, 44, 50	97–98, 103–104
Coordination/subordination	3, 23, 48	83–84, 89–98
Modification	24, 35, 38	145–153
Parallelism	2, 27	154–156
USAGE		
Subject-verb agreement	4, 9, 11, 18, 21, 31, 33, 37	51–59, 62–73
Verb tense/form	5, 13, 20	51–61, 101–102
Pronoun reference/antecedent agreement	22, 25, 34, 39, 46	38–42, 157–165
MECHANICS		
Capitalization	8, 43	29, 34–35, 177–178
Punctuation (commas)	15, 16, 26, 28, 29, 49	31, 87, 93, 96, 183–185
Spelling (possessives, contractions, and homonyms)	1, 6, 30	43, 179–182

Part II: Evaluation Guidelines

If at all possible, give your instructor your essay to evaluate. You will find his or her objective opinion helpful in deciding whether you are ready for the actual GED. If this is not possible, have another student evaluate your paper. If you cannot find another student to help you, review your paper yourself. If you do this, it is usually better to let your paper sit for a few days before you evaluate it. This way you will experience your essay much the same way a first-time reader will experience it. Whoever reads your paper, that person should use the GED Essay Scoring Guide to evaluate your essay and give it a score.

After scoring your essay, think about ways that you can improve your writing. Think about the following questions:

1. After you read your topic, did you plan your answer, jotting down ideas for your essay? Was this process easy or hard? If gathering your ideas seemed hard, review Chapter 9 of this book.

2. Did you take time to organize your ideas before you began writing? Was this process easy or hard? For help on organizing your ideas, review Chapter 10.

3. Were you able to write a clear introduction to your essay? Did the introduction clearly indicate the organization of the rest of the essay? For more information on this aspect of writing, see pages 255–258 in Chapter 11.

4. As you were writing your essay, were you able to compose body paragraphs that stated main ideas and supported them with plenty of details? For more information on this aspect of writing, see pages 259–264 in Chapter 11.

5. Were you able to write a clear concluding paragraph for your essay? For help in this area, see pages 265–266 in Chapter 11.

6. After you finished writing, did you revise your essay to improve its content and organization? If you want help in this area, see pages 276–292 in Chapter 12.

7. After you finished writing, did you revise your essay to improve its control of spelling, punctuation, and so on? If you want help in this area, see pages 293–294 in Chapter 12.

LANGUAGE ARTS, WRITING, PART II

Essay Scoring Guide

	1 Inadequate	2 Marginal	3 Adequate	4 Effective
	Reader has difficulty identifying or following the writer's ideas.	**Reader occasionally has difficulty understanding or following the writer's ideas.**	**Reader understands the writer's ideas.**	**Reader understands and easily follows the writer's expression of ideas.**
Response to the Prompt	Attempts to address prompt but with little or no success in establishing a focus.	Addresses the prompt, though the focus may shift.	Uses the writing prompt to establish a main idea.	Presents a clearly focused main idea that addresses the prompt.
Organization	Fails to organize ideas.	Shows some evidence of an organizational plan.	Uses an identifiable organizational plan.	Establishes a clear and logical organization.
Development and Details	Demonstrates little or no development; usually lacks details or examples or presents irrelevant information.	Has some development but lacks specific details; may be limited to a listing, repetitions, or generalizations.	Has focused but occasionally uneven development; incorporates some specific detail.	Achieves coherent development with specific and relevant details and examples.
Conventions of EAE	Exhibits minimal or no control of sentence structure and the conventions of Edited American English (EAE).	Demonstrates inconsistent control of sentence structure and the conventions of EAE.	Generally controls sentence structure and the conventions of EAE.	Consistently controls sentence structure and the conventions of EAE.
Word Choice	Exhibits weak and/or inappropriate words.	Exhibits a narrow range of word choice, often including inappropriate selections.	Exhibits appropriate word choice.	Exhibits varied and precise word choice.

PRACTICE TEST

Questions 9–16 refer to the following passage.

Registering with the U.S. Selective Service System

(A)

(1) All male citizens of the United States and male immigrant aliens living in the United States and it's territories must register with the Selective Service System within 30 days of their eighteenth birthday. (2) This registration is the process by which the government collects names and addresses of young men in case a national emergency requires quick expansion of the armed forces. (3) Registering with the Selective Service does not mean you are joining the military or that you will be drafted. (4) No one can be drafted into the military unless ordered by Congress and the President; in fact, no one have been drafted since 1973.

(B)

(5) There are two ways to register. (6) The easy way is to register online by going to www.sss.gov and completed the forms provided there. (7) The other way to register is to pick up a form at any post office or your town hall. (8) Be sure to fill out either form correctly, providing all requested information. (9) Failure to register is a felony. (10) Failing to register results in a loss of certain benefits. (11) These benefits include student financial aid, being government employment, and government-sponsored job training.

(C)

(12) Within two months of registering, you should receive a Registration Acknowledgment Card in the mail. (13) Keep this card in a safe place, as it offers proof of your compliance with the law. (14) If you do not receive this notification it is very important that you contact the Selective Service System immediately, either by phone or online. (15) The law also requires you to let the Selective Service know of any address changes so that you can be reached without delay.

(D)

(16) You may request these brochures by mail at Box 212, Washington, D.C. 20003. (17) Or you may call 703-605-4100 and ask for SSS booklet No. 101A and 101B. (18) If you need additional information about Selective Service registration, there are two brochures available that explain your responsibilities.

9. Sentence 1: **All male citizens of the United States and male immigrant aliens living in the United States and it's territories must register with the Selective Service System within 30 days of their eighteenth birthday.**

What correction should be made to sentence 1?

(1) replace *it's* with *its*
(2) replace *it's* with *their*
(3) insert a comma after *territories*
(4) replace *their* with *his*
(5) no correction is necessary

10. Sentence 4: **No one can be drafted into the military unless ordered by Congress and the President; in fact <u>no one have been drafted since 1973</u>.**

Which is the best way to write the underlined portion of the text? If the original is the best way, choose option (1).

(1) no one have been drafted since 1973.
(2) and no one have been drafted since 1973.
(3) no one has been drafted since 1973.
(4) no one was drafted since 1973.
(5) no one will be drafted since 1973.

11. **Sentence 6: The easy way is to register online by going to www.sss.gov and completed the forms provided there.**

What correction should be made to sentence 6?

(1) replace *is* with *was*
(2) insert a comma after *www.sss.gov*
(3) replace *completed* with *have completed*
(4) change *completed* to *completing*
(5) no correction is necessary

12. **Sentences 9 and 10: Failure to register is a felony. Failing to register results in a loss of certain benefits.**

The most effective combination of sentences 9 and 10 would include which group of words?

(1) Failure to register and loss of certain benefits
(2) Failure to register is a felony, and failure to register
(3) A felony and a loss, failure to register
(4) Failing and a failure, registering
(5) Failing to register is a felony and results

13. **Sentence 11: These benefits include student financial aid, being government employment, and government-sponsored job training.**

Which is the best way to write the underlined portion of the text? If the original is the best way, choose option (1).

(1) financial aid, being government employment, and
(2) financial aid being government employment, and
(3) financial aid, government employment, and
(4) financial aid, be government employment, and
(5) financial aid, being government employment, but

14. **Sentence 14: If you do not receive this notification it is very important that you contact the Selective Service System immediately, either by phone or online.**

What correction should be made to sentence 14?

(1) replace *If* with *Although*
(2) insert a comma after *notification*
(3) replace *is* with *was*
(4) change *contact* to *contacted*
(5) no correction is necessary

15. **Sentence 15: The law also requires you to let the Selective Service know of any address changes so that you can be reached without delay.**

Which is the best way to write the underlined portion of the text? If you the original is the best way, choose option (1).

(1) know of any address changes so that you can be reached
(2) know of any address changes, so that you can be reached
(3) known of any address changes so that you can be reached
(4) know of any address changes so that, you can be reached
(5) know of any address changes so that you had been reached

16. **Sentence 18: If you need additional information about Selective Service registration, there are two brochures available that explain your responsibilities.**

Which revision should be made to sentence 18?

(1) remove sentence 18
(2) move sentence 18 to the beginning of paragraph C
(3) move sentence 18 to the end of paragraph C
(4) move sentence 18 to follow sentence 16
(5) move sentence 18 to the beginning of paragraph D

PRACTICE TEST

Questions 17–26 refer to the following letter.

May 3, 2001

Dear Ms. Arturo:

(A)

(1) We have received your letter dated April 9 and would like to respond. (2) We understand that you are concerned with the care and service your cat received while visiting the Bayview Veterinary Clinic on April 2 of this year. (3) Your domesticated animal, of the feline species, was observed in our waiting area on the second day of April in the year 2001. (4) Having discussed the matter at great length with the receptionist who were on duty at the time of your visit, as well as Dr. Bloom, we believe we have a fair understanding of the events that took place.

(B)

(5) The Bayview Veterinary Clinic in business in this community for over fifteen years, has always had a policy of treating both people and animals with respect. (6) Our staff works hard to handle all cases in a fare and efficient manner. (7) We know we are not perfect, we are always striving for better performance.

(C)

(8) If you arrived at the clinic on April 2, you certainly should have been informed that there would be a considerable wait before a doctor could see your pet. (9) They had several emergencies that morning that put us behind schedule. (10) We apologize that you were not adequately informed so that you could make a decision to come back at a more convenient time. (11) However, our patient services policy and your contract clearly states that an appointment time will be honored to the best of our ability. (12) Accidents happen and, we are obliged to provide immediate care for those animals whose situation is critical. (13) The two animals who were seen ahead of your cat were both considered in critical condition by the veterinarian on duty. (14) We ask that you try to understand the events of April 2 in light of how you would want your pet cared for in the case of an emergency.

(D)

(15) You are a valued client, Ms. Arturo, and we appreciate the fact that you took the time to right to us. (16) We hope that this response has clarified our position on what happened during your visit. (17) Please do not hesitate to contact us again if we can provide any further explanation for you.

Sincerely,
The Staff of the Bayview Veterinary Clinic

17. Sentence 3: Your domesticated animal, of the feline species, was observed in our waiting area on the second day of April in the year 2001.

Which revision should be made to sentence 3?

(1) move sentence 3 to the beginning of paragraph A
(2) move sentence 3 to follow sentence 1
(3) remove sentence 3
(4) move sentence 3 to the end of paragraph A
(5) move sentence 3 to the beginning of paragraph C

18. Sentence 4: Having discussed the matter at great length with the receptionist who were on duty at the time of your visit, as well as Dr. Bloom, we believe we have a fair understanding of the events that took place.

The most effective revision of sentence 4 would include which group of words?

(1) the receptionist who was
(2) the receptionist who will be
(3) at the time of your visit as well
(4) they believe we have
(5) we believed we have

19. Sentence 5: The Bayview Veterinary Clinic in business in this community for over fifteen years, has always had a policy of treating both people and animals with respect.

What correction should be made to sentence 5?

(1) change *Bayview Veterinary Clinic* to *bayview veterinary clinic*
(2) insert a comma after *Clinic*
(3) change *business* to *Business*
(4) remove the comma after *years*
(5) no correction is necessary

20. Sentence 6: Our staff works hard to handle all cases in a fare and efficient manner.

What correction should be made to sentence 6?

(1) change *works* to *work*
(2) insert a comma after *hard*
(3) replace *fare* with *fair*
(4) insert a comma after *fare*
(5) no correction is necessary

21. Sentence 7: We know <u>we are not perfect, we are always striving</u> for better performance.

Which is the best way to write the underlined portion of the text? If the original is the best way, choose option (1).

(1) we are not perfect, we are always striving
(2) we are not perfect we are always striving
(3) we were not perfect, we were always striving
(4) we are not perfect, but we are always striving
(5) we are not perfect, for we are always striving

22. **Sentence 8: If you arrived at the clinic on April 2, you certainly should have been informed that there would be a considerable wait before a doctor could see your pet.**

    What correction should be made to sentence 8?

    (1) replace *If* with *When*
    (2) replace *If* with *Although*
    (3) remove the comma after *April 2*
    (4) replace *informed* with *inform*
    (5) replace *there* with *their*

23. **Sentence 9: <u>They had</u> several emergencies that morning that put us behind schedule.**

    Which is the best way to write the underlined portion of the text? If the original is the best way, choose option (1).

    (1) They had
    (2) They have
    (3) They will have
    (4) There were
    (5) They're

24. **Sentence 11: However, our patient services policy and your contract clearly states that an appointment time will be honored to the best of our ability.**

    What correction should be made to sentence 11?

    (1) replace *our* with *hour*
    (2) replace *your* with *you're*
    (3) insert a comma after *contract*
    (4) change *states* to *stating*
    (5) change *states* to *state*

25. **Sentence 12: <u>Accidents happen and, we are</u> obliged to provide immediate care for those animals whose situation is critical.**

    Which is the best way to write the underlined portion of the text? If the original is the best way, choose option (1).

    (1) Accidents happen and, we are
    (2) Accidents happen, and we are
    (3) Accidents happened and, we are
    (4) Accidents happened and, we were
    (5) Accidents happened, and you are

26. **Sentence 15: You are a valued client, Ms. Arturo, and we appreciate the fact that you took the time to right to us.**

    What correction should be made to sentence 15?

    (1) remove the comma after *client*
    (2) replace *and* with *but*
    (3) change *appreciate* to *appreciated*
    (4) replace *right* with *write*
    (5) no correction is necessary

Questions 27–35 refer to the following set of instructions.

How to Clean Your Computer

(A)

(1) You should take time to clean your computer, and when dust settles on and within the machine casing, your computer will be less efficient and perform poorly. (2) Before you begin the cleaning process, consult your computer manual for specific instructions that might not be included in these general instructions. (3) Some computers require special cleaning products. (4) For some ordinary soap and water work well. (5) Turn off and unplug the computer and monitor before cleaning it using the steps outlined below.

(B)

(6) To clean the monitor, first spray some mildly soapy water onto a clean cloth. (7) Do not, spray directly onto any part of the monitor! (8) Wipe the monitor's casing, being careful not to let any water drip inside. (9) Using a separate clean cloth, also sprayed with soapy water, wipe the monitor screen. (10) Wipe very gently.

(C)

(11) Now it's time to clean the computer box itself. (12) First, you should be careful to release any static electricity by touching a heavy metal object, such as a chair, desk, or touching a lamp. (13) There's also good reasons not to shuffle your feet across any carpeting as you work. (14) Next, opening the casing in whatever manner your computer's operating manual recommends. (15) Using a can of compressed air with a plastic extension straw, your computer can be gently but effectively dusted. (16) Be sure you do not touch any part of the circuit board, but try to get air into all nooks and crannies. (17) Finally, close your computer up tightly according to directions.

27. Sentence 1: **You should take time to clean your computer, and when dust settles on and within the machine casing, your computer will be less efficient and perform poorly.**

    The most effective revision of sentence 1 would begin with which group of words?

    (1) Take time to clean your computer because when dust settles
    (2) You should take time to clean your computer so that dust settles
    (3) Taking time to clean your computer, dust settles
    (4) Even though you take time to clean your computer, dust settles
    (5) To take time to clean your computer, dust settles

28. Sentence 4: **For some ordinary soap and water work well.**

    What correction should be made to sentence 4?

    (1) replace *For* with *Four*
    (2) replace *some* with *sum*
    (3) insert a comma after *some*
    (4) change *work* to *works*
    (5) no correction is necessary

29. Sentence 5: Turn off and unplug the computer and monitor before cleaning it using the steps outlined below.

What correction should be made to sentence 5?

(1) replace *before* with *although*
(2) replace *it* with *them*
(3) change *using* to *used*
(4) change *using* to *use*
(5) no correction is necessary

30. Sentence 7: <u>Do not, spray directly</u> onto any part of the monitor!

Which is the best way to write the underlined portion of the text? If the original is the best way, choose option (1).

(1) Do not, spray directly
(2) Does not, spray directly
(3) You do not, spray directly
(4) Do not spray, directly
(5) Do not spray directly

31. Sentences 9 and 10: Using a separate clean cloth, also sprayed with soapy water, wipe the monitor screen. Wipe very gently.

The most effective combination of sentences 9 and 10 would include which group of words?

(1) Gently wipe the monitor screen,
(2) To wipe the monitor screen very gently
(3) Wipe very gently and use a separate
(4) Using, spraying, and wiping
(5) Use a gentle separate clean cloth

32. Sentence 12: First, you should be careful to release any static electricity by touching a heavy metal object, such as a <u>chair, desk, or touching a lamp.</u>

Which is the best way to write the underlined portion of the text? If the original is the best way, choose option (1).

(1) chair, desk, or touching a lamp.
(2) chair desk or touching a lamp.
(3) chair desk, or touching a lamp.
(4) chair, desk, or lamp.
(5) chair desk or lamp.

33. Sentence 13: <u>There's also good reasons</u> not to shuffle your feet across any carpeting as you work.

Which is the best way to write the underlined portion of the text? If the original is the best way, choose option (1).

(1) There's also good reasons
(2) There's also good reasons,
(3) They're also good reasons
(4) Theirs also good reasons
(5) There are also good reasons

34. Sentence 14: Next, opening the casing in whatever manner your computer's operating manual recommends.

What correction should be made to sentence 14?

(1) remove the comma after *Next*
(2) change *opening* to *opened*
(3) change *opening* to *open*
(4) change *computer's* to *computers*
(5) no correction is necessary

35. Sentence 15: Using a can of compressed air with a plastic extension straw, <u>your computer can be gently but effectively dusted</u>.

Which is the best way to write the underlined portion of the text? If the original is the best way, choose option (1).

(1) your computer can be gently but effectively dusted.

(2) you can gently but effectively dust your computer.

(3) you're computer can be gently but effectively dusted.

(4) your computer can be, gently but effectively, dusted.

(5) your computer can be gentle but effectively dusted.

PRACTICE TEST

Questions 36–44 refer to the following passage.

Do Men and Women Speak the Same Language?

(A)

(1) If you're a woman have you ever wondered why your boyfriend or husband won't ask for directions even after he's been driving around lost for hours? (2) If you're a man, have you ever wondered why the women in your life want to talk about relationships even when the relationships are going fine? (3) Believing that men and women speak different languages, there's research that says you may be right. (4) The reasons and ways these two genders communicate are often strikingly different. (5) Here are some basic principles that seem to define how people learn to communicate. (6) Many young boys think that the main purpose for talking is to give information. (7) These boys grow up believing that the person without information is somehow inferior to the person who has information. (8) Young girls, on the other hand, may grow up believing that the reason to talk is to build emotional closeness. (9) These girls feel that them can deepen a relationship by talking. (10) Therefore, it's not surprising that when these girls and boys grow up and try to communicate with one another, they often end up confused disappointed, or angry.

(B)

(11) For example, as a man circles the same block for the tenth time, his wife should not automatically think that they are trying to be difficult. (12) Instead, she might consider the insecurity her husband is feeling in that moment. (13) Likewise, when a woman asks probing questions about a relationship, a man does not have to feel that she is "looking for trouble." (14) Instead, she might be seeking additional intimacy and understanding.

---

36. **Sentence 1: If you're a woman have you ever wondered why your boyfriend or husband won't ask for directions even after he's been driving around lost for hours?**

    What correction should be made to sentence 1?

    (1) replace *If* with *Although*
    (2) replace *you're* with *your*
    (3) insert a comma after *woman*
    (4) replace *have you* with *has he*
    (5) replace *he's* with *his*

37. **Sentence 3: <u>Believing that men and women speak different languages, there's</u> research that says you may be right.**

    Which is the best way to write the underlined portion of the text? If the original is the best way, choose option (1).

    (1) Believing that men and women speak different languages, there's
    (2) Believing that men and women speak different languages, they're
    (3) Believe that men and women speak different languages, there's
    (4) If you believe that men and women speak different languages, there's
    (5) If they believe that men and women speak different languages, there's

38. Which revision would make paragraph A more effective?

Begin a new paragraph

(1) with sentence 3
(2) with sentence 4
(3) with sentence 5
(4) with sentence 7
(5) with sentence 8

39. Sentences 6 and 7: Many young boys think that the main purpose for talking is to give information. These boys grow up believing that the person without information is somehow inferior to the person who has information.

The most effective combination of sentences 6 and 7 would include which group of words?

(1) Many young boys tend to grow up thinking and believing that information is
(2) Many young boys tend to think and believe about information
(3) Growing up, many boys who are young and believing
(4) Many young boys, thinking that the main purpose for talking is to give information, grow
(5) These boys, many young and growing up, tend to believe that information

40. Sentence 9: These girls feel that them can deepen a relationship by talking.

What correction should be made to sentence 9?

(1) change *feel* to *felt*
(2) change *feel* to *feels*
(3) change *them* to *they*
(4) change *them* to *they're*
(5) change *talk* to *talked*

41. Sentence 10: Therefore, it's not surprising that when these girls and boys grow up and try to communicate with one another, they often end up confused disappointed, or angry.

What correction should be made to sentence 10?

(1) change *it's* to *its*
(2) change *grow* to *grew*
(3) remove the comma after *another*
(4) change *end* to *ended*
(5) insert a comma after *confused*

42. Which sentence below would be most effective at the beginning of paragraph B?

(1) Psychologists believe that the key to effective communication between genders is respect for differences.
(2) What should you do if you cannot communicate well?
(3) All kinds of problems arise between genders, and these problems are almost impossible to overcome.
(4) The communication issue is only one of the many stumbling blocks of modern relationships.
(5) What strategies have been proven ineffective in handling communication between men and women?

43. Sentence 11: For example, as a man circles the same block for the tenth time, his wife should not automatically think that they are trying to be difficult.

What correction should be made to sentence 11?

(1) remove the comma after *example*
(2) remove the comma after *time*
(3) change *think* to *thought*
(4) replace *they are* with *he is*
(5) no correction is necessary

44. Sentence 13: Likewise, when a woman asks probing questions about a relationship, a man does not have to feel that she is "looking for trouble."

What correction should be made to sentence 13?

(1) replace *when* with *although*
(2) replace *asks* with *asked*
(3) remove the comma after *relationship*
(4) replace *does* with *did*
(5) no correction is necessary

Questions 45–50 refer to the following letter.

November 16, 2001

Dear Valued Customer:

(A)

(1) It is with deep regret that I write to inform you that as of December 31 of this year, Chen's Cleaners will no longer be in business. (2) My wife and I, co-owners of this business have taken many months to make this difficult decision. (3) This letter is intended to help you understand our decision and to answer some of the questions you may have. (4) Regarding our closing procedures.

(B)

(5) The main reason we are closing our doors at this time is the skyrocketing rents charged in this neighborhood. (6) Rental agreements can be confusing if you do not pay attention. (7) We simply could not manage our other expenses while keeping up with our rising rent payment.

(C)

(8) As you know, we tried raising prices, but even that was not enough.

(D)

(9) We plan to finish services on all garments brought to us before December 15, we will not accept any more clothes after that date. (10) Our customers will have until December 30 to pick up their items, and we suggest you do this as early in December as possible. (11) Any articles left in the store after December 30 will be donated to a local shelter. (12) As our contracts state, we are not responsible for clothing that is not picked up.

(E)

(13) My wife and I apologize for any inconvenience we cause. (14) Many people have come by the store and wished us well, and for that we thank you. (15) Because we have enjoyed our 10 years in this location, and we are sorry to have to close at this time.

Sincerely,
John Chen

45. Sentence 2: My wife and <u>I, co-owners of this business have taken</u> many months to make this difficult decision.

Which is the best way to write the underlined portion of the text? If the original is the best way, choose option (1).

(1) I, co-owners of this business have taken
(2) I co-owners of this business have taken
(3) I, co-owners of this business, have taken
(4) I, co-owners of this business has taken
(5) I, co-owners of this business have been taking

46. Sentences 3 and 4: This letter is intended to help you understand our decision and to answer some of the questions <u>you may have. Regarding</u> our closing procedures.

Which is the best way to write the underlined portion of the text? If the original is the best way, choose option (1).

(1) you may have. Regarding
(2) you may have and regarding,
(3) we may have. Regarding
(4) you may have regarding
(5) you may have. To regard

47. Sentence 6: Rental agreements can be confusing if you do not pay attention.

Which revision should be made to sentence 6?

(1) move sentence 6 to the end of paragraph A
(2) move sentence 6 to the beginning of paragraph B
(3) move sentence 6 to follow sentence 7
(4) move sentence 6 to the beginning of paragraph E
(5) remove sentence 6

48. Sentence 8: As you know, we tried raising prices, but even that was not enough.

Which revision should be made to sentence 8?

(1) move sentence 8 to the end of paragraph A
(2) move sentence 8 to the beginning of paragraph B
(3) move sentence 8 to the end of paragraph B
(4) move sentence 8 to the beginning of paragraph E
(5) remove sentence 8

49. Sentence 9: We plan to finish services on all garments brought to us before <u>December 15, we will not accept</u> any more clothes after that date.

Which is the best way to write the underlined portion of the text? If the original is the best way, choose option (1).

(1) December 15, we will not accept
(2) December 15 we will not accept
(3) december 15, we will not accept
(4) December 15, and we will not accept
(5) December 15, we did not accept

50. Sentence 15: <u>Because we have enjoyed our ten years in this location, and we</u> are sorry to have to close at this time.

Which is the best way to write the underlined portion of the text? If the original is the best way, choose option (1).

(1) Because we have enjoyed our ten years in this location, and we
(2) Because we have enjoyed our ten years in this location, we
(3) Although we have enjoyed our ten years in this location, and we
(4) Because we will enjoy our ten years in this location, and we
(5) Because we have enjoyed our ten years in this location and we

Answers are on page 357.

Language Arts Writing, Part II

Essay Directions and Topic

Look at the box on the following page. In the box is your assigned topic. You must write on the assigned topic ONLY.

You will have 45 minutes to write on your assigned essay topic. You may return to the multiple-choice section after you complete your essay if you have time remaining in this test period.

Pay attention to the following features as you write:

- Well-focused main points
- Clear organization
- Specific development of your ideas
- Control of sentence structure, punctuation, grammar, word choice, and spelling

As you work, be sure to do the following:

- Do not leave pages blank.
- Write legibly **in ink**.
- Write on the assigned topic.
- Write your essay on a separate sheet of paper.

--- TOPIC ---

Every year companies spend millions of dollars to advertise their products and services. We see advertising everywhere. What are the effects of advertising on modern life?

In your essay, state the effects of advertising on modern life. You may describe the positive effects, the negative effects, or both. Give specific examples to back up your ideas.

Part II is a test to determine how well you can use written language to explain your ideas.

In preparing your essay, you should take the following steps:

- Read the **DIRECTIONS** and the **TOPIC** carefully.

- Plan your essay before you write. Use scratch paper to make any notes.

- After you finish writing your essay, reread what you have written and make any changes that will improve your essay.

Your essay should be long enough to develop the topic adequately.

Evaluation guidelines are on page 360.

PRACTICE TEST
Answer Key

1. (4) The verb form *being* makes no sense in this sentence. The future tense *will be* and the second-person *you* are correct.

2. (1) The subject of the sentence is plural—*stores*. The singular noun *neighborhood* is part of an interrupting prepositional phrase.

3. (3) The original sentence contains a dangling modifier—*once inside*. This answer corrects the error.

4. (2) The passage is written in the present tense, so *is* is the correct verb, not the past-tense *was*.

5. (2) The subject of this inverted sentence is plural—*people*. The correct verb is *are*, not *is*.

6. (5) The antecedent of the pronoun is *stores*, so the plural pronoun *their* is correct.

7. (2) The common noun *holiday* should not be capitalized since it is not a specific title.

8. (2) Do not put a comma between two elements of a compound object.

9. (1) The contraction *it's* is incorrect in this sentence. Use the possessive *its* instead.

10. (3) The subject *No one* is singular, so the verb *has* is correct, not *have*, which agrees with a plural subject. The past progressive tense remains correct.

11. (4) The correct verb is the gerund *completing*, which is parallel to the other verb in the compound, *going*.

12. (5) This answer combines the two sentences correctly and gets rid of unnecessary repetition.

13. (3) The original sentence contains a series that is not parallel. This answer corrects the error.

14. (2) A comma is needed after a dependent clause that precedes an independent clause. *If you do not receive this notification* is a dependent clause.

15. (1) This sentence is correct as written.

16. (5) This sentence makes a good topic sentence and should be the first reference to the brochures. It should come first in the paragraph.

17. (3) The content and tone of this sentence do not fit in this letter. The formal language is unlike the rest of the writing. The sentence also repeats sentence 2.

18. (1) The subject of the verb is the singular *receptionist*. The correct way to write the clause is *receptionist who was*.

19. (2) The modifying phrase *in business in this community for over fifteen years* must be set off with commas before and after it.

20. (3) The homonym *fair* means *equitable* or *just*, and it is the correct choice in this sentence.

21. (4) The original sentence contains a comma splice. To correct it, add a conjunction after the comma. To show contrast, *but* is the best choice.

22. (1) The correct conjunction to use is *When*. The conjunction *If* indicates condition, which makes no sense in this letter.

23. (4) The original sentence contains the vague pronoun reference *they*.

24. (5) The subject of the sentence is plural; therefore the correct verb choice is *state*.

25. (2) In a compound sentence, the comma should precede the conjunction.

26. (4) The homonym *right* is incorrect. Use *write* instead.

27. (1) This answer shows the best way to rewrite the original sentence without error or repetition. The conjunction shows cause and effect.

28. (3) The introductory phrase *For some* should be followed by a comma.

29. (2) The pronoun refers to the compound object *computer and monitor*. Therefore, the plural *them* is correct, not the singular *it*.

30. (5) The original sentence shows an example of comma overuse. There is no reason to put a comma after *Do not*.

31. (1) This choice correctly combines both sentences without repetition.

32. (4) The original sentence contains nonparallel structure. This answer correctly lists three nouns—*chair, desk, lamp*.

33. (5) The subject of this inverted sentence is *reasons*, a plural noun. Therefore, *There are* is correct, not *There is (There's)*.

34. (3) The original text is a sentence fragment. By changing *opening* to *open*, you correct the error.

35. (2) There is a dangling modifier in the original sentence. *Using a can of compressed air with a plastic extension straw* should modify a person, *you*. The computer is not using the air, but *computer* is what the phrase modifies in the original sentence.

36. (3) A comma must follow the dependent clause *If you're a woman*.

37. (4) The original sentence contains a dangling modifier. Change it to a dependent clause with *you*.

38. (3) This sentence tells what follows in the rest of the paragraph. It would make a good topic sentence for a separate paragraph.

39. (4) This sentence correctly combines two sentences by making one a modifying phrase.

40. (3) The subject pronoun *they* is the correct form, not the object pronoun *them*.

41. (5) Commas are needed after each item in a series—*confused, disappointed, or angry*.

42. (1) The sentences that follow in this paragraph give examples of how men and women can respect one another. This answer offers the best statement of this main idea.

43. (4) The correct pronoun is *he*, referring to *a man*. The verb becomes singular—*is*—to agree with it.

44. (5) This sentence is correct as written.

45. (3) The appositive *co-owners of this business* should have a comma preceding it and a comma following it.

46. (4) This sentence corrects the fragment in sentence 4.

47. (5) Confusion over rental payments is not a topic for this paragraph or letter. Removing this sentence improves the writing.

48. (3) This sentence belongs in the same paragraph as the other sentences about expenses. It works better at the end because it is not a topic sentence.

49. (4) Adding the conjunction *and* corrects the comma splice in the original sentence.

50. (2) This answer turns the second part of a fragment into an independent clause.

PRACTICE TEST
Part I: Evaluation Chart

On the following chart, circle the number of any item you answered incorrectly. Next to each group of item numbers, you will see the pages you can review to learn how to answer the items correctly. Pay particular attention to reviewing skill areas in which you missed half or more of the questions.

Skill Area	Item Number	Review Pages
ORGANIZATION		
Text divisions	38, 48	120–126
Topic sentences	42	115–119
Unity/coherence	16, 17, 47	127–133
SENTENCE STRUCTURE		
Complete sentences, fragments, and sentence combining	31, 34, 39, 46, 46, 50	19–24, 83–104
Run-on sentences/comma splices	21, 49	86–88, 96
Wordiness/repetition	12, 49	97–98, 103–104
Coordination/subordination	22, 44	83–84, 89–98
Modification	3, 35, 37	145–153
Parallelism	13, 32	154–156
USAGE		
Subject-verb agreement	2, 5, 10, 18, 24, 33	51–59, 62–73
Verb tense/form	1, 4, 11	51–61, 101–102
Pronoun reference/antecedent agreement	6, 23, 29, 40, 43	38–42, 157–165
MECHANICS		
Capitalization	7	29, 34–35, 177–178
Punctuation (commas)	8, 14, 15, 19, 25, 28, 30 36, 41, 45	31, 87, 93, 96, 183–185
Spelling (possessives, contractions, and homonyms)	9, 20, 26	43, 179–182

Part II: Evaluation Guidelines

If at all possible, give your instructor your essay to evaluate. You will find his or her objective opinion helpful in deciding whether you are ready for the actual GED. If this is not possible, have another student evaluate your paper. If you cannot find another student to help you, review your paper yourself. If you do this, it is usually better to let your paper sit for a few days before you evaluate it. This way you will experience your essay much the same way a first-time reader will experience it. Whoever reads your paper, that person should use the GED Essay Scoring Guide to evaluate your essay and give it a score.

After scoring your essay, think about ways that you can improve your writing. Think about the following questions:

1. After you read your topic, did you plan your answer, jotting down ideas for your essay? Was this process easy or hard? If gathering your ideas seemed hard, review Chapter 9 of this book.

2. Did you take time to organize your ideas before you began writing? Was this process easy or hard? For help on organizing your ideas, review Chapter 10.

3. Were you able to write a clear introduction to your essay? Did the introduction clearly indicate the organization of the rest of the essay? For more information on this aspect of writing, see pages 255–258 in Chapter 11.

4. As you were writing your essay, were you able to compose body paragraphs that stated main ideas and supported them with plenty of details? For more information on this aspect of writing, see pages 259–264 in Chapter 11.

5. Were you able to write a clear concluding paragraph for your essay? For help in this area, see pages 265–266 in Chapter 11.

6. After you finished writing, did you revise your essay to improve its content and organization? If you want help in this area, see pages 276–292 in Chapter 12.

7. After you finished writing, did you revise your essay to improve its control of spelling, punctuation, and so on? If you want help in this area, see pages 293–294 in Chapter 12.

LANGUAGE ARTS, WRITING, PART II

Essay Scoring Guide

	1	2	3	4
	Inadequate	**Marginal**	**Adequate**	**Effective**
Response to the Prompt	**Reader has difficulty identifying or following the writer's ideas.**	**Reader occasionally has difficulty understanding or following the writer's ideas.**	**Reader understands the writer's ideas.**	**Reader understands and easily follows the writer's expression of ideas.**
	Attempts to address prompt but with little or no success in establishing a focus.	Addresses the prompt, though the focus may shift.	Uses the writing prompt to establish a main idea.	Presents a clearly focused main idea that addresses the prompt.
Organization	Fails to organize ideas.	Shows some evidence of an organizational plan.	Uses an identifiable organizational plan.	Establishes a clear and logical organization.
Development and Details	Demonstrates little or no development; usually lacks details or examples or presents irrelevant information.	Has some development but lacks specific details; may be limited to a listing, repetitions, or generalizations.	Has focused but occasionally uneven development; incorporates some specific detail.	Achieves coherent development with specific and relevant details and examples.
Conventions of EAE	Exhibits minimal or no control of sentence structure and the conventions of Edited American English (EAE).	Demonstrates inconsistent control of sentence structure and the conventions of EAE.	Generally controls sentence structure and the conventions of EAE.	Consistently controls sentence structure and the conventions of EAE.
Word Choice	Exhibits weak and/or inappropriate words.	Exhibits a narrow range of word choice, often including inappropriate selections.	Exhibits appropriate word choice.	Exhibits varied and precise word choice.

Additional Essay Topics

Directions: Use these GED essay topics to get additional practice. Make sure you follow all the steps of the writing process to develop strong five-paragraph essays. Time your work so that you finish in 45 minutes. Use the GED Essay Scoring Guide to evaluate your work and figure out ways you can continue to improve.

── TOPIC 1 ──

Even though fear and anxiety are unpleasant emotions, many people spend money to watch horror movies. What makes horror movies so appealing?

In your essay, tell why you think people like to watch horror movies. Use specific reasons and examples in your response.

── TOPIC 2 ──

Though air travel has improved our lives in many ways, some people think it has created new problems. Do you think that air travel has improved modern life?

In your essay, explain whether you believe air travel has improved life. You may describe positive effects, negative effects, or both. Use specific reasons and examples in your response.

── TOPIC 3 ──

Why do people always want more money, no matter how much money they already have?

In your essay, tell why people always want more money, regardless of their financial position. Explain the reasons for your response.

--- T O P I C 4 ---

American society is a mixture of races, religions, and customs, which have brought benefits but also created problems not found in countries where citizens have similar backgrounds. What are the effects that our mixture of backgrounds has had on American society?

In your essay, explain the effects that our mixture of backgrounds has had on American society. Give specific examples to back up your reasoning.

--- T O P I C 5 ---

More and more mothers of young children are entering the workforce. As a result, these children are spending large amounts of time in daycare centers or with babysitters. How do you think this child-care arrangement affects small children as compared to children whose mothers stay at home?

In your essay, compare and contrast how you think this child-care arrangement affects small children versus children whose mothers stay at home. Give specific reasons to back up your ideas.

--- T O P I C 6 ---

In every society in the world, ceremonies are used to mark certain events, such as marriages, deaths, and birthdays. Why, do you think, are ceremonies so important to people?

In your essay, explain why ceremonies are so important to people. Use specific examples to support your reasons.

Answer Key

Chapter 1

Exercise 1, page 20

1. F   Time on our hands. *(What about it?)*
   S   We have time on our hands.
2. S   The overtired baseball team finished its practice.
   F   The overtired baseball team next to the bus. *(What about the team?)*
3. F   While you were sleeping on the couch. *(What happened?)*
   S   While you were sleeping, we took your picture.
4. F   The mileage on your car. *(What about the mileage?)*
   S   The mileage on your car is low.
5. S   Emmanuel works at the front desk.
   F   Emmanuel at the front desk of the hotel. *(What about Emmanuel?)*
6. F   The idea you had. *(What about the idea?)*
   S   The idea sounds good.

Exercise 2, page 22

Part A
1. Daniel and his son usually do the housework.
2. The task has been completed.
3. We plan to visit the cemetery on Saturday.
4. Fruits and vegetables are more healthful than candy.
5. Taxes can take a large chunk out of a paycheck.

Part B
Sample answers:
1. My friends *(S)* always will be there.
2. When she graduated, her parents *(S)* threw her a party.
3. The copying machine out back is broken *(P)*.
4. Sasha thought we would never get the work done *(P)*.
5. Several copies of the memo disappeared *(P)*.

Part C
Sample answers:
1. The final pages of the book were written yesterday.
2. The supervisor liked what he saw. *(sentence)*

3. The woman was hurrying away from the car.
4. My wife worries about the future.

Exercise 3, page 24

Part A
1. Until you reach Huntington Station.
2. The largest source of revenue for the organization.
3. When you see him around the office.
4. If you are able to plan ahead and do some of your own research.

Part B
    Finding time for **yourself is** an important part of a healthful life. You may be neglecting your own **needs if** you are constantly focused on the needs of other people. Research shows that people who set aside time to do what they enjoy are actually better spouses, friends, and **coworkers than** those who spend all their time accommodating others.

Exercise 4, page 26

1. *simple subject:* countries; *verb:* have been *(linking)*
2. *simple subject:* we; *verb:* hiked *(action)*
3. *simple subject:* employee; *verb:* quit *(action)*
4. *simple subject:* Time; *verb:* seems *(linking)*
5. *simple subject:* banner; *verb:* hung *(action)*
6. *simple subject:* January; *verb:* arrived *(action)*
7. *simple subject:* member; *verb:* owned *(action)*
8. *simple subject:* procedures; *verb:* will be *(linking)*

Exercise 5, page 28

1. Mary will take this phone call.
   subject: Mary; *verb:* will take
2. (You) obey the rules of the game, please.
   subject: you; *verb:* obey
3. Several comments were written on the page.
   subject: comments; *verb:* were written
4. The pictures of your building are here.
   subject: pictures; *verb:* are
5. (You) don't tell me your ideas yet, Ms. Walton.
   subject: You; *verb:* don't tell
6. The supervisor did arrive.
   subject: supervisor; *verb:* did arrive

7. (You) think about your plans for the job.
   subject: you; *verb:* think
8. More effort should be in this.
   subject: effort; *verb:* should be

Exercise 6, page 29

If you are between the ages of 45 and 75, you may want to buy whole life insurance at an affordable **rate**. Have you considered the future of your **dependents? You** probably want them to be **covered if** you become ill or incapacitated. Call our toll-free **number. Hurry!**

Exercise 7, page 30

1. *subject:* Marika and Leroy; *verb:* joined
2. *subject:* you; *verb:* find or sit
3. *subject:* line; *verb:* forms and exits
4. *subject:* energy and commitment; *verb:* are needed

Exercise 8, page 31

Managers and salespeople will arrive tomorrow. Please be sure that **offices,** conference **rooms,** and lounges are neat and tidy. The documents for the **meeting** should be prepared by the end of today. Everyone will need **to** greet our colleagues, attend all meetings, and join us for dinner tomorrow night. This conference promises to be the best ever!

Exercise 9, page 33

Thank you for your **letter**, which we received on **Monday**. We appreciate it when our **customers** let us know their **thoughts** about our **products**.

As you know, we here at **The Dairy Company** work hard to make excellent dairy **products**. We believe our **yogurt, butter, cheese,** and **salad dressings** are of excellent **quality**. Each **employee** here does his or her best **work** to ensure top **quality**.

Unfortunately, we do make **mistakes**. The **yogurt** you purchased at your local **grocery store** was mislabeled. The **label** should have read "Raspberry/Banana" instead of simply "Raspberry." We are sorry that you had to throw away all six **cups** of **yogurt** because of this **problem**.

As an **apology** to you, **Ms. Williams**, we have enclosed a **coupon** with this **letter**. Take this **coupon** to a **store** near your **home** and you will receive 12

cups of your favorite **flavors**.

Again, we are sorry for the **trouble**. Please have a good **day**.

Exercise 10, page 35

Part A
1. months
2. Senator; office
3. building; Building.
4. Japanese; door
5. winter

Part B

Shopping for **groceries** can be a quick errand to grab some **milk**. Or it can be an exhausting **day** in the aisles of **Saveway Grocery Store**, in which you do hundreds of math calculations in order to save a few **dollars**. **Writing** the week's grocery list before you leave **home** can help you buy only what you need. Without a list, you may end up buying on impulse—an extra pint of **ice** cream that you really don't need, for example. In addition, the **Sunday** newspaper usually carries lots of valuable coupons that will help you save money. **Fifty** cents off a bottle of **Clorox** bleach can go a long way toward a lower grocery bill, especially if you are not choosy about what kind of **laundry bleach** you use.

Exercise 11, page 37

Part A
1. The newspaper's weather report says it will rain.
2. The girls' argument ended when their mother called.
3. The town's pool is closed for cleaning.
4. Marcus's dog is a Labrador retriever.
5. The Binders' apartment is down the street.
6. Women's clothing is often impractical.

Part B
To: All Night-Shift **Employees**

This **shift's** performance this past week has not been of high quality. The **manager's** office was not vacuumed last night, and the **halls** have not been vacuumed all week. Our **contracts** clearly state that this **shift's** responsibilities include vacuuming. Please do better on next **week's** shift.

Exercise 12, page 38

1. cookies
2. Les

3. Rob
4. Susan and Rob
5. clerk
6. shelves

Exercise 13, page 40

Part A
1. We
2. their
3. its
4. your
5. her
6. ours

Part B
1. She
2. him
3. My
4. it
5. them; their
6. your
7. her
8. They

Exercise 14, page 41

1. her   (*Keep an eye on* **her**.)
2. he   (*Where did* **he** *go after work?*)
3. him and me   (*Flu hit* **him**. *Flu hit* **me**.)
4. They   (**They** *will be at the conference.*)
5. he   (**He** *spoke.*)
6. us   (*They met* **us**.)
7. me   (*Give the check to* **me**.)
8. them   (*A new apartment would give* **them** *more space.*)

Exercise 15, page 42

My wife and **I** would like to complain about the poor condition of the apartment complex. **Your** superintendent here, Mrs. Mitchell, is not doing **her** job very well at all.

The hallways are never swept, and we can see dust and dirt all over **them**. We have told Mrs. Mitchell about the hallways, but when will **she** clean them? Both **she** and her son seem lazy.

In addition the garbage sits in **its** bin for more than a week, smelling up the building incredibly. The stench really bothers my wife and **me**. Mrs. Mitchell and her son should take **their** job more seriously.

You or **she** must take care of this problem, Mr. Howe. Otherwise, **we** will have to start looking for a new apartment. Please be considerate of **your** tenants. We do not want to move.

Exercise 16, page 44

It's a common problem, say **doctors**. People are not getting enough healthful sleep. "There's growing concern," reports Dr. John Santiago of North Medical Center, "that stress and unhealthful **habits** are preventing many people from getting the sleep they need to function well." The good news, however, is that **there's** a lot you can do about it.

First of all, doctors advise, pay attention to **your** sleep patterns. Do you stay up late reading in bed, then have difficulty falling asleep? Or do you fall asleep quickly, only to awaken several **times** a night? The person **who's** aware of his or her sleeping patterns is already on the track to a better night's sleep.

Surprisingly enough, what you eat can affect how you sleep. If **you're** the kind of person who eats a large, spicy dinner accompanied by beer or wine, there's evidence that **your** sleep may be affected. "**It's** simple," states Dr. Santiago. "Your body is like a machine. One system affects another." His advice is to eat smaller **meals** throughout the day rather than one huge one shortly before bed. In addition, he says, alcohol creates sleep disturbances. "**Its** sedative qualities induce sleep unnaturally," says the doctor.

What about people who sleep too much? "**Their's** is sometimes a more serious problem," states Dr. Santiago. "A person who sleeps a lot during the day may have some kind of physical illness that he's unaware of. Or perhaps depression is the cause. Either way, **it's** a problem that a **doctor's** appointment will help solve."

Editing Practice, page 45

Are you planning on retirement soon? Or are you changing jobs? If so, think about **your** financial needs. You might consider a lump-sum distribution from your **employer**. This is a popular course of **action taken** by many people. But is it a wise **move**?

Financial experts across the **country** believe there is a better way. With a rollover IRA you can avoid **taxes**, IRS **penalties**, and unnecessary paperwork. Here's what Arthur C. Evans of **Chicago, Illinois**, says about his MajorBank rollover IRA: "I **received** personalized attention from a retirement specialist. **He** turned out to be a real help to my wife and **me when** we needed investment advice."

Without a rollover IRA, **you're** risking up to 35

percent of **your** savings to **federal** and state taxes. In addition, **there** might be early withdrawal penalties. Call MajorBank **now to** get your free brochure.

Chapter Review, page 46

1. (2) The possessive pronoun *its* does not use an apostrophe. The contraction *it's (it is)* does.
2. (4) The subject pronoun *she* is correct since it is part of the compound subject of the verb *were*.
3. (3) The possessive pronoun *their* is correct; *they're* is the contraction meaning *they are*.
4. (4) Sentence 8 is a fragment.
5. (2) A comma should come after the first two items in a series.
6. (3) Sentence 11 is actually a fragment. Join the two groups of words together to make a complete sentence.
7. (1) Detroit is the name of a city; it should be capitalized.
8. (4) The word *countries* is not a proper noun; it should not be capitalized.
9. (3) *Hartford Daily News* is the title of a newspaper; each word should be capitalized.
10. (4) The possessive pronoun *your* is needed to show possession of the noun *company*.
11. (5) The original is actually a sentence fragment. Adding the subject *I* and changing the verb to agree with it makes a complete sentence.
12. (4) Two subject pronouns are needed since they are the subject of *get*.
13. (4) Avoid shifting pronouns from *one* to *I*.
14. (2) The contraction *it's*, meaning *it is*, is correct.
15. (1) A comma between the subject and predicate is incorrect.

Chapter 2

Exercise 1, page 53

Part A
1. will mail *(tomorrow)*
2. satisfied *(in 1990)*
3. arrives *(every day; takes)*
4. dipped *(last month)*
5. skips *(usually; makes up)*
6. dips *(each day)*
7. will begin *(later this morning)*
8. likes *(always; sees)*

Part B
Sample answers:
1. During 1999 many computer programmers prepared for the millennium.
2. Next month my son will prepare for his exams.
3. When my friend was younger, she played with dollhouses.
4. Every day I try to exercise.
5. When I think about myself, I get anxious.
6. Before I die, I want to write a novel.

Exercise 2, page 54
1. will be flying
2. am thinking
3. will be leaving
4. was doing

Exercise 3, page 56
1. had cleaned
2. has worked
3. talked
4. will have passed
5. had
6. will make

Exercise 4, page 59

Part A
1. (has) gone
2. saw
3. (have) run
4. brought
5. laid
6. came
7. were
8. ('s—has) run
9. sit
10. am

Part B
We have **come** to the end of our fiscal year, and it **is** now my pleasure to announce our budget results. Although we **ran** over on some expenses, I am happy to report that we **did (or have done)** well. We have reached our sales goals for the year! With that happy news it is clear that by next September we **will have** become leaders in the company. Congratulations on a job well done.

Last year at this time, as you may recall, things **did** not look so rosy. We **were** in debt, and the president of our division **had** predicted disaster. So we should be proud of what we **have** done and **raise** our expectations even higher for next year.

Exercise 5, page 61

I **am** writing to you to request a letter of recommendation for a manager's job for which I am applying at the Downtown Sports Arena. I believe I **am** a perfect candidate for this position, and I think you will be able to say something positive about my qualifications.

As you know, I was a basketball instructor in your program from January 1999 until January 2000. I **was** a great member of your team. The kids in my class and my fellow instructors liked me and admired me. If you check my employment record, you will find that I **took** only one sick day that year and was never late for work. In fact, on many occasions, I **worked** overtime when the other instructors didn't show up for work.

I hope to become a manager for the Downtown Sports Arena, and I think I **will do** a good job as a manager there. If you are willing to write a recommendation for me, I will be very grateful. I **have** seen that you are a good person, and I enjoyed working for you.

Exercise 6, page 63

1. doesn't
2. were
3. live
4. doesn't
5. jogs
6. don't
7. have
8. is
9. looks
10. think

Exercise 7, page 65

Part A
1. wants
2. stop
3. check
4. provides
5. provide
6. are
7. offer
8. interfere

Part B

An ulcer **is** a sore on the lining of your stomach or small intestine. Stress and spicy food **do** not cause an ulcer, but they do irritate it. Actually, either an infection or some medicines **cause** ulcers. Recognizing the symptoms of an ulcer and knowing what to do if you have one **are** important steps toward feeling better.

We **don't** know how people acquire the bacteria that can cause ulcers. However, research **shows** that long-term use of nonsteroidal anti-inflammatory medicines can cause ulcers. Also, older men **are** at higher risk of developing intestinal ulcers, while older women develop more stomach ulcers. Both cigarettes and alcohol **are** also contributing factors.

Exercise 8, page 67

Part A
1. are (*glasses*)
2. is (*photograph*)
3. Do (*we*)
4. take (*[You]*)
5. are (*things*)
6. doesn't (*government*)
7. aren't (*doctors*)
8. put (*[You]*)

Part B

Are Americans becoming more interested in physical fitness? There **are** many indications that they are. There **has** been an increase in the popularity of biking, swimming, and hiking. There **are** many companies that offer free use of gyms for their employees. They **find** that it saves more money on health insurance than it costs them to provide wellness programs. **Do** you do anything special to keep in shape? What fitness activities **are** you interested in?

Exercise 9, page 70

1. seem
2. are
3. have
4. are
5. appears
6. has
7. helps
8. look
9. were
10. starts

Exercise 10, page 73

Part A

1. wants *(Everyone)*
2. were *(None)*
3. melts *(Some)*
4. understand *(Most)*
5. arrive *(Few)*
6. has *(Someone)*
7. bites *(one)*
8. attends *(Neither)*

Part B

Our communications class would like to invite you to speak to our department this spring. Many **have** spoken of your valuable experience and excellent skills. It would be an honor to have you share your expertise. Everyone hopes you can fit us into your busy schedule.

Our class is studying media influences on popular culture. Anything related to this topic **is** a good idea for your talk. Since no one has spoken about the upcoming local elections, you may be interested in addressing this topic. Or perhaps you'd rather speak about the more general topic of the Internet. Either **is** fine with us.

Please call me at 555-1313 to discuss this matter further, Ms. Howard. Someone is always in the office. Thank you.

Editing Practice, page 74

Job satisfaction for all employees **is** possible when you work at it. As a manager you are responsible for making sure employees stay on the job and perform well. Here **are** some steps you can take to ensure job satisfaction in your department.

Step 1: Be clear about what the job is. Everyone wants to know exactly what he or she is expected to do each day. Don't add or take away tasks unless you **discuss** it with the employee first.

Step 2: Recognize excellent performance. You can do this in writing or speech. Either **is** acceptable as long as the employee gets the message clearly. Praise and support **make** an employee feel that you value the work he or she does.

Step 3: Include all employees in the decision-making process as much as possible. Why **don't** workers always follow the rules you've set? Often it is because they **do** not feel any ownership of those rules. Allowing them to help establish guidelines can go a long way toward job satisfaction.

Chapter Review, page 75

1. (2) The verb *do* agrees with the subject of the sentence, *you*.
2. (3) The past-tense *were* is consistent in this passage.
3. (5) No correction is necessary.
4. (2) This is a command. The understood subject is *you*. The verb that agrees with *you* does not end in *s*.
5. (1) Change the order of the words to find the subject: *People are there.*
6. (4) The subject is plural, so use *are*, not *is*.
7. (2) The subject of the sentence is *he*, and the correct verb is *doesn't*.
8. (4) Watch out for the prepositional phrases *of working* and *with children*. The actual subject of the sentence, *joy*, is singular.
9. (5) The verb that agrees with the subject *you* is *know*, not *knows*.
10. (1) The subject of the sentence is *speed and accuracy*, a compound. Therefore, the verb *are* is correct.
11. (4) The prepositional phrase *in management* does not contain the subject of the sentence. The subject is the indefinite pronoun *those*, which agrees with *want*.
12. (2) The sentence refers to an action that will take place in the future.
13. (2) The verb *has* agrees with the subject *everybody*.
14. (4) The subject *anyone* is a singular indefinite pronoun that agrees with *is*.
15. (3) The future perfect-tense *will have completed* is correct. Note the clue words *by the end of next month*.

Cumulative Review, page 79

1. (3) Try placing the subject before the verb: *dogs are*, not *dogs is*.
2. (2) Joining the two phrases into one makes a complete sentence.
3. (2) Change the order of the words in the sentence to find the simple subject: *Good reasons have to be there.*

4. (3) Watch out for the prepositional phrase *of dogs* when you are looking for the subject of the sentence. The simple subject is singular—*reason*.

5. (2) As it stands, this group of words is a fragment. Adding the subject and verb *they follow* makes it a complete sentence.

6. (4) This passage is in the present tense, so use *is* here.

7. (3) Remember that the possessive pronoun does not use an apostrophe.

8. (5) The possessive *their* is correct, not the contraction *they're*, which means *they are*.

9. (4) The possessive pronoun *your* is correct, not the contraction *you're* (*you are*).

10. (1) The clue words *next week* indicate that the action will take place in the future, so *will head* is correct.

11. (4) *Ohio* is the name of a specific state, so it should be capitalized.

12. (2) The indefinite pronoun *no one* is the subject, and it agrees with the verb *was*.

13. (3) When a compound subject is joined by *neither . . . nor*, the verb should agree with the subject closer to it—in this case *I*.

14. (1) The subject of the sentence is plural—*pointers*.

15. (5) The second group of words is a fragment; add it to the first group of words to make a complete sentence.

Chapter 3

Exercise 1, page 85

Part A

Sample answers:

1. The phone was ringing, **so** the assistant answered it.

2. It was time for us to go, **and** the waitress got our coats.

3. Your résumé looks impressive, **but** we have no job openings at the moment.

4. I did not like the computer class, **nor** did I like the keyboard class.

5. Please bring a pen, **or** you will have nothing with which to write.

6. The staff always reads the memo board carefully, **for** it contains important information.

Part B

Sample answers:

1. The Amadeos wanted a new car, but they could not afford one.

2. He wanted to be respected, yet he was behaving very badly.

3. Tua is studying computer science, for she'd like a job in an office.

4. We enjoy your company, so we want to invite you for dinner sometime.

5. The supervisor did not like the girl's attitude, nor did he appreciate her rude remarks.

6. The painters arrived early, and they stayed late.

7. The club needs new members, so it is looking for suggestions.

8. The Internet is a useful tool, yet not all Americans have equal access to it.

Exercise 2, page 86

1. The weather has been terrible, **so** the hotel parties have all been indoors.

2. We expect your company to investigate these complaints, and we want to hear from you before Friday so we can finally resolve this matter. **If** we do not hear from you, we will have to call a lawyer.

3. The manager told us he would be here early, **but** he arrived close to midnight.

4. We do not plan to come to the meeting, **nor will we** be at the conference.

Exercise 3, page 88

Part A

1. A cup of coffee and a piece of toast were all she ate today. *(correct)*

2. A cup of coffee, a piece of toast, and an orange were all she ate today.

3. Tuan asked for an application, and he sat down to fill it out.

4. Tuan asked for an application and sat down to fill it out. *(correct)*

5. Julio plans to become a mechanic, and Michael wants to be a teacher.

6. Julio plans to become a mechanic and a father. *(correct)*

7. Job openings are available in shipping, accounting, and filing.

8. The employee looked for a solution to the problem and found one. *(correct)*
9. The employee looked for a solution to the problem, and she found one.
10. This letter should be typed up and sent to all customers on our mailing list. *(correct)*

Part B

Thank you for your **letter and** your résumé. We are happy to hear of your **interest, enthusiasm,** and excitement.

The officers here at GenerCo, Inc., have looked over your **file,** and we have decided we are unable to offer you a job at this time. We are impressed by your résumé and **qualifications,** but there is not a position here that matches your skills. We need a **clerk and** an accountant, and your experience is not in these areas.

We hope that you will continue your job **search,** and we'd like to hear from you again when you have gained more experience. Again, thank you for your **interest, enthusiasm,** and good effort.

Exercise 4, page 92

Part A
Sample answers:
1. Please plan to fill out some forms **when** you see the doctor.
2. **So that** we can serve you better, we have a toll-free number.
3. **Even though** it was raining, the picnic was held outside.
4. **Since** it was raining, the picnic was held inside.
5. The contract has expired **because** it is past December 31.
6. With that résumé, you will find a job **wherever** you want to live.
7. I am planning to come **although** you do not want me to.
8. **Even though** you do not want me to, I am planning to come.

Part B
Sample answers:
1. I planned to go back to school, although it turned out that I never did.
2. The office is empty while the doctor is on vacation.
3. The man signed the papers so that his son could be released from the hospital.

4. Since your order never shipped, we will refund your money.

Exercise 5, page 93

Part A
1. The senator was met with hostility wherever he traveled that day. *(correct)*
2. After he gave this speech for the tenth time, he finally knew it by heart.
3. We want new offices even though these are closer to home. *(correct)*
4. Because her prices are lower, the vendor will supply the food.

Part B

Although many of you already have this **information, I** need to clarify a policy. When an employee takes a **vacation, his** or her supervisor must fill out a #20A form. We have fewer problems with **payroll when** everyone follows this procedure. You can let me **know if** you have any concerns or questions about this form. Thank you.

Exercise 6, page 95

1. This memo serves as a reminder that your rent has not been paid for the past six months. We will give your name to a collection **agency <u>if</u>** you do not provide full payment by May 1. Also, <u>whenever</u> you realize that you will be late with your **payment, it** is a good idea to notify us at once.
2. I have not paid my rent for six **months <u>because</u>** the landlord has not repaired the leaky roof yet. <u>Although</u> I have not **paid, I** have been keeping the rent in escrow for later. <u>When</u> you have finally taken care of the **roof, I'll** release the funds. <u>If</u> you need further information, please call me.
3. No repairs will be made on the <u>roof</u> **<u>until</u>** you have paid your back rent. <u>If</u> you had put your complaint in writing **sooner, we** could have solved this problem long ago. Please send a check now for $1,234 to my attention.
4. I will agree to send the money I **owe <u>when</u>** I have an agreement in writing that the roof will be repaired. Water from last night's rainstorm is dripping onto my living room **floor <u>as</u>** I sit writing this letter to you. <u>If</u> I hear from **you, I** will proceed with the payments.
5. This document outlines the schedule for roof repair. The project will **begin <u>as</u> <u>soon as</u>** you sign this letter and mail it back to me. I understand

your concern in this **matter although** I wish you had alerted me earlier to the problem. You have acted **unprofessionally, as** if you expected me to read your mind.

Exercise 7, page 96

1. We would like to order **even though** the store is out of stock.
2. The music sounded lovely, **so** she turned up the volume.
3. When you are ready, please let me know. *(correct)*
4. Mr. Enright blew the whistle, **and** the team stood still.
5. Sondra wanted a job, **but** she got a vacation.
6. The meeting was called to order, **and** we were asked to sit down.

Exercise 8, page 98

Sample answers:

1. The data-entry clerks will be unable to work since the computers are down.
2. You should call Mr. Chun, for you need a letter of recommendation.
3. I learn quickly on the job, but I have little experience.
4. Although we are understaffed today, all of those lawns need to be mowed.
5. Citizenship is a responsibility, so people should exercise their right to vote.
6. Buy now because our prices are at an all-time low!

Exercise 9, page 100

1. (4) Winnie packed up the last crate so that she could ship it out.
2. (1) Exio Company lost business, but it had a good growth plan.
3. (2) The vandals kicked in the door, but they didn't steal anything.
4. (3) When the clock struck twelve, the guests began to leave.

Exercise 10, page 102

1. (2) The first verb in the sentence is past tense; therefore, the past-tense *was paid* is correct.
2. (3) The conjunction *whenever* with the present tense means something that is always true. The present-tense *carry* shows the correct verb sequence.
3. (4) The second verb in the sentence is in the continuous past tense. The past-tense *slept* is in the correct sequence of tenses.
4. (1) The sentence is correct as written. A past perfect tense is in sequence with the past-tense *circulated*.

Exercise 11, page 104

1. Using computers, getting along well with people, and working with numbers are skills I have.
2. Parties & Company decorated the room, provided entertainment, and prepared the food.
3. When my supervisor arrives at work, she reads the newspaper, makes a pot of coffee, and gets on the phone to talk to her sister. If we do not interrupt her, she then does the crossword puzzle.
4. To keep your finances in good order, you need to write down every penny you spend and anticipate future expenses.

Editing Practice, page 105

Part B

Do you have trouble falling asleep at **night**, or do you wake up several times during the night? Insomnia, or unsatisfying sleep patterns, can affect all aspects of your life. Here are some tips to help you get relief **if** you are suffering from this malady.

1. Try to go to bed at the same time every night. Most adults find that somewhere between 9 P.M. and 11 P.M. is a healthy bedtime, but people can vary quite a bit.
2. Limit your use of alcohol and **caffeine before** you go to sleep. These substances throw off your natural body rhythms. In addition, eating fatty or spicy foods shortly before bedtime is unwise **because** these foods require extra work on the part of your body.
3. Exercise regularly. Exercise **gets your body ready for sleep, releases natural relaxation chemicals in your body, and helps relieve insomnia**.
4. Use your bedroom for sleeping purposes only. Eating, reading, or watching TV in bed "teaches" your body that it is not time to **rest even** though you might be tired.

Chapter Review, page 106

1. (2) Joining these two groups of words corrects the sentence fragment beginning with *because*. No comma is necessary when the dependent clause comes after the independent clause.
2. (3) A comma should separate the two clauses when the dependent clause comes first in the sentence.
3. (5) No correction is necessary.
4. (4) The paragraph is past tense. The future tense makes no sense here.
5. (1) Combining elements or ideas in a series gets rid of the wordy repetition of the original sentence.
6. (2) Remember that *however* is not a conjunction and cannot be used as one. *But* connects the two independent clauses correctly.
7. (3) The original conjunction, *so*, implies that there is a cause-and-effect relationship between the two actions, which there is not. Instead, the second clause just offers additional information, so *and* is an appropriate conjunction.
8. (3) Joining the fragment beginning with *if* forms a complete sentence. No comma is necessary because the dependent clause follows the independent clause.
9. (3) The only error in the original sentence is the inclusion of a comma after the independent clause. No comma is necessary here.
10. (1) Look closely at the compound here. The sentence contains a compound predicate, but it is not a compound sentence. Therefore, a comma before *and* is incorrect.
11. (5) No correction is necessary.
12. (1) There is no contrast relationship between the two clauses, so *although* is incorrect. A time relationship using the conjunction *when* is correct.
13. (4) The two clauses have a cause-and-effect relationship, and the conjunction *so* preceded by a comma is correct.
14. (3) Using the conjunction *and* to join a fragment to a complete sentence is an appropriate way to correct the error.
15. (3) This option effectively gets rid of the unnecessary repetition and wordiness of the original sentence.

Cumulative Review, page 111

1. (4) The noun *country* is not a proper noun and therefore should not be capitalized.
2. (2) The original sentence contains a comma splice. Separating it into two sentences is an effective way to correct the error.
3. (3) The subject of the sentence is *advertising*, a singular subject. Therefore, the verb *is* is correct.
4. (5) This option correctly joins the fragment to a complete sentence. No comma is necessary since the dependent clause follows the independent clause.
5. (5) The document is written in the present about events of the future. The future tense is correct here.
6. (5) No correction is necessary.
7. (4) Remember not to be confused by a *here* or *there* phrase. The subject of this sentence is *samples*, a plural noun. Therefore, *are*, not *is*, is the correct verb form.
8. (3) The document discusses an action that will happen in the future. No form of the past tense works here.
9. (2) The subject of the sentence is not *recommendation*. It is *things*, a plural noun. The correct verb is *are*.
10. (1) The possessive pronoun *your* is correct here, not the contraction meaning *you are*.
11. (4) The first verb of the sentence is in the past tense. The past-tense *were* is correct here.
12. (3) This sentence combines repetitive and wordy phrases into one smooth sentence.
13. (2) There is no contrast in the relationship between the two clauses. The time conjunction *when* correctly represents the relationship.
14. (3) The indefinite pronoun *no one* is the subject of the sentence, and it is singular. Therefore, *wants* is the correct verb form.
15. (2) The subject of the sentence is *morale and productivity*, a compound subject. Therefore, the verb *improve* is correct.

Chapter 4

Exercise 1, page 116

1. effective
2. ineffective

3. effective
4. ineffective
5. ineffective
6. ineffective

Exercise 2, page 118

1. (2) There are several things you can do to make study time more productive.
2. (3) A PureH$_2$0 water filtration system is your family's best source of drinking water.
3. (5) Here are our procedures for helping a coworker who has been burned.
4. (1) The following information provides the details for the Johnson deck.
5. (3) We are requesting a meeting to discuss these important problems in the company.

Exercise 3, page 122

1. (2) with sentence 5
2. (3) with sentence 4
3. (2) with sentence 6
4. (3) with sentence 7
5. (2) with sentence 5

Exercise 4, page 126

1. (2) move sentence 4 to the beginning of paragraph C

Exercise 5, page 130

1. (4) remove sentence 4
   (*This information about a hardware store has nothing to do with the changes at Linden Pharmacy.*)
2. (1) move sentence 6 to the end of paragraph A
   (*This sentence works as a summary statement to what was written about in the first paragraph. Moving it enables paragraph B to start with the first change in Linden Pharmacy policy.*)
3. (4) remove sentence 10
   (*This sentence about poor financial planning does not belong in a paragraph about how a pharmacy plans to bill its customers.*)
4. (3) move sentence 14 to the beginning of paragraph C
   (*This sentence is a good topic sentence for paragraph C, as it states what will be discussed in all the supporting sentences that follow.*)

Exercise 6, page 133

1. *cross out* This old lady is driving me nuts.
   (*The topic and tone do not belong in a business letter.*)
2. *cross out* Just be the dummy you are and ask.
   (*The tone of this sentence is disrespectful and unnecessary.*)
3. *cross out* The consequence of remaining immobile and indecisive on the complex decision of whether or not to construct a center in which all of our citizens may have the opportunity to recreate is that our town will no longer be able to entertain the possibility of said center.
   (*The tone of this sentence is inappropriately formal and stiff for this casual paragraph, written in an informal manner.*)
4. effective
5. effective

Editing Practice, page 134

I'd like to set up a meeting to discuss our business relationship with you. We have worked together for two years now, and I think it is time to consider what works and what does not work. Then we can agree on how to proceed with future contracts.

There are three major topics we need to address, as I see it. Of course, if you have other ideas, we can certainly discuss these as well. We have an excellent relationship that is worth taking care of.

The first topic that needs to be addressed is maintenance scheduling. Our current contract requires two monthly inspection and maintenance calls; my staff and I believe that one per month would be adequate. It would be beneficial to all of us if we could agree on an effective schedule.

The second subject I'd like to discuss is personnel. Unfortunately, some of your technicians are rude and uncooperative. They have actually threatened several of my tenants in the past. ~~What a huge pain in the neck they are, man!~~ We'd like you to assure us that all of your staff will meet or exceed your own high expectations.

Finally, the cost factor of our current agreement needs discussing. Your services are excellent, but there are other less expensive businesses that might be of equal or better quality. Unless we can get a reduction in price, we may be forced to look elsewhere.

Please call my office, Mr. Otis, at your convenience. We look forward to working out these issues so that we may have a continued business relationship in the future. ~~I call 'em like I see 'em is all I can say!~~ My best to you and your staff.

Chapter Review, page 135

1. (5) A sentence about finding a lawn mower does not belong in a piece about selecting the right paint.
2. (2) This sentence makes a good topic sentence for paragraph C. All of the sentences in paragraph C discuss the differences between oil- and water-based paints.
3. (5) The tone and word choice of this sentence are inappropriate.
4. (2) The sentences in paragraph D are about paint color. This answer is the only topic sentence that mentions color.
5. (2) This sentence begins a discussion of another factor in the selection of paint—shine. This is a good place to start a new paragraph.
6. (2) This sentence belongs in the introductory paragraph, the paragraph that tells what the whole piece of writing is about.
7. (1) The main idea of this piece of writing is reasons to support Enviroworld. The idea of supporting other causes does not belong.
8. (2) This sentence is not a good topic sentence, and it should not come first in the paragraph. Moving it to follow sentence 10 makes logical sense.
9. (2) This sentence changes the topic from children and grandchildren to cost. This is a good topic sentence for all the supporting sentences that follow.
10. (3) The supporting sentences of paragraph E list ways to donate to Enviroworld. This sentence makes an effective topic sentence for the paragraph.

Cumulative Review, page 139

1. (4) The word *Religious* is not a proper noun and does not require a capital letter.
2. (1) This revision corrects the sentence fragment error; the verb form *are* agrees with the plural noun *instructions*.
3. (5) This sentence follows logically from the topic sentence of paragraph B.
4. (4) This sentence calls for the possessive pronoun *your*, not the contraction *you're*, which means *you are*.

5. (4) This sentence does not relate to the topic of how to request to vote by mail. The sentence is not relevant and should be deleted from the paragraph.
6. (2) This version cuts down on wordiness and makes the sentence easier to understand. The original sentence contains lots of repetition.
7. (3) This revision corrects the sentence fragment error; no comma is needed before *to make*.
8. (2) These two independent clauses require a conjunction to correct the comma splice error.
9. (1) The understood subject of a command is *you*, which requires a plural verb not ending in *s* by the rules of subject-verb agreement.
10. (4) December is the specific name of a month; as a proper noun, it must be capitalized.
11. (5) The original sentence is a run-on. One way to correct a run-on is to make two separate, complete sentences.
12. (3) This sentence has nothing to do with the subject of the letter, which is selling winter merchandise.
13. (2) The original sentence uses the subordinating conjunction *although*, which incorrectly implies a contrast. The conjunction *because* is more appropriate since a cause-effect relationship is expressed here.
14. (5) This sentence is an effective concluding sentence for paragraph D. It does not make sense as a first, or topic, sentence.
15. (5) The original sentence contains the possessive noun *store's*, which does not make any sense. The correct noun is the plural *stores*.

Chapter 5

Exercise 1, page 146

Sample answers:

1. **Carefully**, the carpenter tossed the scrap wood into a corner of the room.
2. Unfortunately, the program is **disorganized**.
3. The workers **rapidly** assembled a prototype for the exhibition.
4. Mary reminded me that red felt-tip markers are **usually** needed at the meeting.
5. Did you make reservations for a **late** lunch on

Wednesday?

6. **Fortunately**, the student discovered his mistake.

7. **Enthusiastically**, the orchestra began its sold-out concert.

8. Several times last year, the committee avoided a **huge** problem by planning ahead.

9. When will we be able to see the **spectacular** video, Mr. Alsbach?

10. **Additional** time is needed to complete the work we've begun together.

Exercise 2, page 148

Part A

1. The governor called out the National Guard to prevent looting after the shopping-mall fire.

2. The campers were awakened by a bear rummaging through their backpacks.

3. Shouting and whistling approval, the crowd gave Slime Green a standing ovation.

4. By driving an alternate route, the trucker avoided the weigh station.

Part B

Sample answers:

1. The child, **looking both ways first**, crossed the street.

2. The package arrived **sooner than expected**.

3. **Later than expected**, the package arrived.

4. Chris stared in horror at the tarantula **as it crawled closer to Josh.**

Exercise 3, page 150

1. Feeling totally overworked, the workers were delighted to get the news of a holiday.

2. Paul felt a large blob of bubble gum stuck under his chair.

3. Larry stared gloomily at his wheat field destroyed by hail.

4. The outraged prisoner, screaming for freedom, was led to his cell by a guard.

5. Harry found his glasses hidden under a pile of newspapers.

6. With a stern warning, the traffic officer handed me a ticket.

7. Eager to hire top technicians, Internet companies are giving many people large bonuses.

8. The beautiful woman, wearing her newest dress, walked with her husband.

Exercise 4, page 152

Sample answers:

1. As the technician threaded the machine, the spool slipped to the floor.

2. Because the train was departing on track 12, the commuter anxiously rushed ahead.

3. The bill will be $90.40 when you buy a new calculator.

4. As the machine crossed over the hedge, a wheel fell off.

5. Since we have received your check, a new bill will be sent out.

6. I was crying inconsolably, so the tears just kept flowing long after the movie ended.

Exercise 5, page 153

1. The winner of our customer contest, a teenage boy, will get the grand prize.

2. The program, a new documentary about Africa, was shown last night.

3. Renew.com, an Internet company, has been purchased by a larger company.

4. Howard, our neighbor across the street, sells life insurance.

5. This office, the site of our monthly meetings, has inspired us all.

6. Time, the healer of all wounds, has been passing very slowly.

Exercise 6, page 156

Part A

1. A parent needs to be ~~patient~~ and a firm disciplinarian.
   A parent needs to be a patient person and a firm disciplinarian.

2. Eating good food, ~~to swim~~ in the ocean, and sleeping are great vacation activities.
   Eating good food, swimming in the ocean, and sleeping are great vacation activities.

3. The featured speaker was unprepared, rude, and ~~a disappointment~~ during our annual conference.
   The featured speaker was unprepared, rude, and disappointing during our annual conference.

4. We can solve math problems by adding, subtracting, ~~multiplication~~, and dividing.
   We can solve math problems by adding, subtracting, multiplying, and dividing.

5. Why does Ms. Santorelli treat the staff like slaves but ~~she acts~~ as if she is the world's nicest boss?

Why does Ms. Santorelli treat the staff like slaves but act as if she is the world's nicest boss?

6. The movers <u>lifted the desks from the truck, carried them into the building, and</u> ~~they~~ placed them in offices.

The movers lifted the desks from the truck, carried them into the building, and placed them in offices.

Part B

Due to your hard work, dedication, and ~~being diligent~~ **diligence**, this past week was one of Interior Hotel's best ever. Our rooms were fully booked, and we received no customer complaints. The entire management team thanks you for your efforts. In honor of your teamwork, we plan to give an extra paid day off next month, ~~offering~~ **to offer** a free night's stay at any of our partner hotels, and to schedule a celebration banquet over the holiday season. Thank you again for all you do for the hotel, management, and each other.

Exercise 7, page 158

1. With the growing technology industry, **many companies will** need more and more skilled workers in the months ahead.
2. The manager told **my colleague** that my colleague would need to travel to Houston at least once a month.
3. correct
4. Sam and Ted got into a terrible argument after **Ted** called **Sam** a liar.
5. correct
6. In the memo, **management** says that there is a hiring freeze in effect until the first of the year.
7. The files and the disks were late getting to the office because **the files** had been lost in our warehouse.
8. As **Susan** approached, the woman behind the desk said, "May I help you?"

Exercise 8, page 162

Part A
1. its *(company)*
2. her *(woman)*
3. their *(sons)*
4. it is *(problem)*
5. They *(runners)*
6. their *(all)*
7. her *(boss)*

8. he begins *(man)*
9. its *(company)*
10. his or her *(Everyone)*

Part B

The easiest way to get to the conference center is by either car or by subway. If you are driving from the south, try to hook up with <u>someone</u> from the office. ~~They'll~~ **He'll (or She'll)** appreciate a ride. Take I-92 to Exit 14 and bear left at the end of the ramp. When you get to Linset Street on your right, take it for about 5 miles. <u>Everyone</u> should park ~~their~~ **his or her** car in the back lot.

If you want to take the subway, use the Purple Line toward South Station. <u>Most</u> subway cars post ~~its~~ **their** destination clearly on the display window. When you get to South Station, switch trains and take the Blue Line toward Englewood. The <u>company</u> will be sure that ~~their~~ **its** shuttle bus is there to pick you up.

Exercise 9, page 165

Part A
1. I *(My)*
2. their *(Most)*
3. he or she *(person)*
4. he sees *(George)*
5. their *(Animals)*

Part B

If you want to build a bookcase, first decide what kind of lumber **you want** to use. Then measure the place where you plan to put the bookcase. When you go to the lumberyard, the salesperson will help you figure out how much wood to buy. When you get it home, remeasure everything, using pencil to make marks on the wood. Then cut where you have put **your** pencil marks. Assemble the wood pieces with nails or glue. **You** may want to use both for added strength.

Editing Practice, page 166

We, the citizens of this town, need to take back control of our streets. Crime has been increasing at an unprecedented rate over the past several years, and it is time for us to put a stop to **it. When we were** growing up, our doors were never locked. We worked, shopped, and played without worrying whether our homes would be vandalized or robbed. Nowadays, one cannot leave **one's** house without locking it up tight as a drum.

What can we do? First of all, we can get to know **our** neighbors again. If someone comes to our door and asks us to watch **his (or her)** home while he is away, we should say yes! Keep an eye out for people who act suspiciously around our neighborhoods, and report **them** to the police. Let's take care of each other's property as if it were our own.

Second, support our local police. A police officer in this town works hard for a living, and **he (or she) deserves** respect from the community. Please consider attending the annual Police Officers' Ball, usually held in November. It is a night of great entertainment, good cheer, and ~~very friendly~~ **friendship**. **If you are** unable to go, **you can** at least buy a ticket to support the cause.

Last, use the power of your vote to elect councilmen and councilwomen who care about controlling crime. After being in office for over 10 years, **Councilman McHenry needs to step down**. He has consistently been in favor of reducing police salaries, cutting back on neighborhood youth programs, **and letting** criminals get off with light sentences. McHenry has to go!

Chapter Review, page 167

1. (2) The renaming phrase *once bulky and expensive machines* must be set off with a comma before and after it.
2. (2) The pronoun *they* is vague; it does not have a proper antecedent. A good substitute is *some educators*.
3. (4) The original sentence does not contain parallel structure. The three elements are *analyze, select*, and *decide*.
4. (1) The antecedent is *children*, so the pronoun must agree in number (plural) and person (third)—*they*.
5. (5) This sentence is correct as written.
6. (4) The antecedent to the pronoun in the underlined phrase is *person*. Therefore, the third-person singular *he* is correct.
7. (5) The phrase *as well as* connects the two ideas without any repetition. Deleting *having* makes the compound predicate parallel.
8. (3) The original sentence does not contain parallel structure. The four items in the series are *buy, remodel, sending*, and *take*. If you replace *sending* with *send*, the elements will be parallel.
9. (2) The passage uses the second person throughout; therefore, the third-person pronoun *his* is incorrect.
10. (5) The original sentence contains a dangling modifier: *shopping for this type of loan*. This correction gets rid of any confusion and matches the rest of the passage in terms of pronoun reference.
11. (2) The pronoun *we* is not correct since the rest of the passage uses the second-person pronoun, *you*.
12. (4) To make the series *tax deductible, low cost, and an easy loan* parallel in structure, you should replace *an easy loan* with simply the adjective *easy*.
13. (3) The pronoun *one* is third person, unlike the second person used throughout the passage. Correct it by substituting *you*.
14. (2) The renaming phrase *a government-secured loan* tells more about the subject, *the HUD loan*. It must be set off with commas from the rest of the sentence.
15. (1) The antecedent to the pronoun is *Federal Housing Authority*, a singular noun. Therefore, the singular pronoun *its* is correct, not the plural *their*.

Cumulative Review, page 172

1. (3) The subject of the clause is *bus service*, a singular noun. Therefore, the verb *provide* is incorrect. This answer corrects this error while keeping the possessive *yours* in the correct form.
2. (2) This answer correctly joins the two sentences without any unnecessary repetition.
3. (5) The original sentence contains a dangling modifier. The *suitcases* did not wait for what seemed like hours. This answer adds a subject, *we*, for the modifying phrase to describe.
4. (3) This sentence makes an excellent topic sentence for paragraph C, so it should begin that paragraph. All the sentences that follow support this main idea.
5. (1) The conjunction *and* joins two independent clauses in this sentence and requires a comma after *station*.

6. (3) The original sentence incorrectly implies a contrasting relationship by using the conjunction *yet*. The relationship that should be expressed is one of cause and effect, so *yet* should be replaced with *so*.

7. (3) The possessive form *their* is correct. *They're* is a contraction meaning *they are*.

8. (5) To make the series *an explanation, apologizing, and some monetary recompense* parallel in structure, replace *apologizing* with the noun *an apology*.

9. (2) The subject of the sentence is a compound formed with *both . . . and. Are*, the verb that agrees with a plural subject, is correct.

10. (5) This answer choice makes the sentence parallel in structure without any unnecessary repetition.

11. (2) This sentence is irrelevant. It does not belong in a paragraph about ways to light a charcoal fire.

12. (5) This sentence is correct as written.

13. (4) The original sentence is wordy and redundant. Answer choice (4) gets rid of the extra words.

14. (3) The original sentence contains a comma splice. By adding the conjunction *because* after the comma, you correct the error.

15. (4) The contraction *you're* is not a proper noun and therefore should not be capitalized.

Chapter 6

Exercise 1, page 178

Part A
1. river, United States
2. cities
3. Thursday
4. winter
5. town hall

Part B
June 5, 2001
To: Ms. Sanders
From: Renée Armstrong
I would like to request the following days off: Monday, **July** 6, **Thursday, August** 10, and two **days** in September that I have not yet chosen. My **mother** has been sick, and I need the time off to help care for her. Since I will have to travel to **South** Carolina on these dates, simply an afternoon off is not sufficient.

Please let me know, **Ms.** Sanders, if these dates are okay with you.

Exercise 2, page 182

Part A
1. right
2. affect
3. passed
4. all ready
5. whether
6. through
7. break
8. principal
9. new
10. too

Part B
This report summarizes the sales events we have planned for the month of January. It was decided that all holiday merchandise **already** marked down will be sold for an additional 25 percent off. Our **whole** inventory of men's and women's clothing will be 30 percent off, now **through** February 1. **It's** important for all employees to be present to help with labeling. Customers should be informed that **their** discounts will be taken at the register. This coming **week** will be an important one for the sales department.

Exercise 3, page 185

1. The change order requested that the part be measured, polished, and shipped.
   Rule # 1
2. The train will depart as soon as all passengers are aboard.
   Rule # 6
3. Martha's manager, a great guy, is planning to retire next year.
   Rule # 3
4. The kitchen was out of potatoes, so the assistant chef went to the market.
   Rule # 4
5. Although the meeting is in Philadelphia, a teleconference is planned as well.
   Rule # 5
6. Please set up all the folding chairs so that there is room for everyone.
   Rule # 6
7. Immediately, the fire department was called to the scene.
   Rule # 2

8. My uncle, my brother, and my stepfather all work for United Companies.
    Rule # 1

9. Sandra wants to see the new movie, but we would like to go out to eat.
    Rule # 4

10. Ms. Ortega, an immigrant from Chile, came to our class yesterday.
    Rule # 3

Editing Practice, page 186

Here is the information about the support group meeting that will take place on **Saturday**, June 2, this year. Please try to be there, for we will be discussing some very important issues all day. **There** will be lots of opportunities to visit with old friends and meet new ones. We will **talk, laugh, and** work together in support of each other's growth and development.

First of all, the meeting will be held at the Western Conference Center on Foley Avenue from 8:00 A.M. until 4:00 P.M. If you have not **registered, please** send your $25 registration fee to Mrs. Eileen Smith. Paying at the door is also an option, although the fee will then be $30. You should park in the lot to the right of the **building**.

To get to the conference center, travel north on Route 60 until you see signs for Millwood. Take Exit **12 and** bear right at the blinking yellow light. Go approximately 4 **miles, turn** left onto Brook **Street, and** take your first right onto Main Street. The conference center is on **your** left.

It is a good idea to bring your own beverages for the **day and** cash for lunch. We plan to get **through** our morning agenda by noon to enjoy a group-sponsored buffet lunch. Several **breaks** are also scheduled throughout the day.

Chapter Review, page 187

1. (2) The homonym *it's*, meaning *it is*, makes sense in this sentence—*It is holiday time.*
2. (3) The noun *kitchen* is not a proper noun and should not be capitalized.
3. (1) Items in a series must be separated by commas.
4. (3) The clause *If the turkey is very juicy* is a dependent clause, and since it comes first in the sentence, a comma should follow it.
5. (4) This option correctly places a comma between the items in a series—*soggy, pasty,* and *undercooked.*

6. (5) The homonym *meat* makes more sense here.
7. (1) A comma should be placed after the introductory phrase *As a final step.*
8. (4) The phrase the *residence of my grandmother* is an appositive and must be separated by commas.
9. (2) The two parts of the compound subject should not be separated with a comma.
10. (3) The homonym *knew*, past tense of *know*, is correct here.
11. (4) All words of this title should be capitalized— *Department of Human Services.*
12. (1) Placing a comma after *room* is correct because *room* is part of a series joined by *and.*
13. (5) The homonym *hear*, meaning *to listen*, is incorrect. *Here*, meaning *in this place*, is the correct choice.
14. (2) The possessive pronoun *your* is correct, not the contraction *you're*, meaning *you are.*
15. (5) The word *community* is not a proper noun and therefore should not be capitalized.

Cumulative Review, page 191

1. (2) This sentence consists of two clauses joined by *and.* A comma should be placed before the conjunction.
2. (4) The plural possessive pronoun *their* does not agree with the singular antecedent *worker.* *Workers* is the best choice.
3. (3) To make all three elements of the series parallel, the word *to* must be deleted—*read, sign, return.*
4. (4) This sentence refers to the complaint copy. It belongs in the first paragraph.
5. (5) Sentence 8 is a fragment. The best way to join it to sentence 7 and keep all elements parallel is to write all three elements as adverbs.
6. (5) The past tense makes no sense here. The future *will be* is correct.
7. (1) This choice correctly joins the two sentences together, showing a cause-effect relationship.
8. (4) The plural pronoun *they* cannot correctly refer back to the singular noun *Someone.* This answer correctly uses singular pronouns joined by *or.*
9. (2) The subject of this inverted sentence is *reasons*, a plural noun. Therefore, the verb *are* is correct, not *is.*

10. (2) This option correctly places the modifying phrase closer to the noun it is describing.
11. (3) This choice moves the dependent clause to the beginning of the sentence.
12. (5) The correct homonym here is *affect*.
13. (3) Because this sentence introduces the main idea of the supporting sentences, it is an excellent topic sentence for the paragraph.
14. (3) The subject of the sentence is singular, *enrollment*, and the verb *has* shows correct subject-verb agreement.
15. (4) The possessive pronoun *yours* does not have an apostrophe.

Chapter 7

There are no exercises in Chapter 7.

Chapter 8

Exercise 1, page 213

Part A
1. d
2. c
3. a
4. b

Part B
3 Write
1 Gather ideas
4 Revise
2 Organize

Exercise 2, page 215

1. c
2. b
3. a

Exercise 3, page 216

1. introduction
2. body paragraph
3. body paragraph
4. body paragraph
5. conclusion

Chapter 9

Exercise 1, page 222

1. *Topic:* Economy cars vs. SUVs
   How you will respond: Compare and contrast
2. *Topic:* Why people overeat
   How you will respond: State causes and effects

Exercise 2, page 223

Sample answers:
1. SUVs are safer, more comfortable, and more attractive than economy cars.
2. People overeat because there is too much stress and boredom in their lives.

Exercise 3, page 225

Go over your idea list with another student or your instructor.

Exercise 4, page 227

Go over your idea map with another student or your instructor.

Writing a GED Essay, page 228

Use the ideas in Raising Your Score to evaluate your answers. Go over your answers with another student or your instructor. Figure out ways to think of a better idea list the next time you write.

Chapter 10

Exercise 1, page 233

1. comparison and contrast *(more)*
2. cause and effect *(bad)*
3. comparison and contrast *(better)*
4. order of importance *(most important)*
5. cause and effect *(causes)*

Exercise 2, page 234

1. Presidents of the United States (most recent to least recent)
   6 Gerald Ford
   4 Ronald Reagan
   3 George H.W. Bush
   1 George W. Bush

<u>2</u> Bill Clinton
<u>5</u> Jimmy Carter
2. Steps for starting a car at night
   <u>4</u> Turn on the headlights.
   <u>1</u> Open the door, get in, and close the door.
   <u>3</u> Turn the key in the ignition.
   <u>2</u> Put the key in the ignition.
   <u>5</u> Put the car in gear and start driving.
3. How to bake a cake using a mix
   <u>3</u> Pour the mixture into a greased cake pan.
   <u>4</u> Bake at 350 degrees for about 30 minutes.
   <u>1</u> Put the mix, two eggs, and 1/3 cup of oil in a bowl.
   <u>5</u> Cool completely before frosting.
   <u>2</u> Mix the ingredients.
4. My trip to the airport
   <u>1</u> Got up early.
   <u>6</u> Walked to the gate and got on my flight.
   <u>2</u> Ate breakfast and took a shower.
   <u>3</u> Took a cab to the subway stop.
   <u>5</u> Got off the train at the airport stop.
   <u>4</u> Got on the train.

Exercise 3, page 235

Show your completed paragraph to your instructor or another student.

Exercise 4, page 236

There are many possible ways to order these ideas. Share your ordered list with your instructor or another student. Talk about why you ordered it in this way. Why do you believe that this is the best way to order the list?

Exercise 5, page 236

Show your completed paragraph to your instructor or another student.

Exercise 6, page 237

There are many possible ideas you can gather for each of these topics. Show your idea lists to your instructor or another student. Explain why you answered the way you did. Make sure that all of the ideas are about the topic.

Exercise 7, page 238

Show your completed chart to your instructor or another student.

Exercise 8, page 240

There are many ways to arrange the groups in this idea map by order of importance. One way would be based on historical importance. You might begin with Dallas, then talk about the state capital, and then discuss the Alamo. Go over your idea map with another student or your instructor.

Exercise 9, page 244

Ideas/Supporting Details
Dental problems

Eating a lot of sugar causes tooth decay.

If children drink soda instead of milk, they won't get calcium for strong teeth.

Physical and emotional problems

Children who eat a lot of sweets may get fat.

Children who eat a lot of sweets may become hyperactive.

Lack of nutrients

Usually sweets lack vitamins.

Usually sweets lack protein.

~~Ice cream, candy, cookies, and cake are delicious.~~

Outlining
I. Dental problems
   A. Eating a lot of sugar causes tooth decay
   B. If children drink soda instead of milk, they won't get calcium for strong teeth
II. Physical and emotional problems
   A. Children who eat a lot of sweets may get fat
   B. Children who eat a lot of sweets may become hyperactive
III. Lack of nutrients
   A. Usually sweets lack vitamins
   B. Usually sweets lack protein

Exercise 10, page 247

Items to Discuss	Roommate	Living Alone
Cost	With a roommate, you can share the rent. With a roommate, you can split the cost of utilities.	Living alone, you have to pay the rent and utilities by yourself.
Housekeeping	You can share cleaning duties with a roommate.	
Friendship	When you have a roommate, you always have a friend to talk to. If you are lucky, you and your roommate will become friends.	It's lonely to live alone.

~~I once had three roommates in a small apartment~~.

Exercise 11, page 251

You need to add at least one idea to *Housekeeping: Living Alone.* One idea might be that if you live alone, you have to take care of all the housework yourself. Go over your idea with another student or your instructor.

Writing a GED Essay, page 251

Use the ideas in Raising Your Score to evaluate your answers to the exercise. Go over your answers with another student or your instructor. Figure out ways that you can organize your idea list better the next time you write an essay.

Chapter 11

Exercise 1, page 258

1. a. Pastimes
   b. There are many different kinds of pastimes.
   c. *Thesis:* My three favorite pastimes are walking in the park, reading good books, and going to the movies. *Main ideas of body paragraphs:* walking in the park, reading good books, and going to the movies.

2. a. Getting a GED
   b. There are many good reasons for getting a GED.
   c. *Thesis:* Passing the GED test will help me get a better job, make my husband feel proud of me, and help me feel better about myself. *Main ideas of body paragraphs:* better job, proud husband, and better feelings about self.

3. a. Life in small towns
   b. Life is good in small towns.
   c. *Thesis:* There are three things that make small-town life attractive: your life is simple and not congested, you know all your neighbors, and you feel safe. *Main ideas of body paragraphs:* life is simple, you know everyone, and you feel safe.

Exercise 2, page 262

Sample answers:
1. There are many good things we can do with the money from the property tax increase that we just voted in.
2. Every exercise develops a different part of the body.
3. Tyrone's mornings are always busy.

Exercise 3, page 263

Sample answers:
1. c; Stores sell a lot of candy around Valentine's Day.

   Many retail stores take advantage of holidays to boost their sales. For example, supermarkets usually promote picnic supplies around the Fourth of July, and you can always count on huge candy displays around Halloween. Another big season for candy occurs around Valentine's Day. In November supermarkets sell lots of Thanksgiving supplies, such as turkey, cranberry sauce, and pumpkins.

2. a; People love Chinese food like chow mein.

   American food is enriched by traditional foods from many different countries. For example, many Mexican foods are popular these days. People also love to eat Japanese foods such as sushi and Chinese food like chow mein. Different kinds of sausages imported from Germany are another popular food enjoyed by many Americans.

3. a; Make sure that the transmission is in good working order.

   You should always examine a used car carefully before you buy it. Start by checking the number of miles on the odometer, and look at the tires for even wear. If these features seem okay, you can also have a mechanic check the engine and the transmission to make sure everything is in good working order.

4. b; You can take an aerobics class at the rec center.

   There are many ways to get exercise. You can do something as simple as going for a walk in your neighborhood. If you want do to something a little more active, you can swim in Lakeside Park, or you can ride your bicycle on the bike trail. Even if you don't want to be outdoors, you can still exercise by taking an aerobics class at the rec center.

Exercise 4, page 266

1. a
2. b
3. b
4. a

Writing a GED Essay, page 268

Use the ideas in Raising Your Score to evaluate your answers to the exercise. Go over your answers with another student or your instructor. Figure out ways that you can improve your writing style the next time you write an essay.

Chapter 12

Exercise 1, page 275

Essay 1: This essay probably deserves a 1. There is not much development or support, and there is no clear pattern of organization. In addition, there are a lot of errors in Edited American English.

Essay 2: This essay probably deserves a 2. It has some development and organization but lacks a clear introductory paragraph and a strong conclusion. The writer seems to list ideas rather than develop them

fully, and there are a number of errors in Edited American English. As a result, the reader occasionally has trouble following the writer's ideas.

Exercise 2, page 278

1. *cross out* In contrast, cats usually do not pay attention when people come home.
   (The paragraph is about dogs. The information about cats is irrelevant.)
2. *cross out* I saw a good W. C. Fields movie on TV last night.
   (W. C. Fields came up in the paragraph because his picture is on a U.S. stamp. The fact that one of his movies was on TV is irrelevant.)
3. *cross out* Always keep all your medical supplies away from children so that they cannot accidentally take an overdose.
   (The paragraph is about medical supplies everyone should have at home. Though reminding people to keep medicine out of children's reach is good advice, it is not relevant to this essay.)

Exercise 3, page 281

Sample answers:
1. City life is more stressful than farm life because the city's extra noise, crowded conditions, and pollution make relaxing very difficult.
2. correct
3. In my opinion, the federal government wastes taxpayers' money by spending it on overpriced goods like $200 hammers.
4. The automobile is one of the most useful inventions of this century. It has made transportation cheaper and more accessible to a broad cross section of the population.
5. I believe that water pollution is a serious environmental problem in this country because it contaminates our drinking water and poisons our fish and wildlife.
6. correct
7. Elementary school children should be required to learn a foreign language because it teaches them about a culture other than their own.
8. correct

Exercise 4, page 283

Sample answers:

1. My grandfather dropped out of high school because he wanted to earn money to help his mother, who was raising six children on her own.
2. For instance, we could find out what happened in our families during the Great Depression of the 1930s.
3. For example, assembly line workers often find their work dull because they do the same thing over and over.
4. Day after day, you read about stories in magazines and newspapers about rich film stars getting divorced or being hooked on alcohol or drugs.
5. For example, fires can spread very fast when buildings are close together.

Exercise 5, page 285

Sample answers:

1. Standing in the ticket line of the downtown bus terminal, the tired traveler burst into tears when she discovered that her wallet had been stolen by a pickpocket.
2. The increase in abandoned buildings, litter-covered streets, and gang-related activity in the north part of the city has caused many families to move to better-kept areas in the city and suburbs.
3. The performer played a mellow jazz tune on his saxophone as the rush-hour crowds passed by him on their way to the train station.
4. Bob angrily asked his mother why she wouldn't extend his curfew after midnight now that he was 17.
5. The weekend before Christmas, Lakeside Mall was packed with people hurrying to buy all their gifts for family and friends.
6. Due to the drought this past summer, the price of fresh fruit and vegetables has nearly doubled from what it was last year.

Exercise 6, page 287

Sample answers:

1. However,
2. In addition,
3. In addition,
4. Otherwise,

5. Second, Next, *or* Then,
6. , on the other hand, *or* , however,

Exercise 7, page 289

Sample answer:

High school students should not be allowed to drive for several reasons. **First, they** are not mature enough to handle the responsibility. Every Friday night, one teenager I know downs a six-pack of beer and then challenges his classmates to drag race down Main Street.

Second, cars detract from schoolwork. Most students who own cars work to pay for gas and insurance. They spend less time on schoolwork, which should be their primary concern.

Finally, cars give high school students too much freedom. Instead of cruising the streets looking for parties to crash or girls to pick up, they should be with their families, where more adult supervision is provided.

Exercise 8, page 290

Sample answer:

Frank was annoyed with Lisa because **she** never became angry with him. Whenever Frank complained to **his girlfriend** about anything, **she** apologized to **him** instead of becoming angry in return. Frank found it impossible to have a good argument with Lisa because **she** refused to **disagree**. Lisa's **attitude** simply made Frank even **madder** than **he** was to begin with.

Exercise 9, page 292

Part A

Sample answers:

1. The dress is made of blue cotton.
2. We finally found an apartment that is large but inexpensive.
3. I'm going to order a large pizza.
4. The silver dollars were worth at least $50 each.
5. We are going to the store to buy some milk, eggs, and cheese.

Part B

Sample answer:

Today's heating costs are dangerously high for poor people. Retired people must rely on a fixed income. Their social security checks just aren't large enough to cover higher utility bills when the weather is cold. Congress should pass a bill to assist people in this situation.

Exercise 10, page 294

1. She **passed** the GED test in 2001.
2. Mary Elizabeth **was** late today.
3. I do not like cheese. **However,** I love yogurt.
4. Ms. **G**reene is going to the supply room to get some paper.
5. I went to the store to **buy** some supplies.
6. Jerome is my best friend.
7. My uncle is going to visit me in Chicago next year.
8. **I don't** like to go swimming in the morning.
9. The girl who was hit by a car **was rushed to the hospital**.
10. The painters cleaned **their** equipment after they finished painting the house.

Writing a GED Essay, page 295

Part A

Go over your ratings with another student or your instructor and compare them to the examples in this chapter.

Part B

Go over your revisions with another student or your instructor.

Part C

Go over your corrections with another student or your instructor.

Chapter 13

Exercise 1, page 298

1. a
2. c
3. b
4. b

Exercise 2, page 304

1. d
2. c

3. a
4. d
5. a
6. b
7. b
8. c

Exercise 3, page 306

Parts A, B, and C

Go over your completed essay with another student or your instructor. Use the GED Essay Scoring Guide to evaluate your essay. Figure out ways that you can work more effectively in the future.

Writing a GED Essay, page 310

Go over your completed essay with another student or your instructor. Use the ideas in Raising Your Score to evaluate your essay. Figure out ways that you can work more effectively in the future.

Glossary

A

action verb   a verb that describes the action in a sentence.
> Marion Jones <u>sprinted</u> across the finish line.

active verb   a verb that shows the subject doing the action.
> Hector <u>mowed</u> the lawn.

adjective   a word that describes a noun or pronoun.
> The <u>talented</u> actress walked up to the podium to accept her Academy Award.

adverb   a word that describes a verb.
> The getaway car sped <u>quickly</u> down the highway.

agreement in number   a correct sentence structure in which a pronoun and an antecedent are both singular or both plural.
> Emily and Bill went shopping to buy an anniversary present for <u>their</u> parents.

antecedent   the word or words that a pronoun refers to in a sentence.
> <u>Emily and Bill</u> went shopping to buy an anniversary present for their parents.

appositive   a type of modifying phrase that supplies additional information about a noun or pronoun in a sentence; an appositive must be set off from the rest of the sentence with commas.
> Mr. Burns, <u>my boss</u>, is going on vacation for two weeks.

B

body paragraphs   the second, third, and fourth paragraphs in a five-paragraph essay; each body paragraph expresses an idea that supports the main idea of the essay.

brainstorming   a technique used to gather ideas in which the writer lists ideas as they come to him or her.

C

cause and effect   a pattern of organization that lists the reasons why something occurred or predicts the possible results if an event or action takes place.

circling   a technique used to organize an idea list in which the writer draws circles to show how the ideas go together in groups.

circular reasoning   a style of writing in which the writer mistakenly restates an opinion in other words instead of providing a specific reason to support the opinion.
> Brad Pitt is the best-looking movie star in the world. No other actor is as handsome as he is.

clause   a group of words containing a subject and a verb; two clauses are used to create a compound or complex sentence.
> <u>I am flying to Tokyo tomorrow</u>, but <u>my husband is flying to Mexico City</u>.

clustering   a technique used to gather ideas in which the writer arranges ideas on an idea map to show how they relate to the main idea of the essay.

comma splice   a sentence consisting of two clauses joined by a comma without a conjunction; a comma splice is considered an error in sentence structure.
> Erin went to the hospital, she was in labor.

command   a sentence that tells someone to do something; the subject of a command is always understood to be *you*.
> Go upstairs to your room now!

comparison and contrast   a pattern of organization that shows how things are alike and different.

complex sentence   a sentence that contains a dependent clause connected to an independent clause.
> Joe and Felicia bought the couch while it was still on sale.

compound sentence a sentence that contains two independent clauses joined by a coordinating conjunction.

> Regina is going to a local college, but her sister is going to college in another state.

compound subject a subject that consists of two or more simple subjects.

> The <u>cat</u> and <u>dog</u> chased each other around the house.

compound verb a predicate that consists of two or more verbs.

> The cat <u>chased</u> the dog and <u>scratched</u> him on the face.

concluding paragraph the fifth and final paragraph in a five-paragraph essay; the concluding paragraph summarizes the essay and gives a final idea about the topic.

coordinating conjunction a word used to connect independent clauses in a compound sentence.

> Regina is going to a local college, <u>but</u> her sister is going to college in another state.

D

dangling modifier a word or phrase that has no word to describe in a sentence.

> <u>Typing furiously</u>, the paper was finished just in time for class.

dependent clause a clause that depends on another clause in order to make sense; a dependent clause makes up part of a complex sentence.

> Joe and Felicia bought the couch <u>while it was still on sale</u>.

diction the word choice in a sentence, paragraph, or essay.

direct address a noun set off by commas that refers to the subject in a sentence; a direct address is never the subject of the sentence.

> <u>Charlie</u>, please hand me the remote control.

E

essay a group of related paragraphs about one topic.

F

first person a category of writing that refers to the speaker or writer.

> <u>I</u> must be more cautious when <u>I</u> am out alone late at night.

fragment see **sentence fragment**.

future continuing tense a verb tense used to show an ongoing action in the future.

> I <u>will be traveling</u> all over the world for the next few months.

future perfect tense a verb tense used to show an action that will be completed by a specified time in the future.

> By summertime, I <u>will be finished</u> with my travels.

future tense a simple verb tense used to show an action that has not yet taken place but will take place in the future.

> I <u>will travel</u> to Costa Rica tomorrow.

G

gathering ideas the first step in the writing process in which the writer figures out the main idea of the essay and makes a list of supporting details.

H

here or there statement a sentence that starts with the word *here* or *there*; the subject comes after the verb in a *here* or *there* statement.

> Here comes the Martinez family!

homonym two or more words that sound alike but are spelled differently and have different meanings.

> I <u>hear</u> that you have been promoted.
> Report <u>here</u> tomorrow to start your new job.

I

idea map see **clustering**.

indefinite pronoun a pronoun that does not name a specific person or thing.

> <u>Someone</u> has broken my favorite glass!

independent clause a clause that can stand alone as a complete sentence; two independent clauses are used to create a compound sentence.

> <u>Regina is going to a local college</u>, but <u>her sister is going to college in another state</u>.

introductory paragraph the first paragraph of a five-paragraph essay; the introductory paragraph indicates the issue the essay is going to address and states the main idea.

irregular verb a verb that does not follow a familiar pattern in order to form a different tense.

> I <u>have</u> a doctor's appointment today.
> I <u>had</u> a doctor's appointment yesterday.

linking verb a verb that links the subject of a sentence to words that describe or rename it.

> The child <u>is</u> sick.

M

main idea the point of view that an essay discusses or develops.

modifier see **adjective**.

modifying phrase a group of words that describes another word in a sentence.

> Yesterday's snowfall beat last year's record <u>by nine inches</u>.

N

noun a word that labels a person, place, thing, or idea.

> The <u>girl</u> drove her <u>car</u> into a <u>tree</u>.

O

order of importance a pattern of organization that lists ideas from least to most important.

organizing the second step in the writing process in which the writer makes sure there are enough supporting details, ensures that the details are all about the main idea, and puts ideas in an order that makes sense.

outlining a technique used to organize ideas in which the writer lists group names and supporting details in the order that they'll appear in the essay.

P

paragraph a group of sentences that develops a central point or main idea.

parallel structure a correct form of sentence structure in which all elements of a compound sentence have the same form.

> The runner <u>stretched</u> out her muscles, <u>ran</u> a warm-up lap, and <u>took</u> her place at the starting line.

passive verb a verb that shows the subject being acted upon.

> The lawn <u>was mowed</u> by Hector.

past continuing tense a verb tense used to show a past action that continued for some time.

> We <u>were studying</u> for the GED Test.

past participle the form of a verb used in all the perfect tenses; in regular verbs, the past participle is formed by adding *ed* or *d* to the base form; in irregular verbs, the past participle is usually an entirely new word.

> By the time the guests arrived, Sophie had <u>finished</u> decorating for the party.
> Lucinda and Ramon had <u>been</u> married for five years by the time they had their first child.

past perfect tense a verb tense used to show an action that took place before a specified time in the past.

> By the time the guests arrived, Sophie <u>had finished</u> decorating for the party.

plural noun a noun that names more than one person, place, thing, or idea.

> The <u>leaves</u> have fallen from all the <u>trees</u> in the neighborhood.

possessive noun a noun that shows possession of something; a possessive noun usually ends in *'s*.

> <u>Dina's</u> car was stolen last night.

predicate the part of a sentence that tells the reader what the subject is or does.

> The employees <u>entered the conference room</u>.

prepositional phrase a word group that starts with a preposition and ends with a noun or pronoun; a prepositional phrase describes another word in the sentence.

> The Elliott family just bought a house <u>on a lake</u>.

present continuing tense a verb tense used to show an ongoing action that is happening now.

> The man at the corner <u>is selling</u> newspapers.

present perfect tense a verb tense used to show an action that started in the past and continues into the present or has just been completed.

> My grandparents <u>have lived</u> in Chicago since 1938.

pronoun a word that takes the place of a noun in a sentence.

> Jane went to the store so <u>she</u> could buy some milk.

proper noun a noun that names a specific person, place, or thing; a proper noun is generally capitalized.

> <u>Ralph</u> and his daughter are going to look at colleges in <u>California</u>.

Q

question a sentence that asks something; at least part of the verb in a question comes before the subject.

> Can we finish this discussion at another time?

R

regular verb a verb that follows a familiar pattern, such as adding *ed* to the base to form a past tense.

> Madeline <u>looks</u> like the girl in the photo in the newspaper.
> Madeline <u>looked</u> at the photo in the newspaper.

renaming phrase see **appositive**.

revising the fourth and final step in the writing process, in which a writer reviews and corrects an essay.

run-on sentence a sentence consisting of too many clauses; a run-on sentence is considered an error in sentence structure.

> Jerry went to the grocery store I went home.

S

second person a category of writing that refers to the audience or reader.

> <u>You</u> must be more cautious when <u>you</u> are out alone late at night.

sentence a group of words that contains a subject and predicate and expresses a complete thought; the sentence is the basic building block of clear, effective writing.

> I passed the test.

sentence fragment a group of words that does not fulfill the three requirements of a complete sentence.

> Hoping I would pass the test.

sequence of tenses the logical relationship between verbs in a sentence.

> When you have completed this book, you will be prepared for the Language Arts, Writing Test.

simple past tense a verb tense used to show an action that occurred at a specified time in the past.

> Last year, I <u>decided</u> to get my GED.

simple present tense a verb tense used to show an action or state of being that is happening now or happens regularly.

> She <u>walks</u> her dog every day.

simple subject the key word in the subject of a sentence that tells the reader whom or what the sentence is about.

> The blue <u>dress</u> looks nice on you.

subject the part of a sentence that tells the reader whom or what the sentence is about.

> <u>The blue dress</u> looks nice on you.

subject-verb agreement the process of choosing a present-tense verb to match a singular or plural subject.

> <u>She has</u> $3,000 in her bank account.
> <u>They have</u> $5,000 in their bank account.

subordinating conjunction a word that joins a dependent clause to an independent clause.

> Joe and Felicia bought the couch <u>while</u> it was still on sale.

supporting sentence a sentence in a paragraph that gives more information about the main idea presented in the topic sentence.

synonym a word or phrase that has nearly the same meaning as another word.

> Will you please stop making such a <u>racket</u>? The <u>noise</u> is driving me crazy!

T

tense the time showed by a verb.

> I <u>eat</u> pizza for dinner on Tuesday.
> I <u>ate</u> pizza for dinner on Tuesday.
> I <u>will eat</u> pizza for dinner on Tuesday.

thesis statement a sentence that previews the content and organization of an essay by stating the topic and main idea of each of the three body paragraphs; the thesis statement is usually the last sentence in the introductory paragraph.

third person a category of writing that refers to the person, thing, or group spoken about.

> <u>She</u> must be more cautious when <u>she</u> is out alone late at night.

tightening a technique used to reduce the number of words in an essay without losing important ideas; tightening makes writing clearer and more forceful.

time order a pattern of organization that lists ideas in the order in which they occurred.

tone the style in which a sentence or paragraph is written.

topic sentence a sentence in a paragraph that tells what the rest of the paragraph is about; the topic sentence is often the first sentence in a paragraph.

transition a word or group of words that help a reader follow the writer's thoughts from sentence to sentence and paragraph to paragraph.

> Elsa wanted to buy the table. <u>However</u>, she didn't have enough money in her purse.

V

verb the key word in the predicate of a sentence that tells what the subject is or does.

> The employees <u>entered</u> the conference room.

verbal phrase a modifying phrase that uses a verbal form to describe a noun.

> <u>Swinging her long hair from side to side</u>, the girl skipped down the street.

W

writing the third step in the writing process in which the writer uses an organized idea list to write an essay.

Index